D0002683

CONTENTS

120 600

ACKNOWLEDGMENTS

WHEN WRITING a book, one is continually reminded of how collaborative such a project always is. I would like to acknowledge gratefully the College Preparatory School of Oakland, California, for not only employing but also encouraging me. The English department was especially invaluable in this regard. Thanks to my spirited departmental colleagues: Julie Anderson, Joy Crisman, Richard Cushman, John Faggi, Larissa Parson, Nancy Steele, and Andrea Tinnemeyer, who was instrumental in this book's undertaking. Thanks to the technology department, which helped ensure that I secured word to page. Thanks to my students, whose questions, quips, and insights inspire my own studies of literature. Thanks to the Oakland Public Library and the Steinbeck Center at San Jose State University, both of which provided textual resources and useful answers. For his guidance and quick responses, thanks to my editor, Jeff Soloway. For their unparalleled bonhomie, thanks to Max Delgado, Bruno and Lucy Zicarelli, Ingrid Adamson-Smith, and all Smiths great and small. Thanks to my excellent friends who cannot, will not, and do not stop rocking. A hearty thanks to my parents, Judy and John Kordich, for their cheering huzzahs and vital support. And an operatic thanks goes to Douglas Smith, whose bibliographical enthusiasm and editorial gumption helped bring this book to fruition. This book is, with love, for him.

—*Catherine J. Kordich*

SERIES
INTRODUCTION

BLOOM's How to Write about Literature series is designed to inspire students to write fine essays on great writers and their works. Each volume in the series begins with an introduction by Harold Bloom, meditating on the challenges and rewards of writing about the volume's subject author. The first chapter then provides detailed instructions on how to write a good essay, including how to find a thesis; how to develop an outline; how to write a good introduction, body text, and conclusions; how to cite sources; and more. The second chapter provides a brief overview of the issues involved in writing about the subject author and then a number of suggestions for paper topics, with accompanying strategies for addressing each topic. Succeeding chapters cover the author's major works.

The paper topics suggested within this book are open-ended, and the brief strategies provided are designed to give students a push forward on the writing process rather than a roadmap to success. The aim of the book is to pose questions, not answer them. Many different kinds of papers could result from each topic. As always, the success of each paper will depend completely on the writer's skill and imagination.

INTRODUCTION
by Harold Bloom

HOW TO WRITE ABOUT JOHN STEINBECK

THE COMMON reader, hearing John Steinbeck mentioned, has to think of and about *The Grapes of Wrath*. Steinbeck was endlessly prolific, but *The Grapes of Wrath* is his most famous work. As befits this series, I will emphasize questions and problems that necessarily relate to writing about Steinbeck's principal novel.

This approach partly relieves me from dealing with the sad issue of whether *The Grapes of Wrath* is now a period piece, rather than a permanent aesthetic achievement. I cannot resolve this issue anyway, because I am of two minds. Yet my inward conflict in itself can help us in learning how to write about *The Grapes of Wrath*. Steinbeck's prose style was inadequate for a novelist, though not for a writer of screenplays. His scripts for Alfred Hitchcock's *Lifeboat* (1944) and Elia Kazan's *Viva Zapata!* (1952) are better written than his own fiction, but of course may have been doctored. More interesting to me is that Nunnally Johnson's screenplay for John Ford's *The Grapes of Wrath* (1940) is clearly more eloquent and memorable than Steinbeck's own novel (1939), perhaps because Steinbeck's *The Grapes of Wrath* is akin to Eugene O'Neill's plays and Theodore Dreiser's novels. All three naturalistic expressionists gave us works that are stronger in dramatic gesture and as myth than they are in prose rhetoric and in the portrayed inwardness of their protagonists.

I have just reread Steinbeck's novel and reseen Ford's film, after being away from them for a decade. Aesthetically the film is superior, just as Sir Laurence Olivier's movie of *Sister Carrie* is better than Dreiser's book, where frequently the prose makes me wince. And yet I am not much of a film fan and greatly prefer reading novels, plays, poems, and stories. I find reading O'Neill a struggle, though a good production of *Long Day's Journey into Night* moves me. It is germane that the best filmed Shakespeare I have seen are Akira Kurosawa's *Throne of Blood* (*Macbeth*) and *Ran* (*King Lear*), even though not a word of Shakespeare's magnificent art of language was involved. Of Shakespeare, anyone can observe accurately than he excelled all other writers, wherever and whenever, as a thinker, an artist of beauty, and an inventor of the human. Even with the language withdrawn, thought and character survive. Steinbeck was an anxious imitator of Ernest Hemingway's prose style, modified somewhat by rather awkwardly handled cadences of the King James Bible. *The Grapes of Wrath* is a flawed novel that nevertheless survives, at least until and for now. Why? Is Steinbeck a master of myth, or of human gesture? Yes and no, no and yes.

Revolutionary politics are irrelevant to Steinbeck's novel, which has a very poor grasp of Marxist dialectics, if indeed any at all. As a writer on the Left in the 1930s and after, Steinbeck was far closer to an American native anarcho-syndicalism than to an imported Marxism. Tom Joad, his mother, and the Emersonian martyred preacher Jim Casy could have found a home with the Wobblies, Big Bill Haywood's Industrial Workers of the World, whose Christlike martyr was Joe Hill. Even American anarcho-syndicalism was too radical for Steinbeck himself, though not for Tom and Ma Joad and Jim Casy.

It is in such characters finally that I would locate the focus of how to write about Steinbeck in *The Grapes of Wrath*, where he is at his mixed best. Tom Joad, Ma, and Jim Casy, though their psyches are barely sketched by Steinbeck, all possess enough mythic force to get away from their frequently confused and inhibited creator. This is made possible by gesture, muted utterance, but most of all by Steinbeck's talent for communicating a kind of love, both familial and group, that transcends individual desires.

In writing about *The Grapes of Wrath*, it is wise to concede that Steinbeck knew almost nothing about Okies or indeed about Oklahoma. As sociology or social culture, *The Grapes of Wrath* is absurd. Perhaps Steinbeck should have set it all in California, the only culture he knew, but he felt he needed the dust bowl. Floyd Watkins, in *In Time and Place*

(1977), demonstrated this, though his unfavorable comparison of the Joads to the Bundrens of William Faulkner's *As I Lay Dying* is hardly fair. If I had to choose the greatest and most original novel by a 20th-century American, it would have to be *As I Lay Dying*, where fantasy and folkways merge into the highest kind of imaginative vision, as they do in the best of Herman Melville and Nathaniel Hawthorne. In proximity to Faulkner's masterpiece of phantastmagoria, *The Grapes of Wrath* shrivels away to not much.

To write about *The Grapes of Wrath*, you need to yield to the real pathos of Steinbeck's myth, which is as devoid of Faulkner's mythic grandeur as it is of Hemingway's stoic eloquence. Accept Steinbeck with all his limitations, and then go on from there, even as the Joads go on.

HOW TO WRITE
A GOOD ESSAY

WHILE THERE are many ways to write about literature, most assignments for high school and college English classes call for analytical papers. In these assignments, you are presenting your interpretation of a text to your reader. Your objective is to interpret the text's meaning in order to enhance your reader's understanding and enjoyment of the work. Without exception, strong papers about the meaning of a literary work are built upon a careful, close reading of the text or texts. Careful, analytical reading should always be the first step in your writing process. This volume provides models of such close, analytical reading, and these should help you develop your own skills as a reader and as a writer.

As the examples throughout this book demonstrate, attentive reading entails thinking about and evaluating the formal (textual) aspects of the author's works: theme, character, form, and language. In addition, when writing about a work, many readers choose to move beyond the text itself to consider the work's cultural context. In these instances, writers might explore the historical circumstances of the time period in which the work was written. Alternatively, they might examine the philosophies and ideas that a work addresses. Even in cases where writers explore a work's cultural context, though, papers must still address the more formal aspects of the work itself. A good interpretative essay that evaluates Charles Dickens's use of the philosophy of utilitarianism in his novel *Hard Times*, for example, cannot adequately address the author's treatment of the philosophy without firmly grounding this discussion in the book itself. In other words, any analytical paper about a text, even

1

one that seeks to evaluate the work's cultural context, must also have a firm handle on the work's themes, characters, and language. You must look for and evaluate these aspects of a work, then, as you read a text and as you prepare to write about it.

WRITING ABOUT THEMES

Literary themes are more than just topics or subjects treated in a work; they are attitudes or points about these topics that often structure other elements in a work. Writing about theme therefore requires that you not just identify a topic that a literary work addresses but also discuss what that work says about that topic. For example, if you were writing about the culture of the American South in William Faulkner's famous story "A Rose for Emily," you would need to discuss what Faulkner says, argues, or implies about that culture and its passing.

When you prepare to write about thematic concerns in a work of literature, you will probably discover that, like most works of literature, your text touches upon other themes in addition to its central theme. These secondary themes also provide rich ground for paper topics. A thematic paper on "A Rose for Emily" might consider gender or race in the story. While neither of these could be said to be the central theme of the story, they are clearly related to the passing of the "old South" and could provide plenty of good material for papers.

As you prepare to write about themes in literature, you might find a number of strategies helpful. After you identify a theme or themes in the story, you should begin by evaluating how other elements of the story—such as character, point of view, imagery, and symbolism—help develop the theme. You might ask yourself what your own responses are to the author's treatment of the subject matter. Do not neglect the obvious, either: What expectations does the title set up? How does the title help develop thematic concerns? Clearly, the title "A Rose for Emily" says something about the narrator's attitude toward the title character, Emily Grierson, and all she represents.

WRITING ABOUT CHARACTER

Generally, characters are essential components of fiction and drama. (This is not always the case, though; Ray Bradbury's "August 2026: There

Will Come Soft Rains" is technically a story without characters, at least any human characters.) Often, you can discuss character in poetry, as in T. S. Eliot's "The Love Song of J. Alfred Prufrock" or Robert Browning's "My Last Duchess." Many writers find that analyzing character is one of the most interesting and engaging ways to work with a piece of literature and to shape a paper. After all, characters generally are human, and we all know something about being human and living in the world. While it is always important to remember that these figures are not real people but creations of the writer's imagination, it can be fruitful to begin evaluating them as you might evaluate a real person. Often you can start with your own response to a character. Did you like or dislike the character? Did you sympathize with the character? Why or why not?

Keep in mind, though, that emotional responses like these are just starting places. To truly explore and evaluate literary characters, you need to return to the formal aspects of the text and evaluate how the author has drawn these characters. The 20th-century writer E. M. Forster coined the terms *flat* characters and *round* characters. Flat characters are static, one-dimensional characters who frequently represent a particular concept or idea. In contrast, round characters are fully drawn and much more realistic characters who frequently change and develop over the course of a work. Are the characters you are studying flat or round? What elements of the characters lead you to this conclusion? Why might the author have drawn characters like this? How does their development affect the meaning of the work? Similarly, you should explore the techniques the author uses to develop characters. Do we hear a character's own words, or do we hear only other characters' assessments of him or her? Or, does the author use an omniscient or limited omniscient narrator to allow us access to the workings of the characters' minds? If so, how does that help develop the characterization? Often you can even evaluate the narrator as a character. How trustworthy are the opinions and assessments of the narrator? You should also think about characters' names. Do they mean anything? If you encounter a hero named Sophia or Sophie, you should probably think about her wisdom (or lack thereof), since *Sophia* means "wisdom" in Greek. Similarly, since the name *Sylvia* is derived from the word *sylvan,* meaning "of the wood," you might want to evaluate that character's relationship with nature. Once again, you might look to the title of the work. Does Herman Melville's "Bartleby, the Scrivener" signal anything about Bartleby himself? Is Bartleby adequately defined by his job as scrivener? Is this part of Melville's point? Pursuing questions like these can help you develop thorough papers about characters from psychological, sociological, or more formalistic perspectives.

WRITING ABOUT FORM AND GENRE

Genre, a word derived from French, means "type" or "class." Literary genres are distinctive classes or categories of literary composition. On the most general level, literary works can be divided into the genres of drama, poetry, fiction, and essays, yet within those genres there are classifications that are also referred to as genres. Tragedy and comedy, for example, are genres of drama. Epic, lyric, and pastoral are genres of poetry. Form, on the other hand, generally refers to the shape or structure of a work. There are many clearly defined forms of poetry that follow specific patterns of meter, rhyme, and stanza. Sonnets, for example, are poems that follow a fixed form of 14 lines. Sonnets generally follow one of two basic sonnet forms, each with its own distinct rhyme scheme. Haiku is another example of poetic form, traditionally consisting of three unrhymed lines of five, seven, and five syllables.

While you might think that writing about form or genre might leave little room for argument, many of these forms and genres are very fluid. Remember that literature is evolving and ever changing, and so are its forms. As you study poetry, you may find that poets, especially more modern poets, play with traditional poetic forms, bringing about new effects. Similarly, dramatic tragedy was once quite narrowly defined, but over the centuries playwrights have broadened and challenged traditional definitions, changing the shape of tragedy. When Arthur Miller wrote Death of a Salesman, many critics challenged the idea that tragic drama could encompass a common man like Willy Loman.

Evaluating how a work of literature fits into or challenges the boundaries of its form or genre can provide you with fruitful avenues of investigation. You might find it helpful to ask why the work does or does not fit into traditional categories. Why might Miller have thought it fitting to write a tragedy of the common man? Similarly, you might compare the content or theme of a work with its form. How well do they work together? Many of Emily Dickinson's poems, for instance, follow the meter of traditional hymns. While some of her poems seem to express traditional religious doctrines, many seem to challenge or strain against traditional conceptions of God and theology. What is the effect, then, of her use of traditional hymn meter?

WRITING ABOUT LANGUAGE, SYMBOLS, AND IMAGERY

No matter what the genre, writers use words as their most basic tool. Language is the most fundamental building block of literature. It is essential that you pay careful attention to the author's language and word choice as you read, reread, and analyze a text. Imagery is language that appeals to the senses. Most commonly, imagery appeals to our sense of vision, creating a mental picture, but authors also use language that appeals to our other senses. Images can be literal or figurative. Literal images use sensory language to describe an actual thing. In the broadest terms, figurative language uses one thing to speak about something else. For example, if I call my boss a snake, I am not saying that he is literally a reptile. Instead, I am using figurative language to communicate my opinions about him. Since we think of snakes as sneaky, slimy, and sinister, I am using the concrete image of a snake to communicate these abstract opinions and impressions.

The two most common figures of speech are similes and metaphors. Both are comparisons between two apparently dissimilar things. Similes are explicit comparisons using the words *like* or *as*; metaphors are implicit comparisons. To return to the previous example, if I say, "My boss, Bob, was waiting for me when I showed up to work five minutes late today—the snake!" I have constructed a metaphor. Writing about his experiences fighting in World War I, Wilfred Owen begins his poem "Dulce et decorum est," with a string of similes: "Bent double, like old beggars under sacks, / Knock-kneed, coughing like hags, we cursed through sludge." Owen's goal was to undercut clichéd notions that war and dying in battle were glorious. Certainly, comparing soldiers to coughing hags and to beggars underscores his point.

"Fog," a short poem by Carl Sandburg provides a clear example of a metaphor. Sandburg's poem reads:

The fog comes
on little cat feet.

It sits looking
over harbor and city
on silent haunches
and then moves on.

Notice how effectively Sandburg conveys surprising impressions of the fog by comparing two seemingly disparate things—the fog and a cat.

Symbols, by contrast, are things that stand for, or represent, other things. Often they represent something intangible, such as concepts or ideas. In everyday life we use and understand symbols easily. Babies at christenings and brides at weddings wear white to represent purity. Think, too, of a dollar bill. The paper itself has no value in and of itself. Instead, that paper bill is a symbol of something else, the precious metal in a nation's coffers. Symbols in literature work similarly. Authors use symbols to evoke more than a simple, straightforward, literal meaning. Characters, objects, and places can all function as symbols. Famous literary examples of symbols include Moby-Dick, the white whale of Herman Melville's novel, and the scarlet *A* of Nathaniel Hawthorne's *The Scarlet Letter.* As both of these symbols suggest, a literary symbol cannot be adequately defined or explained by any one meaning. Hester Prynne's Puritan community clearly intends her scarlet *A* as a symbol of her adultery, but as the novel progresses, even her own community reads the letter as representing not just *adultery,* but *able, angel,* and a host of other meanings.

Writing about imagery and symbols requires close attention to the author's language. To prepare a paper on symbolism or imagery in a work, identify and trace the images and symbols and then try to draw some conclusions about how they function. Ask yourself how any symbols or images help contribute to the themes or meanings of the work. What connotations do they carry? How do they affect your reception of the work? Do they shed light on characters or settings? A strong paper on imagery or symbolism will thoroughly consider the use of figures in the text and will try to reach some conclusions about how or why the author uses them.

WRITING ABOUT HISTORY AND CONTEXT

As noted above, it is possible to write an analytical paper that also considers the work's context. After all, the text was not created in a vacuum. The author lived and wrote in a specific time period and in a specific cultural context and, like all of us, was shaped by that environment. Learning more about the historical and cultural circumstances that surround the author and the work can help illuminate a text and provide you with productive material for a paper. Remember, though, that when you write analytical papers, you should use the context to illuminate the text. Do not lose sight of your goal—to interpret the meaning of the literary work. Use historical or philosophical research as a tool to develop your textual evaluation.

Thoughtful readers often consider how history and culture affected the author's choice and treatment of his or her subject matter. Investigations into the history and context of a work could examine the work's relation to specific historical events, such as the Salem witch trials in 17th-century Massachusetts or the restoration of Charles to the British throne in 1660. Bear in mind that historical context is not limited to politics and world events. While knowing about the Vietnam War is certainly helpful in interpreting much of Tim O'Brien's fiction, and some knowledge of the French Revolution clearly illuminates the dynamics of Charles Dickens's *A Tale of Two Cities,* historical context also entails the fabric of daily life. Examining a text in light of gender roles, race relations, class boundaries, or working conditions can give rise to thoughtful and compelling papers. Exploring the conditions of the working class in 19th-century England, for example, can provide a particularly effective avenue for writing about Dickens's *Hard Times.*

You can begin thinking about these issues by asking broad questions at first. What do you know about the time period and about the author? What does the editorial apparatus in your text tell you? These might be starting places. Similarly, when specific historical events or dynamics are particularly important to understanding a work but might be somewhat obscure to modern readers, textbooks usually provide notes to explain historical background. These are a good place to start. With this information, ask yourself how these historical facts and circumstances might have affected the author, the presentation of theme, and the presentation of character. How does knowing more about the work's specific historical context illuminate the work? To take a well-known example, understanding the complex attitudes toward slavery during the time Mark Twain wrote *Adventures of Huckleberry Finn* should help you begin to examine issues of race in the text. Additionally, you might compare these attitudes to those of the time in which the novel was set. How might this comparison affect your interpretation of a work written after the abolition of slavery but set before the Civil War?

WRITING ABOUT PHILOSOPHY AND IDEAS

Philosophical concerns are closely related to both historical context and thematic issues. Like historical investigation, philosophical research can provide a useful tool as you analyze a text. For example, an investigation into the working class in Dickens's England might lead you to a topic on the philosophical doctrine of utilitarianism in *Hard Times*. Many other works explore philosophies and ideas quite explicitly. Mary Shelley's famous novel *Frankenstein*, for example, explores John Locke's tabula rasa theory of human knowledge as she portrays the intellectual and emotional development of Victor Frankenstein's creature. As this example indicates, philosophical issues are somewhat more abstract than investigations of theme or historical context. Some other examples of philosophical issues include human free will, the formation of human identity, the nature of sin, or questions of ethics.

Writing about philosophy and ideas might require some outside research, but usually the notes or other material in your text will provide you with basic information and often footnotes and bibliographies suggest places you can go to read further about the subject. If you have identified a philosophical theme that runs through a text, you might ask yourself how the author develops this theme. Look at character development and the interactions of characters, for example. Similarly, you might examine whether the narrative voice in a work of fiction addresses the philosophical concerns of the text.

WRITING COMPARISON AND CONTRAST ESSAYS

Finally, you might find that comparing and contrasting the works or techniques of an author provides a useful tool for literary analysis. A comparison and contrast essay might compare two characters or themes in a single work, or it might compare the author's treatment of a theme in two works. It might also contrast methods of character development or analyze an author's differing treatment of a philosophical concern in two works. Writing comparison and contrast essays, though, requires some special consideration. While they generally provide you with plenty of material to use, they also come with a built-in trap: the laundry list. These papers often become mere lists of connections between the works. As this chapter will discuss, a strong thesis must make an assertion that you want to prove or validate. A strong comparison/contrast thesis, then, needs to comment on the significance of the similarities and differences you observe. It is not enough merely to assert that the works contain similarities and differences. You might, for example, assert why the similarities and differences are important and explain how they illuminate the works' treatment of theme. Remember, too, that a thesis should not be a statement of the obvious. A comparison/contrast paper that focuses only on very obvious similarities or differences does little to illuminate the connections between the works. Often, an effective method of shaping a strong thesis and argument is to begin your paper by noting the similarities between the works but then to develop a thesis that asserts how these apparently similar elements are different. If, for example, you observe that Emily Dickinson wrote a number of poems about spiders, you might analyze how she uses spider imagery differently in two poems. Similarly, many scholars have noted that Hawthorne created many "mad scientist" characters, men who are so devoted to their science or their art that they lose perspective on all else. A good thesis comparing two of these characters—Aylmer of "The Birth-mark" and Dr. Rappaccini of "Rappaccini's Daughter," for example—might initially identify both characters as examples of Hawthorne's mad scientist type but then argue that their motivations for scientific experimentation differ. If you strive to analyze the similarities or differences, discuss significances, and move beyond the obvious, your paper should move beyond the laundry list trap.

PREPARING TO WRITE

Armed with a clear sense of your task—illuminating the text—and with an understanding of theme, character, language, history, and philosophy, you are ready to approach the writing process. Remember that good writing is grounded in good reading and that close reading takes time, attention, and more than one reading of your text. Read for comprehension first. As you go back and review the work, mark the text to chart the details of the work as well as your reactions. Highlight important passages, repeated words, and image patterns. "Converse" with the text through marginal notes. Mark turns in the plot, ask questions, and make observations about characters, themes, and language. If you are reading from a book that does not belong to you, keep a record of your reactions in a journal or notebook. If you have read a work of literature carefully, paying attention to both the text and the context of the work, you have a leg up on the writing process. Admittedly, at this point, your ideas are probably very broad and undefined, but you have taken an important first step toward writing a strong paper.

Your next step is to focus, to take a broad, perhaps fuzzy, topic and define it more clearly. Even a topic provided by your instructor will need to be focused appropriately. Remember that good writers make the topic their own. There are a number of strategies—often called "invention"— that you can use to develop your own focus. In one such strategy, called *freewriting*, you spend 10 minutes or so just writing about your topic without referring back to the text or your notes. Write whatever comes to mind; the important thing is that you just keep writing. Often this process allows you to develop fresh ideas or approaches to your subject matter. You could also try *brainstorming*: Write down your topic and then list all the related points or ideas you can think of. Include questions, comments, words, important passages or events, and anything else that comes to mind. Let one idea lead to another. In the related technique of *clustering*, or *mapping*, write your topic on a sheet of paper and write related ideas around it. Then list related subpoints under each of these main ideas. Many people then draw arrows to show connections between points. This technique helps you narrow your topic and can also help you organize your ideas. Similarly, asking journalistic questions— Who? What? Where? When? Why? and How?—can develop ideas for topic development.

Thesis Statements

Once you have developed a focused topic, you can begin to think about your thesis statement, the main point or purpose of your paper. It is imperative that you craft a strong thesis, otherwise, your paper will likely be little more than random, disorganized observations about the text.

Think of your thesis statement as a kind of road map for your paper. It tells your reader where you are going and how you are going to get there.

To craft a good thesis, you must keep a number of things in mind. First, as the title of this subsection indicates, your paper's thesis should be a statement, an assertion about the text that you want to prove or validate. Beginning writers often formulate a question that they attempt to use as a thesis. For example, a writer exploring the theme of friendship in Steinbeck's *Of Mice and Men* might ask, Why are so many lonely characters skeptical of George and Lennie's friendship? While a question like this is a good strategy to use in the invention process to help narrow your topic and find your thesis, it cannot serve as the thesis statement because it does not tell your reader what you want to assert about friendship. You might shape this question into a thesis by instead proposing an answer to that question: In *Of Mice and Men*, all the characters are driven by the need for friendship, but the story presents friendship as tenuous and therefore rare. The novella ultimately argues that friendship is a nearly impossible achievement for individuals in an otherwise heartless society. Notice that this thesis provides an initial plan or structure for the rest of the paper, and notice, too, that the thesis statement does not necessarily have to fit into one sentence. After discussing George and Lennie's friendship, you could examine the ways in which friendship is presented as rare in this novella and then theorize about what Steinbeck is saying about friendship more generally; perhaps you could discuss how the common need for friendship in light of its seeming impossibility is a flaw of the society in which the story is set.

Second, remember that a good thesis makes an assertion that you need to support. In other words, a good thesis does not state the obvious. If you tried to formulate a thesis about friendship by simply saying, Friendship is important in *Of Mice and Men*, you have done nothing but rephrase the obvious. Since Steinbeck's novella is centered on the two protagonists and their friendship, there would be no point in spending three to five pages supporting that assertion. You might try to develop a thesis from that point by asking yourself some further questions: What does it mean to "have somebody to talk to that gives a damn" about you (Steinbeck 15)? Does the novella seem to indicate that to be a friend is a natural or unnatural phenomenon for this society? Does it present friendship as an advantage in this world of agricultural itinerancy, or is friendship presented as a source of vulnerability? Such a line of questioning might lead you to a more viable thesis, like the one in the preceding paragraph.

As the comparison with the road map also suggests, your thesis should appear near the beginning of the paper. In relatively short papers (three to six pages) the thesis almost always appears in the first paragraph. Some writers fall into the trap of saving their thesis for the end, trying to provide a surprise or a big moment of revelation, as if to say, "TA-DA! I've just proved that in 'The Chrysanthemums' Steinbeck uses clothing to symbolize the protagonist's frustrations with her life." Placing a thesis at the end of an essay can seriously mar the essay's effectiveness. If you fail to define your essay's point and purpose clearly at the beginning, your reader will find it difficult to assess the clarity of your argument and understand the points you are making. When your argument comes as a surprise at the end, you force your reader to reread your essay in order to assess its logic and effectiveness.

Finally, you should avoid using the first person ("I") as you present your thesis. Though it is not strictly wrong to write in the first person, it is difficult to do so gracefully. While writing in the first person, beginning writers often fall into the trap of writing self-reflexive prose (writing *about* their paper *in* their paper). Often this leads to the most dreaded of opening lines: "In this paper I am going to discuss . . ." Not only does this self-reflexive voice make for very awkward prose, it frequently allows writers to boldly announce a topic while completely avoiding a thesis statement. An example might be a paper that begins as follows: "The Chrysanthemums," Steinbeck's most famous story, takes place over an afternoon and evening when Elisa Allen, a farm wife, is visited by a tinker who is looking for work and who flirts with her in an effort to get work. In this paper I am going to discuss how Elisa reacts to him. The author of this paper has done little more than announce a general topic for the paper (the reaction of Elisa to the tinker). While the last sentence might be a thesis, the writer fails to present an opinion about the significance of the reaction. To improve this "thesis," the writer would need to back up a couple of steps. First, the announced topic of the paper is too broad; it largely summarizes the events in the story, without saying anything about the ideas in the story. The writer should highlight what she considers the meaning of the story: What is the story about? The writer might conclude that the tinker's visit serves to reveal Elisa's feelings of isolation and frustration in her life. From here, the author could select the means by which Steinbeck communicates these ideas and then begin to craft a specific thesis. A writer who chooses to explore the symbols of frustration that are associated with Elisa's clothing might, for example, craft a thesis that reads, "The Chrysanthemums" is a story that explores the effects of isolation and frustration on one woman, Elisa Allen, who mistakes the interest of a passing tinker for a true connection. The descriptions of her work, her personal life, and even her clothing show the impact of her feelings of isolation, frustration, and ultimate disappointment.

Outlines

While developing a strong, thoughtful thesis early in your writing process should help focus your paper, outlining provides an essential tool for logically shaping that paper. A good outline helps you see—and develop—the relationships among the points in your argument and assures you that your paper flows logically and coherently. Outlining not only helps place your points in a logical order but also helps you subordinate supporting points, weed out any irrelevant points, and decide if there are any necessary points that are missing from your argument. Most of us are familiar with formal outlines that use numerical and letter designations for each point. However, there are different types of outlines; you may find that an informal outline is a more useful tool for you. What is important, though, is that you spend the time to develop some sort of outline—formal or informal.

Remember that an outline is a tool to help you shape and write a strong paper. If you do not spend sufficient time planning your supporting points and shaping the arrangement of those points, you will most likely construct a vague, unfocused outline that provides little, if any, help with the writing of the paper. Consider the following example.

Thesis: "The Chrysanthemums" is a story that explores the effects of isolation and frustration on one woman,

Elisa Allen, who mistakes the interest of a passing tinker for a true connection. The descriptions of her work, her personal life, and even her clothing show the impact of her feelings of isolation, frustration, and ultimate disappointment.

I. Introduction and thesis

II. Elisa
    A. Work clothes
    B. Toilette/bathing scene
    C. Dress
    D. Frustrations

III. Henry Allen (husband)

IV. Sexual language
    A. Panting

V. Conclusion
    A. Elisa is frustrated and we see this by observing her ideas and her clothing

This outline has a number of flaws. First, the major topics labeled with the Roman numerals are not arranged in a logical order. If the paper's aim is to show how Elisa is frustrated by her personal life, the writer should establish the particulars of that attitude before showing how frustration is evident in her clothing. Similarly, the thesis makes no reference to the husband or to sexual language, but the writer includes each of them as major sections of this outline. As the masculine counterpart of Elisa, the husband may well have a place in this paper, but the writer fails to provide details about his place in the argument. Sexual language, too, though it might be relevant to her frustrations, does not logically merit a major section. The writer could, however, discuss sexual language in another section of the essay. Third, the writer includes the idea of frustrations as one of the lettered items in section II. Letters A, B, and C all refer to specific instances where the symbolism of Elisa's clothing will be discussed; frustrations as an idea does not belong in this list. The writer could argue that frustration is the idea that is illustrated by the clothing (therefore, it is the idea that encompasses all the examples of symbolic clothing), but it itself is not an example of clothing. A fourth problem is the inclusion of a section A in sections IV and V. An outline should not include an A without a B, a 1 without a 2, and so forth. The final problem with this outline is the overall lack of detail. None of the sections provide much information about the content of the argument, and it seems likely that the writer has not given sufficient thought to the content of the paper.

A better start to this outline might be the following:

Thesis: "The Chrysanthemums" is a story that explores the effects of isolation and frustration on one woman, Elisa Allen, who mistakes the interest of a passing tinker for a true connection. The descriptions of her work, her personal life, and even her clothing show the impact of her feelings of isolation, frustration, and ultimate disappointment.

    I. Introduction and thesis

   II. Elisa's feelings of frustration and isolation
      1. In her work
      2. In her relationship with her husband
      3. As demonstrated by her work clothes

  III. Elisa's hope for change and connection
      1. Tinker's visit triggers hope and wonder
      2. Tinker's visit inspires sexual energy
      3. Change and sexual energy clear in bathing scene

  IV. Elisa's hope for change disappointed
      1. No new connection with husband
      2. No connection with tinker
      3. Clothing symbolizes isolation

   V. Conclusion

This new outline would prove much more helpful when it came time to write the paper.

An outline like this could be shaped into an even more useful tool if the writer fleshed out the argument by providing specific examples from the text to support each point. Once you have listed your main point and your supporting ideas, develop this raw material by listing related supporting ideas and material under each of those main headings. From there, arrange the material in subsections and order the material logically.

For example, you might begin with one of the theses cited above: In *Of Mice and Men*, all the characters are driven by the need for friendship, but the story presents friendship as tenuous and therefore rare. The novella ultimately argues that friendship is a nearly impossible achievement for individuals in an otherwise heartless society. As noted above, this thesis already gives you the beginning of an organization: Start by supporting the notion that all the characters long for the rarity of friendship and then explain how Steinbeck presents this longing as prevented by social conditions. You might begin your outline, then, with four topic headings: (1) relationship between George and Lennie as an example of friendship, (2) friendship as necessary for humans, (3) friendship as rare, and (4) friendship as impossible for individuals to sustain in this society. Under each of those headings you could list ideas that support the particular point. Be sure to include references to parts of the text that help build your case.

An informal outline might look like this:

Thesis: In *Of Mice and Men*, all the characters are driven by the need for friendship, but the story presents friendship as tenuous and therefore rare. The novella ultimately argues that friendship is a nearly impossible achievement for individuals in an otherwise heartless society.

1. Friendship shown in relationship between George and Lennie
   - Complex but caring relationship

- George gets frustrated with Lennie
- Lennie adores George
- Their interdependence seen in their dreams for the future
  - Difference from other, lonely workers: "We got a future"
  - Protect each other: "You got me and I got you"
  - Their retelling of their dreams reassures them both

2. Friendship as necessary
   - First note that the characters in the story as desperate for the friendship that George and Lennie share, and all suffer psychologically because they have no friendship in their lives
     - Focus on example of Candy
     - Curley's wife
     - Crooks
   - Candy wants safety, security, peace of mind that comes with friendship
     - Offers to fund the farm if he is allowed to be a part of it: "Maybe if I give you guys my money, you'll let me hoe in the garden even after I ain't no good at it".
     - Sees friendship with George and Lennie as giving him some strength: "And we got fren's, that's what we got."
   - Curley's wife suffers from lack of companionship and kindness
     - "Ain't I got a right to talk to nobody?"
     - Dislikes husband
   - Crooks suffers from lack of companionship because of racism

o "A guy goes nuts if he ain't got nobody. Don't make no difference who the guy is, long's he's with you. I tell ya . . . a guy gets too lonely an' he gets sick"

3. Friendship as rare in this world
   - George and Lennie's friendship is a "symbiotic dependency [that] is hardly understood" (Shillinglaw xx)
     - o The owner of the ranch suspects that George's interest in the slow-witted Lennie is a scam: "You takin' his pay away from him?" When George assures him that he is not, the owner responds, "Well, I never seen one guy take so much trouble for another guy"
     - o Slim also remarks on the rarity of George's and Lennie's friendship, but Slim is admiring: "Ain't many guys travel around together" (34).
   - Set up transition from rarity of friendship to circumstances of the world by Slim's remark about isolation in general: He thinks that it might be fear that is preventing friendships: "Maybe ever'body in the whole damn world is scared of each other" (34).

4. Friendship as impossible for individuals to sustain in this society
   - Individuals wield virtually no power in this world of farm workers; the individual's power is subsumed by the need to be protected by a group
     - o Candy is unable to prevent his dog being put down; Candy's weaknesses

make him choose the group's acceptance
over his pet's life
○ George is, like Candy, unable to
prevent the killing of his friend,
but in this case he is able to spare
his friend the cruelty of the world
(symbolized by the mob that is looking
to lynch Lennie)
• In order to survive, both George and
Candy sacrifice their friends and their
friendships. The implication is that the
bindle stiff's life is too vulnerable to
either maintain friendships or protect
friendships.

Conclusion:
• Final scene suggests how, by losing his
friend, George has also lost his future and
psychological salvation.
• Novella strongly implies that the world
of bindle stiffs working odd jobs in an
agricultural world is a dehumanizing one.
• Novella is also a celebration of the
importance of friendship.

You would set about writing a formal outline with a similar process, though in the final stages you would label the headings differently. A formal outline for a paper that argues the thesis about "The Chrysanthemums" cited above—that the protagonist's frustration and isolation is communicated by her actions, thoughts, and clothing—might look like this:

Thesis: "The Chrysanthemums" is a story that explores
the effects of isolation and frustration on one woman,
Elisa Allen, who mistakes the interest of a passing
tinker for a true connection. The descriptions of her
work, her life, and even her clothing show the impact

of her feelings of isolation, frustration, and ultimate disappointment.

I. Introduction and thesis

II. Elisa's feelings of frustration and isolation
    A. In her work
        1. Hands are "over-eager" and "over-powerful"
        2. Chrysanthemum stems are "too small and easy" for her energy
    B. In her life
        1. Cannot communicate with her husband, whose voice she "starts" at
        2. Longs for the tinker's free lifestyle and the open road
    C. In her clothing
        1. Individuality hidden by boots, huge apron
        2. Identity hidden by hat; pulled "low over face"

III. Elisa's hope for change and human connection
    A. Tinker's visit kindles in her a hope for change in her life and work
        1. His visit inspires her desire to preserve some of change she sensed when they were talking
            a. She suggests that they will meet again in a professional capacity: "You might be surprised to have a rival sometime. I can sharpen scissors, too."
            b. Her desire to follow him communicated as she watches the direction in which he's headed: "There's a glowing there."

      2. Sexual energy derived from visit with tinker

   B. Tinker's visit inspires a symbolically rich toilette and dressing

      1. Bath as a marker of transition, purification, baptism

         a. "tore off soiled clothes"

         b. scrubs body with pumice

         c. appraises figure in mirror

      2. Associations with sexual energy

      3. Sexual awakening also seen in the slow, careful selection of her clothes (including the dress which, the narrator says, is a "symbol of her prettiness")

IV. Elisa's hope for change disappointed

   A. No connection with husband

      1. Their communication remains strained (seen in disastrous jokes)

      2. Anti-erotic diction ("started," "blundered")

   B. No connection with tinker

      1. He throws her gift of chrysanthemums on side of the road

      2. She cannot bring herself to look his way

   C. Clothing symbolizes her isolation

      1. She cries, hidden in the collar of her coat

      2. She had dressed as a vital woman, but is now weeping "like an old woman"

V. Conclusion

   A. How this story comments on the basic human need for connection, work, understanding

        B. Connections to other Steinbeck charac-
           ters
          1. Mary Teller from "The White Quail"
          2. Curley's wife from *Of Mice and Men*

As in the previous example outline, the thesis provided the seeds of a structure, and the writer was careful to arrange the supporting points in a logical manner, showing the relationships among the ideas in the paper.

Body Paragraphs

Once your outline is complete, you can begin drafting your paper. Paragraphs, units of related sentences, are the building blocks of a good paper, and as you draft you should keep in mind both the function and the qualities of good paragraphs. Paragraphs help you chart and control the shape and content of your essay, and they help the reader see your organization and your logic. You should begin a new paragraph whenever you move from one major point to another. In longer, more complex essays you might use a group of related paragraphs to support major points. Remember that in addition to being adequately developed, a good paragraph is both unified and coherent.

UNIFIED PARAGRAPHS

Each paragraph must be centered around one idea or point, and a unified paragraph carefully focuses on and develops this central idea without including extraneous ideas or tangents. For beginning writers, the best way to ensure that you are constructing unified paragraphs is to include a topic sentence in each paragraph. This topic sentence should convey the main point of the paragraph, and every sentence in the paragraph should relate to that topic sentence. Any sentence that strays from the central topic does not belong in the paragraph and needs to be revised or deleted. Consider the following paragraph about how the individual's lack of power in the world of *Of Mice and Men* prevents the keeping of friendships. Notice how the paragraph veers away from the main point that friendships are sacrificed for the sake of survival:

Friendships are difficult to sustain in the world of bindle stiffs. In the world of itinerant workers, the greatest impediment to friendship is the individual's need to survive in a world where the individual has very little power. Curley is always trying to get power by fighting people. Carlson also likes to fight people, and George has a temper. When Candy's old dog is shot it is an example of power: Infirmity makes the dog unpopular in the bunkhouse, and when Carlson offers to euthanize the dog, Candy's need to remain with the group prevents his stopping Carlson. George is unable to save Lennie after his accidental killing of Curley's wife. The same weapon (Carlson's gun) is used to, symbolically, euthanize Lennie. The mob is looking for Lennie to either commit him to an mental institution or lynch him for killing Curley's wife; this mob is heard in the background as George prepares to kill Lennie. As George narrates the story of the farm, the story that always soothed both himself and his friend, the mob's "footsteps" are heard "crashing in the brush" (103). George pulls the trigger just as the other men arrive. George, in effect, does what the mob wanted and thereby saves himself and spares his friend the cruelty Lennie would have suffered at the hands of the mob.

Although the paragraph begins solidly, and the second sentence provides the central idea of the paragraph, the author soon goes on a tangent. If the purpose of the paragraph is to demonstrate that friendships are hard to sustain because of the individual's need to survive in the more powerful group, the sentences about the tempers of Curley, Carlson, and George are tangential here. They may find a place later in the paper, but they should be deleted from this paragraph.

Coherent Paragraphs

In addition to shaping unified paragraphs, you must also craft coherent paragraphs, paragraphs that develop their points logically with sentences that flow smoothly into one another. Coherence depends on the order of your sentences, but it is not strictly the order of the sentences that is important to paragraph coherence. You also need to craft your prose to help the reader see the relationship among the sentences.

Consider the following paragraph about the possibility of friendship in *Of Mice and Men*. Notice how the writer uses the same ideas as the paragraph above yet fails to help the reader see the relationships among the points.

> Slim's theory that the scarcity of friendships is due to fear is half right: Fear might very well lead to distrust and prevent friendships. In the world of migrant workers the greatest barrier to friendship is the need to survive in a world where the individual has very little power. This is evident when Candy's old dog is shot: Infirmity makes the dog unpopular in the bunkhouse, and when Carlson offers to euthanize the dog, Candy's need to remain with the group prevents his stopping Carlson. George is unable to save Lennie after the latter's accidental killing of Curley's wife. The same weapon (Carlson's gun) is used to euthanize Lennie. George has a need to survive, and Lennie's mistake is too grave for George to take care of (George has had to fix Lennie's mistakes in the past). The mob is looking for Lennie to either commit him to an mental institution or lynch him for killing Curley's wife; this mob is heard in the background as George prepares to kill Lennie and thereby prevent any future cruelty the world might do to Lennie. George narrates the story of the farm, the story that always soothed both himself and his friend, and the mob's "footsteps" are heard "crashing in the brush" (103). George pulls the trigger when the other men arrive. George tells them that he has wrestled the gun away from Lennie and killed him; George does what the mob wanted and thereby saves himself and spares his friend the probable lynching Lennie would have suffered at the hands of the mob.

```
George is sacrificing the element of his life that made
it humane: friendship.
```

This paragraph demonstrates that unity alone does not guarantee paragraph effectiveness. The argument is hard to follow because the author fails both to show connections between the sentences and to indicate how they work to support the overall point.

A number of techniques are available to aid paragraph coherence. Careful use of transitional words and phrases is essential. You can use transitional flags to introduce an example or an illustration (*for example, for instance*), to amplify a point or add another phase of the same idea (*additionally, furthermore, next, similarly, finally, then*), to indicate a conclusion or result (*therefore, as a result, thus, in other words*), to signal a contrast or a qualification (*on the other hand, nevertheless, despite this, on the contrary, still, however, conversely*), to signal a comparison (*likewise, in comparison, similarly*), and to indicate a movement in time (*afterward, earlier, eventually, finally, later, subsequently, until*).

In addition to transitional flags, careful use of pronouns aids coherence and flow. If you were writing about *The Wizard of Oz*, you would not want to keep repeating the phrase *the witch* or the name *Dorothy*. Careful substitution of the pronoun *she* in these instances can aid coherence. A word of warning, though: When you substitute pronouns for proper names, always be sure that your pronoun reference is clear. In a paragraph that discusses both Dorothy and the witch, substituting *she* could lead to confusion. Make sure that it is clear to whom the pronoun refers. Generally, the pronoun refers to the last proper noun you have used.

While repeating the same name over and over again can lead to awkward, boring prose, it is possible to use repetition to help your paragraph's coherence. Careful repetition of important words or phrases can lend coherence to your paragraph by reminding readers of your key points. Admittedly, it takes some practice to use this technique effectively. You may find that reading your prose aloud can help you develop an ear for effective use of repetition.

To see how helpful transitional aids are, compare the paragraph below to the preceding paragraph about the fate of friendships in *Of Mice and*

Men's brutal world. Notice how the author works with the same ideas and quotations but shapes them into a much more coherent paragraph whose point is clearer and easier to follow.

> Slim's theory about the scarcity of friendships is, perhaps, half right: Fear might very well lead to distrust and prevent friendships. In the world of migrant workers, though, the greatest impediment to friendship is the individual's need to survive in a world where the individual has very little power. This fact is made evident when Candy's old dog is shot: Infirmity makes the dog unpopular in the bunkhouse, and when Carlson offers (really, threatens) to euthanize the dog, Candy's need to remain with the group prevents his stopping Carlson. George is likewise unable to save Lennie after the latter's accidental killing of Curley's wife. In fact, the same weapon is used to, symbolically, euthanize Lennie. George has a need to survive, and Lennie's mistake is too grave for George to take care of (as George has had to do with Lennie's mistakes in the past). The mob is looking for Lennie to either commit him to an mental institution or, more likely, lynch him for killing Curley's wife; this mob is heard in the background as George prepares to kill Lennie and thereby prevent any future cruelty the world might do to him. As George narrates the story of the farm, the story that always soothed both himself and his friend, the mob's "footsteps" are heard "crashing in the brush" (103). George pulls the trigger just as the other men arrive. George tells them that he has wrestled the gun away from Lennie and killed him; George, in effect, does what the mob wanted and thereby saves himself and spares his friend the probable lynching Lennie would have suffered at the hands of the mob. Of course, by killing his friend, George is also sacrificing the element of his life that made it humane: friendship.

Similarly, the following paragraph from a paper on Elisa's feelings of frustration and isolation in "The Chrysanthemums" demonstrates both unity and coherence. In it, the author argues that Steinbeck draws the story's setting to prepare us to see the oppression Elisa Allen feels.

In "The Chrysanthemums" John Steinbeck tells the story of a farm wife whose life leaves her unsatisfied. She feels frustration because her gender role prevents her from seeing the world beyond the home that she so desires to leave. She is also frustrated that the only outlet for her prodigious creative energy and talent is the garden; that her talent is larger than her outlet is demonstrated by the almost grotesque size of the chrysanthemums she grows. Furthermore, she is frustrated by her distant relationship with her husband. One example of their uneasiness with each other is seen when Elisa "start[s] at the sound of her husband's voice" (2). But even before the reader is introduced to these characters or situations, Steinbeck presents the setting of the story as anticipating these ideas. The first two sentences of the story, in fact, introduce the notion that the physical landscape surrounding the Allen ranch is a site of both oppression and isolation: "The high grey-flannel fog of winter closed off the Salinas Valley from the sky and from all the rest of the world. On every side it sat like a lid on the mountains and made of the great valley a closed pot" (1). The first sentence describes a world that is separated by the "fog" from both the sky and the "rest of the world." This story, then, is going to take place in a world that is all its own, so we should be prepared for a place that feels limited to itself. Before we are even introduced to Elisa Allen, we are prepared to encounter characters who sense the limitations of their world. The second sentence extends the idea of

oppression to one of frustration. The fog sits "like
a lid on the mountains and made of the great valley
a closed pot." Because this is a story about a woman
whose domestic life leaves her frustrated and lonely,
the narrator's use of a decidedly domestic image, a
cooking pot, emphasizes and anticipates one of the
central conflicts in the story: that of a woman who
finds in her domestic responsibilities (cooking being
one of those) an insufficient outlet for her creative
drive. In fact, Elisa's actions show that she is desperate for a life beyond the "closed pot" of her married life.

Introductions

Introductions present particular challenges for writers. Generally, your
introduction should do two things: capture your reader's attention and
explain the main point of your essay. In other words, while your introduction should contain your thesis, it needs to do a bit more work than
that. You are likely to find that starting that first paragraph is one of
the most difficult parts of the paper. It is hard to face that blank page
or screen, and as a result, many beginning writers, in desperation to
start somewhere, start with overly broad, general statements. While it is
often a good strategy to start with more general subject matter and narrow your focus, do not begin with broad sweeping statements such as
Everyone likes to be creative and feel understood. Such
sentences are nothing but empty filler. They begin to fill the blank page,
but they do nothing to advance your argument. Instead, you should try
to gain your readers' interest. Some writers like to begin with a perti-
nent quotation or with a relevant question. Or, you might begin with
an introduction of the topic you will discuss. If you are writing about
Steinbeck's presentation of the effects of frustration in "The Chrysanthemums," for instance, you might begin by talking about how frustration is understood to affect people psychologically. Another common
trap to avoid is depending on your title to introduce the author and the
text you are writing about. Always include the work's author and title in
your opening paragraph.

Compare the effectiveness of the following introductions.

1) Throughout history, people have hated being frustrated. Think how you feel when you're frustrated: It
   makes you kind of crazy, doesn't it? In this story,
   Steinbeck shows Elisa Allen's sense of frustration
   and alienation by focusing on her thoughts, actions,
   and even clothing.

2) Psychologists are well aware that the human psyche,
   or internal self, is a powerful entity: In some ways,
   it is more powerful than the individual of which
   it is a part. The psyche is also a bit of a tyrant;
   it does not like to be ignored or disregarded. The
   power of the psyche is such that an individual who
   tries to circumvent his true nature will, eventually, have to face up to who he is and what he needs.
   For good mental health, Sigmund Freud advised being
   true to your psyche, even if your psyche's impulses
   contradict social niceties. In "The Chrysanthemums,"
   John Steinbeck demonstrates the power of the human
   psyche in the protagonist Elisa Allen, whose psychological struggles are demonstrated in her thoughts,
   actions, and even clothing.

The first introduction begins with a vague, overly broad sentence;
cites unclear, undeveloped examples; and then moves abruptly to the
thesis. Notice, too, how a reader deprived of the paper's title does not
know the title of the story that the paper will analyze. The second introduction works with the same material and thesis but provides more
detail and is consequently much more interesting. It begins by discussing psychological understandings of the psyche, gives specific examples,
and then speaks briefly about one psychologist's philosophy of the individual psyche. The paragraph ends with the thesis, which includes both
the author and the title of the work to be discussed.

The paragraph below provides another example of an opening strategy. It begins by introducing the author and the text it will analyze, and
then it moves on by briefly introducing relevant details of the story in
order to set up its thesis.

John Steinbeck's novella *Of Mice and Men* celebrates the power and poignancy of friendship. The friendship between George and Lennie, the two main characters, is a refuge for them: Their affection and shared dreams are "opposed sharply to the . . . sordid reality of the bunkhouse and the ranch" (Levant 125). George and Lennie reassure themselves of their future and their difference by the often-recited dream they share of a steady home with a farm where they will be self-sufficient and "an' live off the fatta the lan'" (15). The friendship they have is a difference remarked upon by nearly all the people in the story, who are not used to itinerant workers, or "bindle stiffs," sharing the road and a life together. What the events in the novel ultimately demonstrate is that George and Lennie are right about the importance of friendship: Human companionship makes all the difference in life. Those characters who lack friendship—and that would include all the other workers at the ranch—long and suffer for it. In *Of Mice and Men*, all the characters are driven by the need for friendship, but the story presents friendship as tenuous and therefore rare. The novella ultimately presents friendship as a nearly impossible achievement for individuals in an otherwise heartless society.

Conclusions

Conclusions present another series of challenges for writers. No doubt you have heard the old adage about writing papers: "Tell us what you are going to say, say it, and then tell us what you've said." While this formula does not necessarily result in bad papers, it does not often result in good ones, either. It will almost certainly result in boring papers (especially boring conclusions). If you have done a good job establishing your points in the body of the paper, the reader already knows and understands your argument. There is no need to merely reiterate. Do not just summarize your main points in your conclusion. Such a boring and mechanical conclusion does nothing to advance your argument or interest your reader. Consider the following conclusion to the paper about frustration and alienation in "The Chrysanthemums."

In conclusion, Steinbeck presents frustration and isolation as destructive to characters. Elisa is disappointed that she cannot seem to break out of her rut
despite her desire to change her life. Her sadness at
the end of the story indicates that, even when we try
hard, we cannot always change our lives. I guess that
is true for all of us.

Besides starting with a mechanical transitional device, this conclusion
does little more than summarize the main points of the outline (and it
does not even touch on all of them). It is incomplete and uninteresting
(and a little too depressing).

Instead, your conclusion should add something to your paper. A good
tactic is to build upon the points you have been arguing. Asking "why?"
often helps you draw further conclusions. For example, in the paper on
"The Chrysanthemums," you might speculate or explain how Elisa's frustrations speak to what Steinbeck is presenting as a human desire for true
connections with other people, as well as a desire for engaging work.
Scholars often discuss this story as a study in gender roles, and your conclusion could discuss whether the story presents gender roles as natural
or imposed. Another method for successfully concluding a paper is to
speculate on other directions in which to take your topic by tying it into
larger issues. You might do this by envisioning your paper as just one
section of a larger paper. Having established your points in this paper,
how would you build upon this argument? Where would you go next?
In the following conclusion to the paper on "The Chrysanthemums," the
author reiterates some of the main points of the paper but does so in
order to amplify the discussion of the story's central message and to connect it to other texts by John Steinbeck:

In the end, Elisa Allen's growing sense of hope, vitality, and connection is thwarted by her disappointment
in the tinker's callously disposing of the chrysanthemums that she had given him. The flowers represent her
creativity and her sense of self-worth. In his throwing
the flowers away, Elisa must realize that his interest
in the flowers, and in her, was a ruse to get work,
nothing more. That the story ends with Elisa's hiding

her tears from Henry demonstrates not only her sense of loss but also her ongoing isolation from her husband. Steinbeck seems to have acute insight into the psyches of women whose passions overrun the role that society permits; he revisits these frustrated female characters in the short story "The White Quail" and in the novella *Of Mice and Men*. And though Steinbeck's fiction does not offer a solution for the frustration that talented women feel in a male-centered society, his deft portraits lend the situation and the experience understanding and dignity.

Similarly, in the following conclusion to a paper on friendship in *Of Mice and Men*, the author draws a conclusion about what the novella is saying about friendship more broadly.

Ultimately, *Of Mice and Men* is a tale of an unlikely but sustaining friendship that cannot weather the cruelties of a brutal society. George cannot imagine the idyllic farm without Lennie, and when Candy asks if they can still pursue that dream, George responds, "It's all off" (95). To George, it is evident, the notion of a future beyond migrant farm work is impossible to imagine without his friend. That friendships are so rare in this world but are wanted by all suggests that the society in which this story is set prevents human kindness, companionship, and understanding. Because it is set in a specifically agricultural world, one that Steinbeck knew well from his life and work in the Salinas Valley, the novella asserts that the conditions of those who work on farms and are subjected to the demands of harvesting seasons are dehumanizing ones. Individuals who do seasonal work on farms and ranches, the book shows, are denied hope and humanity by their rootlessness and loneliness. George, after shooting his friend, walks away with Slim, who suggests a drink. George's going along with Slim symbolizes that George will replace the true friendship he enjoyed with the oblivion that drinking and, it is suggested, a night in a brothel will afford. Though the novel is set in a specific locale, the values it describes—friendship, love, human connection—are universal ones. By showing the profound sacrifice George makes to survive in the world, the reader is led to think about the sacrifices we all make to survive. Ultimately, Steinbeck's novella encourages us to value the friendships that enrich our common humanity.

Citations and Formatting
Using Primary Sources

As the examples included in this chapter indicate, strong papers on literary texts incorporate quotations from the text in order to support their points. It is not enough for you to assert your interpretation without providing support or evidence from the text. Without well-chosen quotations to support your argument you are, in effect, saying to the reader, "Take my word for it." It is important to use quotations thoughtfully and selectively. Remember that the paper presents *your* argument, so choose quotations that support *your* assertions. Do not let the author's voice overwhelm your own. With that caution in mind, there are some guidelines you should follow to ensure that you use quotations clearly and effectively.

Integrate Quotations:

Quotations should always be integrated into your own prose. Do not just drop them into your paper without introduction or comment. Otherwise, it is unlikely that your reader will see their function. You can integrate textual support easily and clearly with identifying tags, short phrases that identify the speaker. For example:

> The narrator describes Elisa Allen's face as "lean and strong."

While this tag appears before the quotation, you can also use tags after or in the middle of the quoted text, as the following examples demonstrate:

"That sounds like a nice kind of a way to live," says
Elisa.

"It would be a lonely life for a woman, ma'am," the tinker tells Elisa, "and a scary life, too, with animals
creeping under the wagon all night."

You can also use a colon to formally introduce a quotation:

Elisa's pride and enthusiasm is clear: "Oh, those are
chrysanthemums, giant whites and yellows. I raise them
every year, bigger than anybody around here."

When you quote brief sections of poems (three lines or fewer), use slash marks to indicate the line breaks in the poem:

As the poem ends, Dickinson speaks of the power of the
imagination: "The revery alone will do, / If bees are
few."

Longer quotations (more than four lines of prose or three lines of poetry) should be set off from the rest of your paper in a block quotation. Double-space before you begin the passage, indent it 10 spaces from your left-hand margin, and double-space the passage itself. Because the indentation signals the inclusion of a quotation, do not use quotation marks around the cited passage. Use a colon to introduce the passage:

The narrator implies Elisa's repression in the description of her tightly contained garden:

There was a little square sandy bed kept for rooting
the chrysanthemums. With her trowel she turned the
soil over and over, and smoothed it and patted it
firm. Then she dug ten parallel trenches to receive
the sets. Back at the chrysanthemum bed she pulled
out the little crisp shoots, trimmed off the leaves

of each one with her scissors and laid it on a small
orderly pile.

By now, the reader should not have any doubts about
Elisa's reliance on order.

The whole of Dickinson's poem speaks of the
imagination:

> To make a prairie it takes a clover and one bee,
> One clover, and a bee,
> And revery.
> The revery alone will do,
> If bees are few.

Clearly, she argues for the creative power of the
mind.

It is also important to interpret quotations after you introduce them
and explain how they help advance your point. You cannot assume that
your reader will interpret the quotations the same way that you do.

Quote Accurately

Always quote accurately. Anything within quotations marks must be the
author's exact words. There are, however, some rules to follow if you need
to modify the quotation to fit into your prose.

1. Use brackets to indicate any material that might have been
   added to the author's exact wording. For example, if you need to
   add any words to the quotation or alter it grammatically to allow
   it to fit into your prose, indicate your changes in brackets:

   > The tinker's arrival marks a contrast to Eli-
   > sa's controlled world. Elisa "watch[es] to see
   > the crazy, loose-jointed wagon pass by. But it
   > does[n't] pass."

2. Conversely, if you choose to omit any words from the quotation, use ellipses (three spaced periods) to indicate missing words or phrases:

> Soon Elisa throws herself into transplanting the sprouts for the tinker: "She kneel[s] on the ground . . . [and] scoop[s] [the soil] into the bright new flowerpot."

3. If you delete a sentence or more, use the ellipses after a period:

> The narrator describes Elisa's thorough appraising her body: "When she had dried herself she stood in front of a mirror. . . . She turned and looked over her shoulder at her back."

4. If you omit a line or more of poetry, or more than one paragraph of prose, use a single line of spaced periods to indicate the omission:

> To make a prairie it takes a clover and one bee,
> . . . .
> And revery.
> The revery alone will do,
> If bees are few.

Punctuate Properly

Punctuation of quotations often causes more trouble than it should. Once again, you just need to keep these simple rules in mind.

1. Periods and commas should be placed inside quotation marks, even if they are not part of the original quotation:

> Henry's effort with Elisa is clear: "You've got a strong new crop coming."

The only exception to this rule is when the quotation is followed by a parenthetical reference. In this case, the period or comma goes after the citation (more on these later in this chapter):

> Henry's effort with Elisa is clear: "You've got a strong new crop coming" (2).

2. Other marks of punctuation—colons, semicolons, question marks, and exclamation points—go outside the quotation marks unless they are part of the original quotation:

> Why does the narrator say that Elisa's "work with the scissors was over-eager, over-powerful"?

> Elisa interrogates her husband's observation: "Nice? You think I look nice?"

Documenting Primary Sources

Unless you are instructed otherwise, you should provide sufficient information for your reader to locate material you quote. Generally, literature papers follow the rules set forth by the Modern Language Association (MLA). These can be found in the *MLA Handbook for Writers of Research Papers* (sixth edition). You should be able to find this book in the reference section of your library. Additionally, its rules for citing both primary and secondary sources are widely available from reputable online sources. One of these is the Online Writing Lab (OWL) at Purdue University. OWL's guide to MLA style is available at http://owl.english.purdue.edu/owl/resource/557/01/. The Modern Language Association also offers answers to frequently asked questions about MLA style on this helpful Web page: http://www.mla.org/style_faq. Generally, when you are citing from literary works in papers, you should keep a few guidelines in mind.

Parenthetical Citations:

MLA asks for parenthetical references in your text after quotations. When you are working with prose (short stories, novels, or essays) include page numbers in the parentheses:

```
Henry's effort with Elisa is clear: "You've got a strong
new crop coming" (2).
```

When you are quoting poetry, include line numbers:

```
Dickinson's speaker tells of the arrival of a fly:
"There interposed a Fly— / With Blue—uncertain stum-
bling Buzz— / Between the light—and Me—" (12-14).
```

Works Cited Page:

These parenthetical citations are linked to a separate works cited page at the end of the paper. The works cited page lists works alphabetically by the authors' last name. An entry for the above reference to Steinbeck's "The Chrysanthemums" would read:

> Steinbeck, John. "The Chrysanthemums." *The Long Valley*. New York: Penguin, 1995. 1–13.

The *MLA Handbook* includes a full listing of sample entries, as do many of the online explanations of MLA style.

Documenting Secondary Sources

To ensure that your paper is built entirely upon your own ideas and analysis, instructors often ask that you write interpretative papers without any outside research. If, on the other hand, your paper requires research, you must document any secondary sources you use. You need to document direct quotations, summaries or paraphrases of others' ideas, and factual information that is not common knowledge. Follow the guidelines above for quoting primary sources when you use direct quotations from secondary sources. Keep in mind that MLA style also includes specific guidelines for citing electronic sources. OWL's Web site provides a good summary: http://owl.english.purdue.edu/owl/resource/557/09/.

Parenthetical Citations:

As with the documentation of primary sources, described above, MLA guidelines require in-text parenthetical references to your secondary sources. Unlike the research papers you might write for a history class, literary research papers following MLA style do not use footnotes as a means of documenting sources. Instead, after a quotation, you should cite the author's last name and the page number:

"Henry has no gift with words" (McMahan 455).

If you include the name of the author in your prose, then you would include only the page number in your citation. For example:

According to Elizabeth E. McMahan, "Henry has no gift with words" (455).

If you are including more than one work by the same author, the parenthetical citation should include a shortened yet identifiable version of the title in order to indicate which of the author's works you cite. For example:

According to R. S. Hughes, "We can also surmise that Elisa's marriage neither fills her time nor fulfills her desires" (*Short* 24).

Similarly, and just as important, if you summarize or paraphrase the particular ideas of your source, you must provide documentation:

Elisa Allen is frustrated by the company of her unexciting husband; she is seemingly undervalued by both herself and her husband (Hughes, *Short* 23).

Works Cited Page:

Like the primary sources discussed above, the parenthetical references to secondary sources are keyed to a separate works cited page at the end of your paper. Here is an example of a works cited page that uses the examples cited above. Note that when two or more works by the same author are listed, you should use three hypens followed by a period in the subsequent entries. You can find a complete list of sample entries in the *MLA Handbook* or from a reputable online summary of MLA style.

WORKS CITED

Hughes, R. S. *Beyond* The Red Pony: *A Reader's Companion to Steinbeck's Complete Short Stories.* Metuchen, NJ: Scarecrow Press, 1987.

——. *John Steinbeck: A Study of the Short Fiction.* Twayne's Studies in Short Fiction. Boston: Twayne Publishers, 1989.

McMahan, Elizabth E. "'The Chyrsanthemums': Study of a Woman's Sexuality." *Modern Fiction Studies* 14.4 (Winter 1968–69): 451–55.

Plagiarism

Failure to document carefully and thoroughly can leave you open to charges of stealing the ideas of others, which is known as plagiarism, and this is a very serious matter. Remember that it is important to include quotation marks when you use language from your source, even if you use just one or two words. For example, if you wrote, Henry has no gift with words, you would be guilty of plagiarism, since you used McMahan's distinct language without acknowledging her as the source. Instead, you should write: Henry's clumsy communication, his lack of a "gift with words" frustrates Elisa (McMahan 455). In this case, you have properly credited McMahan.

Similarly, neither summarizing the ideas of an author nor changing or omitting just a few words means that you can omit a citation. Jackson J. Benson's biography of John Steinbeck contains the following passage about the stories "The Chrysanthemums" and "Flight":

> This was the author's primary concern and a major theme throughout his fiction—he wanted the reader to discard the blinders of teleology and to see the whole as it really is. Even in short stories, such as "The Chrysanthemums" or "Flight," he is not just telling us about the frustrations of a rancher's wife or the tragic initiation into manhood of a Mexican-American boy, he is also—and for him, more importantly—defining the nature of reality.

Below are two examples of plagiarized passages:

Steinbeck wanted the reader to not be limited by the end
results of life but to see life as it is. By describing
in a nonjudgmental way the events in "The Chrysanthemums" and "Flight," Steinbeck sought to show things not
as they should be but how they are.

"The Chrysanthemums" and "Flight" are two stories where
Steinbeck is showing the whole nature of reality. He did
not want people to be blinded by teleology. Defining
the nature of reality: this was a major theme in all of
his work (Benson 246).

While the first passage does not use Benson's exact language, it does
list the same ideas he proposes as the critical themes behind two
stories without citing his work. Since this interpretation is Benson's
distinct idea, this constitutes plagiarism. The second passage has
shortened his passage, changed some wording, and included a citation, but some of the phrasing is Benson's. The first passage could be
fixed with a parenthetical citation. Because some of the wording in the
second remains the same, though, it would require the use of quotation marks, in addition to a parenthetical citation. The passage below
represents an honestly and adequately documented use of the original
passage:

According to Jackson J. Benson, a major element of
Steinbeck's fiction was the nonteleological description
of events. Steinbeck "wanted the reader to discard the
blinders of teleology and to see the whole as it really
is" (246). Benson sees this approach in "The Chrysanthemums" and "Flight," two stories described by an
objective narrator. In having the narration follow this
style, Benson argues, Steinbeck is trying to define
"the nature of reality" (246).

This passage acknowledges that the interpretation is derived from Benson
while appropriately using quotations to indicate his precise language.

While it is not necessary to document well-known facts, often referred to as "common knowledge," any ideas or language that you take from someone else must be properly documented. Common knowledge generally includes the birth and death dates of authors or other well-documented facts of their lives. An often-cited guideline is that if you can find the information in three sources, it is common knowledge. Despite this guideline, it is, admittedly, often difficult to know if the facts you uncover are common knowledge or not. When in doubt, document your source.

Sample Essay

Ingrid Adamson-Smith

Mr. Zicarelli

English II

October 20, 2006

THE VALUE OF FRIENDSHIP IN *OF MICE AND MEN*

John Steinbeck's novella *Of Mice and Men* celebrates the power and poignancy of friendship. The friendship between George and Lennie, the two main characters, is a refuge for them: Their affection and shared dreams are "opposed sharply to the . . . sordid reality of the bunkhouse and the ranch" (Levant 125). George and Lennie reassure themselves of their future and their difference by the often-recited dream they share of a steady home with a farm where they will be self-sufficient "an' live off the fatta the lan'" (15). The friendship they have is a difference remarked upon by nearly all the people in the story who are not used to itinerant workers, or "bindle stiffs," sharing the road and a life together. What the events in the novel ultimately demonstrate is that George and Lennie are right about the importance of friendship: Human companionship makes all the difference in life. Those characters who lack friendship—and that would include all the workers at the ranch—long and suffer for it. In *Of Mice and Men*, all the characters are driven by the need for friendship, but the story presents friendship as tenuous and therefore rare. The novella ultimately presents friendship as a nearly impossible achievement for an individual in an otherwise heartless society.

The relationship of George and Lennie is shown, at the beginning of the story, to be complicated but ultimately caring. George gets impatient with Lennie, but Lennie's total devotion to George is very clear. He imitates the way George sits, and he tries desperately to remember the instructions that George has given him (such as how to stay out of trouble and where to go should he get into trouble), but Lennie's slowness interferes with his ability to recall simple details. The only details that Lennie can remember are those that have to do with their dream for the future. Lennie knows the particulars of this dream very well, but he likes to hear George "tell about the rabbits" that Lennie will be in charge of on this hypothetical farm (14). George soothes and comforts both Lennie and himself by narrating a story of the stability, self-sufficiency, and safety that they will enjoy on their farm. The story of the farm is perhaps less important than the prelude to the story; the prelude "locates the good life in friendship, not in the material image of the little farm" (Levant 140). George starts his story of their future by describing how they are meant for a future beyond the imaginations of most bindle stiffs:

> Guys like us, that work on ranches, are the lone-liest guys in the world. They got no family. They don't belong no place. . . . They ain't got nothing to look ahead to. . . . With us it ain't like that. We got a future. We got somebody to talk to that gives a damn about us. . . . If them other guys gets in jail they can rot for all anybody gives a damn. But not us. (14)

George's description of the difference of their friendship is picked up by Lennie, who "delightedly" contributes his part of the prelude: *"But not us! An' why?
Because . . . because I got you to look after me, and
you got me to look after you, and that's why"* (italics
in text). The mutual affection between these mismatched
men is rooted in their common dream for the home and
farm, as well as their seeing in each other a bond of
friendship that fights off the petty cruelties of the
world.

The impact of living a life without the benefit of
friendship is expressed by many of the characters who
live on the ranch. Three particular characters, Candy,
Crooks, and Curley's wife, all seem drawn to the mystery of George and Lennie's friendship. Candy's desire
for belonging is perhaps the strongest because he feels
the most vulnerable to the world's lack of interest.
When he hears George's story of the future, Candy wants
to become a part of it so badly that he offers to
fund the farm with his savings: "Maybe if I give you
guys my money, you'll let me hoe in the garden even
after I ain't no good at it" (59). For an old, disabled
ranch worker, the possibility of a home and companionship emboldens him to later defend himself and Lennie
against Curley's criticizing wife: "And we got fren's,
that's what we got" (77). Curley's wife—a character with
no name of her own—is herself isolated and lonely. She
seeks solace in conversation with Lennie. When Lennie
tells her that George has told him not to talk to her,
her outrage and her loneliness are equally clear: "Ain't
I got a right to talk to nobody? Whatta they think I
am, anyways? You're a nice guy. I don't know why I can't
talk to you" (84). The tragedy that will shortly befall
Curley's wife—Lennie's accidental killing of her—makes
even more poignant her seeking conversation and friendship in him. Crooks is another character who is denied
companionship; his race keeps him segregated from the

other men. He too reveals to Lennie the pain of being without friends: "A guy goes nuts if he ain't got nobody. Don't make no difference who the guy is, long's he's with you. I tell ya . . . a guy gets too lonely an' he gets sick" (71). All three of these characters demonstrate a psychological need for friendship and the terrible pain of its absence.

The rarity of friendship in this world is immediately made clear in the story when George and Lennie arrive at the ranch. It is, as Shillinglaw writes, a "symbiotic dependency [that] is hardly understood" (xx). The owner of the ranch suspects that George's interest in the slow-witted Lennie is a scam: "You takin' his pay away from him?" When George asserts that he is not, the owner responds, "Well, I never seen one guy take so much trouble for another guy" (23). Slim, the one wise individual on the ranch, also remarks on the curiosity of friendship among bindle stiffs: "Ain't many guys travel around together" (34). Slim approves of George and Lennie's friendship. He says that more men should travel together and thinks that it might be fear that is preventing friendships: "Maybe ever'body in the whole damn world is scared of each other" (34).

Slim's theory about the scarcity of friendships is, perhaps, half right: Fear might very well lead to distrust and prevent friendships. In the world of migrant workers, though, the greatest barrier to friendship is the need to survive in a world where the individual has very little power. This fact is made evident when Candy's old dog is shot: Infirmity makes the dog unpopular in the bunk house, and when Carlson offers (really, threatens) to euthanize the dog, Candy's need to remain with the group prevents his stopping Carlson. George is likewise unable to save Lennie after the latter's accidental killing of Curley's wife. In fact, the same weapon (Carlson's gun) is used to, symbolically, euthanize Lennie. George has a need to survive, and Lennie's mistake is too grave for George to take care of (as George has had to do with Lennie's mistakes in the past). The mob is looking for Lennie to either commit him to an mental institution or, more likely, lynch him for killing Curley's wife; this mob is heard in the background as George prepares to kill Lennie and thereby prevent any future cruelty the world might do to him. As George narrates the story of the farm, the story that always soothed both himself and his friend, the mob's "footsteps" are heard "crashing in the brush" (103). George pulls the trigger just as the other men arrive. George tells them that he has wrestled the gun away from Lennie and killed him; George, in effect, does what the mob wanted and thereby saves himself and spares his friend the probable lynching Lennie would have suffered at the hands of the mob. Of course, by killing his friend, George is also sacrificing the element of his life that made it humane: friendship.

Ultimately, *Of Mice and Men* is a tale of an unlikely but sustaining friendship that cannot weather the cruelties of a brutal society. George cannot imagine the idyllic farm without Lennie, and when Candy asks if they can still pursue that dream, George responds, "It's all off" (95). To George, it is evident, the notion of a future beyond migrant farm work is impossible to imagine without his friend. That friendships are so rare in this world but are wanted by all suggests that the society in which this story is set prevents human kindness, companionship, and understanding. Because it is set in a specifically agricultural world, one that Steinbeck knew well from his life and work in the Salinas Valley, the novella asserts that the conditions of those who work on farms and are subjected to the demands of harvesting seasons are dehumanizing ones. Individuals who do seasonal work on farms and ranches, the book shows, are denied hope and humanity by their rootlessness and loneliness. George, after shooting his friend, walks away with Slim, who suggests a drink. George's going along with Slim symbolizes that George will replace the true friendship he enjoyed with the oblivion that drinking and, it is suggested, a night in a brothel will afford. Though the novel is set in a specific locale, the values it describes—friendship, love, human connection—are universal ones. By showing the profound sacrifice George makes to survive in the world, the reader is led to think about the sacrifices we all make to survive. Ultimately, Steinbeck's novella encourages us to value the friendships that enrich our common humanity.

WORKS CITED

Benson, Jackson J. *John Steinbeck, Writer.* New York: Penguin, 1984.

Levant, Howard. *The Novels of John Steinbeck: A Critical Study.* Columbia, MO: U of Missouri P, 1974.

Shillinglaw, Susan. Introduction. *Of Mice and Men.* By John Steinbeck. New York: Penguin, 1994. vii–xxv.

Steinbeck, John. *Of Mice and Men.* New York: Penguin, 1994.

HOW TO WRITE
ABOUT STEINBECK

WRITING ABOUT STEINBECK: AN OVERVIEW
Steinbeck's Legacy

JOHN STEINBECK wrote for 50 years. During that time he composed best-sellers, generated considerable controversy, was buffeted by the slings and arrows of mercurial critics, won over generations of readers, and earned the most prestigious recognition granted to writers, the Nobel Prize. But for all his literary accomplishments, he remained a man who remembered the exhaustion following a day in the fields, who sought to understand the alchemy of an old car's transmission, who loved telling stories and being near the ocean, and who always had a garden and at least one dog. Steinbeck's stories show his attention to and love for all of these things, but they also show his tremendous fascination with and affection for other people and other lives. His characters were of varying socioeconomic classes and of diverse ethnic and racial backgrounds, and Steinbeck sought to depict their personal experience of the world with the dignity and honesty that he espoused as necessary for human under-standing. "In every bit of honest writing in the world," he wrote in the late 1930s, "there is a base theme. Try to understand men" (The Martha Heasley Cox Center for Steinbeck Studies).

Steinbeck made understandable the misunderstood. His books depict the experience of the common person, the powerless, and the underdog with conviction, empathy, and poignancy. Steinbeck himself remains an underdog, at least to some critics. These critics find too many quirks in Steinbeck's work, too many odd characters, too many experiments in form, too many ideas, too much feeling, too much (or, sometimes, not enough) symbolism. Steinbeck aficionados counter that those quirks, those oddities, and those situations of highly charged emotion are exactly what make Steinbeck a humane, moving, and great American writer. This book will guide you toward your own analyses of 10 works by this great American author. By so doing, it will also help you learn how to read closely and write about any author.

Anyone reading Steinbeck is rewarded with his portraits of the natural beauty of California and Mexico, of human pettiness and exaltation, of history's legacies, of multifaceted families built and broken, of the myopia of institutions and mobs. Nearly all of these subjects are conveyed in the language of evocative yet earthy American English. His characters have crystallized in the American mindscape, and their situations and lessons can be conjured by the mere mention of their names: Lennie and George, Tom and Ma Joad, Jim Casy, Billy Buck, Doc, Mack and the boys. Their adoption into the American pantheon of memorable characters is a testament to the power of Steinbeck's craft and his insights into the American experience. Out of the mass movements, chaos, and cacophony of the age in which he wrote, he created single characters whose stories helped readers understand the grand scheme of their time. In his fiction and nonfiction he confronted artfully and movingly the social and political events of his era: both world wars, the Great Depression, the labor movement, the Vietnam War, the westward migration, and the demise of small American farms. Steinbeck told stories that made a difference for readers who afterward saw afresh the world around them.

Steinbeck wanted his work to be read and appreciated by the general population, and so it has been both in his native country and worldwide. Steinbeck's books are among the most translated and cherished in American literature. What will probably strike you first about Steinbeck is how accessible his stories are: As a student preparing to write an analysis of his work, you will certainly appreciate the lucidity of his narrations. The more carefully you read his stories, however, the more complexity you will come to recognize in them. *Of Mice and Men* (1937), for instance, is a story that appears to be a simple tragedy about simple people whom fate, unfortunately, brings together. As you read the story more closely, you will recognize that its simplicity belies the rich ideas it contains. This is not to imply that Steinbeck has put the meanings or themes of his story behind a veil that only professors can peer behind. Anyone who takes the time to reflect patiently will realize that *Of Mice and Men* features themes that all people can relate to: themes of friendship, love, home, isolation, and dreams. It is about the role that friendship plays in human experience and the toll that friendlessness takes on the individual experience. The universal significances are evoked in the humble stories.

Steinbeck is an ideal writer to write about. He rewards the careful reader who enjoys discovering insights not immediately apparent, while also welcoming the resistant reader, who quickly becomes aware that a gripping story can also serve as fodder for both personal reflection and good literary analysis. His work offers perpetual returns: If, for instance, you thought you had, in junior high school, mastered a story as simple as *The Red Pony* (1938), you will reread it in college and see there an idea more profound; a clearer, more lyrical voice than you remembered; a formal symmetry that you had not noticed before. Steinbeck proves again and again that his stories are worth second, third, and fourth readings. This volume aims to give you the skills that will make reading and writing about Steinbeck's fiction a generative and rewarding experience.

His Influences

Steinbeck was born in 1902 and raised in Salinas, California, a trading center for the central California agricultural industry 20 miles inland from the Monterey Bay. Both Salinas, where he grew up, and the Monterey Bay, where his family vacationed every year, would forge deep impressions on Steinbeck's imagination. The tales set in the Salinas Valley include the short stories and novels *The Pasture of Heaven* (1932), *In Dubious Battle* (1936), *The Red Pony, Of Mice and Men* (1937), *The Long Valley* (1938), and *East of Eden* (1952). When he could, the young Steinbeck (later, the older one too) would wander the hills around his uncle's ranch or tromp through the meadows, marshes, and farmland that surrounded the city of Salinas. He read the natural world with extraordinary attention, as is seen in the first chapter of *East of Eden:*

On the wide level acres of the valley the topsoil lay deep and fertile. It required only a rich winter of rain to make it break forth in the grass and flowers. The spring flowers in a wet year were unbelievable. The whole valley floor, and the foothills too, would be carpeted with lupins and poppies. Once a woman told me that colored flowers would seem more bright if you added a few white flowers to give the colors definition. Every petal of blue lupin is edged with white, so that a field of lupins is more blue than you can imagine. And mixed with these were splashes of California poppies. These too are of a burning color—not orange, not gold, but if pure gold were liquid and could raise a cream, that golden cream might be like the color of the poppies. When their season was over the yellow mustard came up and grew to a great height. When my grandfather came into the valley the mustard was so tall that a man on horseback showed only his head above the yellow flowers. On the uplands the grass would be strewn with buttercups, with hen-and-chickens, with black-centered yellow violets. And a little later in the season there would be red and yellow stands of Indian paintbrush. These were the flowers of the open places exposed to the sun. (4–5)

In this description of Salinas Valley plant species, we hear the voice of a person who has an eye on the smallest details—the "black" centers of "yellow violets"—of an entire valley of flowers. The narration also places human history in the natural world, with "the mustard . . . so tall that a man on horseback showed only his head above the yellow flowers."

Steinbeck's attention to the details of the land are consistently evident, no matter where his stories are set. He saw the world in a holistic way, so that the landscape and the humans who called it home were organically connected: Each gave rise to the other. This notion of interconnectedness is seen vividly in *Cannery Row* (1945), a novel set in the industrial fish canning district of Monterey. The interconnectedness of people and the land is here rendered through the idea of a tide pool, which serves as a metaphorical microcosm of the human and natural worlds. The details of the tide pool are rendered vividly in this section of a paragraph:

The lovely, colored world is glassed over. Hermit crabs like frantic children scamper on the bottom sand. And now one, finding an empty snail shell he likes better than his own, creeps out, exposing his soft body to the enemy for a moment, and then pops into his new shell. A wave breaks over the barrier and churns the glassy water for a moment and mixes bubbles into the pool, and then it clears and is tranquil and lovely and murderous again. Here a crab tears a leg from his brother. The anemones expand like soft and brilliant flowers, inviting any tired and perplexed animal to lie for a moment in their arms, and when some small crab or little tide-pool Johnnie accepts the green and purple invitation, the petals whip in, the stinging cells shoot tiny narcotic needles into the prey and it grows weak and perhaps sleepy while the searing caustic digestive acids melt its body down. (31–32)

The description of the tide pool in *Cannery Row* is not an elegiac appreciation for the aesthetics of the natural world as is the passage from *East of Eden*. Here Steinbeck is showing that the natural world is complex: not simply beautiful, nor simply brutal, but both of those things simultaneously. It is "tranquil *and* lovely *and* murderous" (italics added). The philosophy of this vision of the natural world, one that saw the world as neither benevolent nor malevolent but a complicated amalgam of all things, is one that Steinbeck would return to many times in his work.

The influence of science and the sea for Steinbeck grew in the 1940s when he began to study marine biology more formally with his close friend Ed Ricketts (1897–1948), a man who was the prototype for many characters, including Doc in *Cannery Row.* Science offered Steinbeck a respite from the acclaim and outrage he was drawing in the wake of the publication of *The Grapes of Wrath* (Shillinglaw, "Steinbeck" 1085). Though it surely appeared odd for a man who had just won the Pulitzer Prize in literature to take up science, considering how fascinated Steinbeck had been with the flora and fauna that composed the world around him, his foray into marine biology makes perfect sense. He would later write about his studies of science in some of his most celebrated nonfiction work, such as *The Log of the Sea of Cortez* (1951).

The natural world is an aspect of Steinbeck's work that you should pay close attention to when you are writing about his works. Personally, nature inspired in Steinbeck a sense of connection with the world; in communicating the world he perceived, Steinbeck enabled others to be sensitive to the wholeness of the world in its positive and negative forms. What you will discover is that his investment in the natural landscape is a constant and that the pleasure he took from seeing and conveying that world never wanes in his fiction. Whether a story is set in the West or elsewhere in the United States, or even in places that were not part of his direct inheritance, such as Europe or Mexico, Steinbeck would set the stage for his human dramas by first accounting for the natural world in which they took place.

Just as Steinbeck read the natural landscape around him, so did he read actual books and with the same passion and attention to detail; reading, then, was another formative influence. His mother had been a schoolteacher, and her story-loving family helped avail the young Steinbeck of the tales of Hans Christian Andersen and *Arabian Nights,* as well as the chivalrous novels of Sir Walter Scott (Shillinglaw and Hearle 5). These stories were popular at that time, so Steinbeck was not the only boy daydreaming of distressed damsels, duels, and honor. The fantastical tales eventually gave way to more sophisticated readings of the Bible, Milton's *Paradise Lost,* and novels by Gustave Flaubert, George Eliot, Fyodor Dostoyevsky, and Thomas Hardy (French 21). Steinbeck had a particular fondness for the stories of King Arthur in Sir Thomas Malory's *Morte d'Arthur,* a book that he would spend his later years studying and translating.

One element of the Arthurian legends that spoke strongly to Steinbeck was their atmosphere of moral conviction, a clear sense of right and wrong. This proves to be another pattern in Steinbeck's work. Some of his most memorable characters are those who are defined by their moral convictions and a desire to see the right thing done even when they personally suffer for it. Characters whose strong moral constitutions define them include Ma Joad and Jim Casy in *The Grapes of Wrath,* Doc in *Cannery Row,* George in *Of Mice and Men,* and Billy Buck in *The Red Pony.* The characters who gain a sense of social responsibility and selflessness are those whose growths are most sympathetic, such as Tom Joad and Rose of Sharon in *The Grapes of Wrath:* Both of those characters begin selfish and acquire, through suffering and loss, a belief in the importance of helping others.

Both of Steinbeck's formative imaginative influences—the landscape and literary idealism—come together in his fictional work. The worlds he knew—those of farms, ranches, and the sea—are elevated by the trans-position of the European heroic mode onto the California landscape. The migrant worker, the bindle stiff, the hired hand, the growing boy are all rendered poignant by the heroic style in which their stories are told. In one early work, *Tortilla Flat* (1935), Steinbeck uses the mock-heroic mode to affectionately portray the *paisanos* of Monterey; this too is the work where he most overtly transplanted the heroic ideal onto a central California population. *Tortilla Flat*, in fact, appropriates the language and form of the King Arthur legends. More generally considered, Stein-beck's early love of literary heroism ensured that his later stories were written with sensitivity and conviction.

Steinbeck's early personal relationships provided another kind of influence on his work. One of the relationships that most influenced Steinbeck was that with his friend Ed Ricketts; Steinbeck's biographer Jackson J. Benson argues that the men had a symbiotic, mutually influ-ential relationship (223). Ricketts was a philosophically-minded marine biologist, raconteur, and charismatic figure in Monterey. Steinbeck and Ricketts shared many days and nights studying the marine life of the Monterey Bay, carousing, and discoursing on the world, history, and their place in the scheme of things. Ricketts and Steinbeck developed a philosophy that perceived the world with dispassion and objectivity (they called it "nonteleological" or "is" thinking). This philosophical approach is evident in works such as *In Dubious Battle* and *Of Mice and Men*. In an instance of kismet, the mythologist Joseph Campbell (1904–87) then lived in Monterey and the three men, Steinbeck, Ricketts, and Campbell, spent a brief but important time together; it was through Campbell that Steinbeck became more aware of the archetypes made famous by Carl Jung (1875–1967). Campbell later said that he "may have learned more from Steinbeck about the relevance of myth than vice versa" (Benson 223). Certainly Campbell's expertise on Jung's theories of psychological archetypes must have informed Steinbeck's understanding of character. The male protagonists of "Flight" (1938), *The Red Pony*, and *The Grapes of Wrath* all experience a hero's quest that closely parallels the arche-typal quests of heroes that both Jung and Campbell discussed in their studies.

The idealism that is integral to mythologies materializes in Steinbeck's stories of working people, such as *In Dubious Battle, Of Mice and Men,* and *The Grapes of Wrath*. All of these books present characters who, despite their economic poverty, are questing for the knowledge and safety of self-sufficiency and a home in the world. While Steinbeck wrote tales that featured members of the proletariat, he was not a proletarian writer, though his idealism and sense of purpose were sometimes mistaken for activism. It is worth noting that Steinbeck's critical reputation took hits from both sides of the proletarian question: Whereas city fathers were so outraged by *The Grapes of Wrath* that book burnings were organized, literary critics and social activists were themselves soon outraged when he did not continue telling stories of economic injustice. Steinbeck bristled at the controversy and political jockeying that *The Grapes of Wrath* inspired, and he was offended by those who tried to pigeonhole his work. The fame and notoriety he experienced after *The Grapes of Wrath* was itself an influence on Steinbeck's work. For an essentially shy man, the vicious criticism that novel attracted compelled him thereafter, in many ways, to retreat from headline topics and return to his first love: a search for universal truths in the telling of stories.

Final Words

In 1962 John Steinbeck was awarded the Nobel Prize in literature, the seventh American recognized by that time. Though Steinbeck had during his career received some of the harshest criticisms from his fellow Americans, he was received in Europe as a great writer. The Swedish Academy stated that Steinbeck had been awarded the prize "for his realistic as well as imaginative writings, distinguished by a sympathetic humour and a keen social perception" (qtd. in Schultz and Li 304).

Before embarking on your own discoveries into Steinbeck's literature, it may be interesting to consider what the man himself felt were the universal roles of literature and writers. Below are excerpts from the acceptance speech he gave when he was awarded the Nobel Prize. With the myriad voices that we hear discussing Steinbeck and his literary legacy, it is important and fitting that you should hear from the writer himself. Before being guided through his works, you might find it edifying to read Steinbeck's own words on literature.

Literature is as old as speech. It grew out of human need for it and it has not changed except to become more needed. The skalds, the bards, the writers are not separate and exclusive. From the beginning, their functions, their duties, their responsibilities have been decreed by our species. . . . The ancient commission of the writer has not changed. He is charged with exposing our many grievous faults and failures, with dredging up to the light our dark and dangerous dreams for the purpose of improvement.

Furthermore, the writer is delegated to declare and to celebrate man's proven capacity for greatness of heart and spirit—for gallantry in defeat, for courage, compassion and love. In the endless war against weakness and despair, these are the bright rally flags of hope and of emulation.

TOPICS AND STRATEGIES

The sample topics provided below are designed to provide you with some ideas for how you might approach writing an essay about a work, or a number of works, by Steinbeck. The subsequent chapters in this volume will describe analytical approaches to single works by Steinbeck; the remainder of this chapter will focus on broader approaches to his works. Many of the samples will give you the titles of some possible works to focus on. Be mindful of the length of your essay when you are deciding on which works, and how many of them, you want to consider discussing. You will want to make sure that you have adequate space to give thorough treatment to each work you talk about in your essay. You are certainly free to select works not mentioned in the sample topics as well. Bear in mind too that if you choose multiple texts, it is important to have a rationale for grouping those texts in your essay. You might choose stories that were written at a certain period in history, or stories that explore similar themes, for example. The following section will offer topics to consider and will also discuss some of the notable elements of Steinbeck's work: the patterns in his use of themes, his construction of character, the history and context of his writing, the philosophy underlying his literature, the many experiments he made with the form of his stories, and his use of symbolism and language. Finally, this chapter will discuss the best ways to make specifically comparative analyses of Steinbeck's work.

Themes

As the discussion about his primary influences above suggests, Steinbeck wrote a great deal about nature and ideals. Much of his work presents the many connections he saw between nature and humans. This connection between people and nature is rendered in one of two ways: through showing how individuals are affected by the natural world or by showing how individuals are themselves a part of nature. This latter characterization of human beings as elements within the natural world is evident in the short stories "Flight" and "The Chrysanthemums" (1938); in the second story's figurative language we see that Elisa Allen demonstrates animal tendencies such as "bar[ing] her teeth." Steinbeck made such connections not to humble humans but to remind us that we are not above the primal instincts that we more readily associate with animals. The theme of the interrelatedness of humans and their natural context is testified to by the fact that nearly all of his stories begin with a description of the place in which they are set.

Steinbeck was interested in the organic connections between people and nature, but what stands out most of all in his writing are the individuals themselves. He was fascinated by how an individual comes to be, as is seen in his many coming-of-age stories such as *The Red Pony*. Some of the themes that recur in Steinbeck's work bespeak a fascination with individuals at odds with themselves or with larger forces. Consider, for example, the experience of the individuals in the labor trilogy: *In Dubious Battle, Of Mice and Men,* and *The Grapes of Wrath.* All three of these books demonstrate how individuals suffer at the hands of larger forces. *The Grapes of Wrath,* for instance, describes the experience of Tom Joad and his family as they are assailed by the ecological, economic, and social disasters that made so many Americans miserable during the dust bowl years. Jim Nolan in *In Dubious Battle,* a novel that describes the human experience during an agricultural strike, is killed by vigilantes and made into a literal prop by his fellow strikers. It is that much more poignant, then, that Jim sought a membership in a group that would give his life meaning. This character's search for purpose takes him into the middle of two groups—the strikers and the growers—whose larger natures overpower and, ultimately, obliterate him. The demands of society also overpower the needs of the individuals in *Of Mice and Men.* To survive in that world of itinerant work, George is forced to sacrifice the friendship that constituted his individuality.

There are less dramatic but just as moving forms of individual alienation in Steinbeck's fiction. Elisa Allen, the protagonist of "The Chrysanthemums," struggles with the social disapproval she perceives. Her industry and strength exceed the expectations of a farm wife, and her barely restrained outrage and frustration pulse palpably; her story demonstrates what happens to individuals who have to internalize feelings deemed socially inappropriate. Social propriety is also an alienating, stultifying force in the stories of *The Red Pony*. There the characters operate in an atmosphere of such artificial restraint that their true selves seem buried beneath their roles as father, son, mother, and hired hand. The vivid natural world of animals, valleys, and mountains contrast sharply with the human world inside the ranch house.

Steinbeck, in other works, demonstrated how social propriety can be gleefully counteracted. Both *Tortilla Flat* and *Cannery Row* promote values that run against the grain of the Protestant work ethic, materialism, and often notions of decency. *Cannery Row,* for instance, has Dora Flood, a brothel madam, acting out of a sense of human kindness and dignity that far exceeds that of the Monterey matrons. "Success" in these works is defined by how good a time one is having, how much leisure one has for philosophical confabulation, how successfully one avoids the bourgeois pitfalls of matrimony and a time clock, and how well one treats one's friends. Friendship and celebrations of friendship are the defining qualities for the characters in these two works, as well as in his more serious works, and friendship proves to be a bonding force that begets an alternative family structure.

Families, both conventional and not, are also important in Steinbeck's work. *The Red Pony* and "The Chrysanthemums" are cautionary tales of oppressive families. Some conventional families are demonstrated to be a source of strength, such as those in *The Grapes of Wrath, The Pearl,* and "Flight." The unconventional families, particularly the fraternal ones, generate as much love, loyalty, and strength as their conventional counterparts. Unconventional families include those in *Of Mice and Men, Tortilla Flat, Cannery Row,* and *In Dubious Battle.* Family in *East of Eden* is an idea, a fact, a practice, and a trap; that novel's depiction of family is complex and often paradoxical, but always a strong entity for its characters.

Sample Topics:

1. **Work:** What does Steinbeck's oeuvre say about work?

Select the story or stories that seem to you to have the most to say about work. Any Steinbeck story will demonstrate something instructive about work, but some especially good choices are "The Chrysanthemums," *The Grapes of Wrath, The Red Pony,* and *In Dubious Battle.* Study closely those characters that seem most accomplished or identified in terms of their work, and note how they are perceived by both the narrator and the other characters. How does work reveal truths about characters? You might notice how often Steinbeck's characters are at their most contented when they are working. There are a number of questions you might ask about work and characters. For instance, how much does work have to do with ambition? How might Steinbeck be commenting on the American Dream by having characters frustrated in their desires for work? How might Steinbeck's characters' desire for work be making a larger commentary on the human need for useful occupation?

2. **Individual and society:** How is the experience of the individual represented in Steinbeck's works?

Begin by selecting one or more works to focus on. Some good choices for this topic include *In Dubious Battle, Of Mice and Men,* and *The Grapes of Wrath.* How is the experience of the individual represented in the work(s) you have chosen? Consider also how individuals seek the protection of society. You might consider how individuals are absorbed or even destroyed by the stronger forces of society. An alternative approach to this topic would be to look for individuals who seek a life beyond the confining forces of society. Books such as *Cannery Row* and *Tortilla Flat,* for instance, both celebrate a counterculture existence.

3. **Family:** What do Steinbeck's works tell us about families?

You might focus on one or more of the following texts: *The Grapes of Wrath, Of Mice and Men, Cannery Row, Tortilla Flat, East of Eden,* or "Flight." Think about how families are created and sustained in these works. What, beyond blood kinship, are family relations built upon? Are created families constructed by mere circumstance, or is there something more profound that draws people together? Consider the value of families for individuals. Do Steinbeck's characters interpret their families as sources of strength, weakness, identity? Use your essay to make a claim that describes and evaluates families in Steinbeck's works.

Characters

Dreamers, philosophers, heroes, misfits—Steinbeck peopled his stories with a variety of character types, and the characters he included in his work help his readers understand what he wanted his works to say. Steinbeck often had a philosophical idea fueling a novel or story, and to that end he often used a philosophically inclined character who would reflect unambiguously on events within the story in a way that allows readers to think more directly about the story's ideas. *The Grapes of Wrath*'s Jim Casy, for instance, is a very philosophical character. Jim had been a preacher, but he relinquished the cloth because he was also unable to quit communing with his more attractive parishioners. In those moments, he reflects in the book, there seemed nothing wrong with this erotic connection, and he doubted his ability to preach against sin when he began to feel that "There ain't no sin." Jim Casy's is a voice of honesty and selflessness, and he has a profound effect on all the members of the Joad family, the newly altruistic Tom Joad especially. Jim Casy is one of Steinbeck's philosophers, and he is also a misfit because his notions of spirituality are technically irreverent. Other philosophers are likewise unusual characters: Doc in *In Dubious Battle*, Doc in *Can-*

nery Row, Slim in *Of Mice and Men.* Steinbeck's philosopher-misfits are in keeping with a literary tradition where the individual most aware of the world and what it needs, is the individual who only has one foot in the world.

Steinbeck wrote movingly about single individuals, but he was also fascinated by the experience of individuals when they are part of a group. He used the Greek word that describes soldiers walking as a single unit into battle, the *phalanx,* as a term that defined his "group-man" idea. Steinbeck was interested in how a single person's fundamental personality traits change radically when he becomes a member of a group. Steinbeck shows the phalanx at work in the frightening scenes of mob violence found in *Of Mice and Men, In Dubious Battle,* and *The Grapes of Wrath* and in stories such as "The Vigilante" (1938).

Another kind of group is that of a brotherhood, and one critic describes this as "Steinbeck's signature fictional relationship . . . male friendship" (Shillinglaw and Hearle 6). Groups of unmarried men abound in *Tortilla Flat, Of Mice and Men, Cannery Row* and other novels. The examples of truly idyllic and tranquil society are those of men who find family where they can and are satisfied by the friendships that sustain them.

Steinbeck also wrote about women, but with far less frequency. This is interesting in terms of his biography because Steinbeck responded to strong, intelligent, inspiring women, such as his agents, his first and third wives, his sisters, and his mother. Of the women who do appear in his work, Ma Joad is the towering figure of feminine heroism: Her altruism and generosity distinguish her throughout *The Grapes of Wrath.* Ma Joad is wise and tenacious and absolutely committed to the family. Two other female characters, who think of everything but family, are Elisa Allen in "The Chrysanthemums" and Cathy Ames in *East of Eden.* The latter character is especially interesting. The narrator calls Cathy a "psychic monster" and appears unable to make any sense of her. Elisa Allen's impulses, on the other hand, though enigmatic, are fathomable, and the narrator's sympathy for her is clear.

Sample Topics:

1. **Female and male characters:** Analyze and evaluate Steinbeck's representations of femininity, masculinity, or both.

For this topic you may choose from any number of Steinbeck's works. "The Chrysanthemums," "The White Quail," and *The Grapes of Wrath* are natural choices for this topic, but looking at the limited female characters in *Cannery Row* and *Of Mice and Men* could also yield very interesting analyses. You might begin such a topic by noting the female and male characters in your chosen work and recording as much as you can about their behaviors and characteristics. Taking notes such as these will lead you to questions about differences between the genders. For instance, how are female and male characters alike or different? Do they ever switch roles (that is, do characters ever take on the characteristics of their opposite gender)? You will want to consider the social context that Steinbeck was writing out of as you consider the representations of femininity and masculinity in your chosen text(s).

2. **Philosophers:** Analyze and evaluate the role of philosophically minded characters in Steinbeck's works.

When you consider all of Steinbeck's fiction, you will notice that his works often feature a character who thinks philosophically about the events going on around him. To answer this topic, you can choose from among the philosophical characters in the novel-length works, such as *The Grapes of Wrath* (Jim Casy), *In Dubious Battle* (Mac or Doc), *Cannery Row* (Doc), or *East of Eden* (Samuel Hamilton or Lee). One approach to this topic could be to consider how the philosophies of these characters compare with one another. Do they have the same values and perspectives? It would also be worthwhile to consider the experiences of these characters in their stories. In what ways are they isolated from the society around them? Do they choose this isolation or is it imposed upon them? Ultimately, what are the costs of being a philosopher in one or more of Steinbeck's works?

3. **Phalanx:** What kind of commentary does Steinbeck's work make about groups of people acting as one?

Steinbeck was interested in the notion of a phalanx, a Greek term that describes a group of men marching together into battle. Steinbeck's interest in this notion of "group-man" appears in his fiction in the many examples of individuals being transformed by their belonging to a larger group. Although many of Steinbeck's books and stories touch on instances of group behavior, "The Vigilante" as well as *In Dubious Battle, Of Mice and Men,* and *The Grapes of Wrath* would be particularly good choices for this topic. You might choose one of the novels and the story or two novels, depending on the length of your essay and the depth of your analysis. Begin by taking notes about how individuals are changed when in group situations (these can include unions, mobs, and, more broadly, social movements). How does the story or novel(s) present these groups of individuals? Are they threatening or galvanizing? Your analysis might find a variety of representations of groups. Based on your findings, reach a conclusion about how a phalanx affects humanity in Steinbeck's works.

History and Context

Steinbeck's belief in the interconnections between the individual and his or her social and natural context must surely apply to Steinbeck the man. To that end, his life in California had a deep influence on him. His fiction speaks to California's idealization as a modern Eden, to its frontier past, and to its anxieties about its identity. Works that most thoroughly investigate the California identity include two stories from the *The Red Pony:* "The Great Mountains" and "The Leader of the People." "The Great Mountains" is an episode in which a very old man from California's Mexican era, Gitano (Spanish for "gypsy"), arrives on the Tiflin ranch. He has returned from a lifetime of wandering to die in his birthplace (which, presumably, he had been banished from upon the Euro-American settlement of California). His arrival is a return of the past to the present and reminds the Americans that their manifest destiny was at the cost of others' destinies. "The Leader of the People" describes the arrival of another old man, Jody's grandfather, a frontiersman who led a wagon train to California. Grandfather remembers vividly his days of adventure and heroism, but with a jaundiced eye he observes the staid, workaday ranch world around him. That Grandfather is as spiritually displaced and out of sorts as Gitano suggests that the Americanization of California was an experience that was mutually unsettling. These stories also testify to the vitality of the past, even after generations pass: Jody, for instance, is concerned that there will never be another time as heroic as those of Gitano and Grandfather. The boy lives in their shadows.

Living in the shadows of the greats of yore is an experience to which the young Steinbeck would have been sympathetic. The heroic tales by Sir Walter Scott and of King Arthur that influenced Steinbeck so strongly as a young boy and man materialize in his 20th-century works. The archaic form of episodic story cycles, for instance, is used by Steinbeck in *The Red Pony*, *The Pastures of Heaven*, *Tortilla Flat*, and *Cannery Row*. The dialogue in *Tortilla Flat* and "Flight" approximates the medieval voices of Arthur and his knights. The Arthurian legends' ideals of honor, reverence, holiness, devotion, and fealty are reworked in *Tortilla Flat*. Steinbeck's own fascination with romantic medievalism constitutes a context that materializes in his fiction.

The social context most readily associated with Steinbeck is the Great Depression of the 1930s and especially the dust bowl refugees. Steinbeck's interest in the experience of migrant labor was long-standing, in part because of the agricultural community in which he was raised. His official experience with the dust bowl migrants was initiated when the *San Francisco News* hired him in 1936 to report on the experience of the waves of refugees coming into California. The desperation and exploitation that Steinbeck saw in the Central Valley outraged him and culminated in his series "The Harvest Gypsies" (1936). Steinbeck continued to study and interview the refugees and fulminate on their experience. This led to *The Grapes of Wrath*, the novel for which he is most justly famous and for which he was sometimes denounced. The novel's criticisms of bankers and growers made Steinbeck a vilified native son of Salinas. Not long after this he moved to New York, where he spent much of the rest of his life. California's cultural context would, however, continue to inform Steinbeck's work, albeit transcontinentally.

Sample Topics:

1. **California:** What do Steinbeck's works say about California as a region and an idea?

Steinbeck was a native son of California, and many of his most renowned stories are set there, so you could choose any number of his works to answer this topic. One way to answer this topic would be by looking at how California is represented in *The Grapes of Wrath* or *East of Eden,* two works that depict how the idea of California motivated immigrants to try their luck there. You might begin by noting the thoughts and dialogue of characters who discuss their dreams of California. Another approach to this topic could examine how residents of California contend with the dream aspects of the state. A third approach might examine how the natural landscape of California is an integral feature in a number of Steinbeck's works. How, for instance, does the natural world act less like a backdrop and more like a character? The story "Flight" is a particularly good example of this phenomenon.

2. **The Great Depression/dust bowl:** Steinbeck is best known for *The Grapes of Wrath,* a novel that chronicles the travails of a family searching for a new beginning west of the dust bowl. What do Steinbeck's works say about this period of American history?

You will want to begin by doing some general background reading on this tumultuous period of American history. Then, choose one or more works written or set in that time period, such as *The Grapes of Wrath* or *In Dubious Battle.* It is a good idea, once you have selected a text to work with, to narrow your focus to a particular historical element. For example, if you decide to write about the historical context of *The Grapes of Wrath,* you might decide to focus on the effect of economic ruin on relationships, either within a family or between individuals. For another example, if you decide to write about the historical context of *In Dubious Battle,* you might decide to focus on the effect that political activism has on families or individuals. Steinbeck was excoriated by many for his depiction of these fraught times, and it could be interesting to consider in what ways his fictional representations sought to produce social change or understanding. Furthermore, it could be worthwhile to analyze more generally what you think Steinbeck was trying to say about the people and the times during this era. With whom does he seem to disagree? What qualities or experiences does he show as valuable and heroic?

3. **The frontier:** What do Steinbeck's works have to say about the western frontier?

Begin answering this topic by doing some background reading, acquiring a basic knowledge of the American West. How did the western frontier energize the American imagination? How did the notions of personal freedom, unlimited land and resources, and adventure associated with the West become a part of the American identity? Examine *The Red Pony* and/or *Of Mice and Men* to determine how Steinbeck is commenting on the effects of the expectations of the frontier. In the case of *The Red Pony,* you could analyze how past adventuring both infuses with pride and stymies the Tiflins, a staid ranching family. In the case of *Of Mice and Men,* you might examine how the itinerant lives of the workers represent the loneliness that the West's freedoms created. Discuss the significance of any differences you uncover between the historical accounts and Steinbeck's fictional works. How do the stories reveal insights not accounted for in histories?

Philosophy and Ideas

Steinbeck's writing reveals how philosophically minded he was. Some scholars have seen in Steinbeck's work an incomplete fusion of philosophy and drama (that is to say, that the philosophy rather sticks out). This is a relative assessment. After all, Steinbeck wanted his ideas to be available and accessible to all readers. Many of his most cherished ideas—such as those about the tyranny of social respectability, about family, about threats to the individual, about the importance of acceptance and freedom and friendship and celebration—were discussed above in the Themes section. One idea dear to Steinbeck that merits discussion here is the philosophical notion of "nonteleological" thinking.

"Nonteleological" thinking is one of the products of the friendship between Steinbeck and Ed Ricketts. Together they aspired to an objective view of the world, a view that would observe with dispassion the world as it was, not as it could or should be. Ricketts coined the term *nonteleological* or "is" thinking to describe this philosophy. In many ways, this "is" thinking, with its lack of a moral mandate, was antithetical to Steinbeck's innate idealism (which wanted to believe in morality, in doing what *should* be done). *In Dubious Battle* and *Of Mice and Men* show the tension between these two very different worldviews; neither book presents clear villains, but they do show the effects of exploitation. Though villainy is indirectly presented, the reader intuits whom to root against.

Sample Topics:

1. **Nonteleological or "is" thinking:** Steinbeck aspired to a philosophy, developed with his friend Ed Ricketts, that sought to represent the world not in moral terms (that is, as things should or could be), but as it is. Where do you see this "is" thinking demonstrated in his works? Does "is" thinking sometimes give way to moral thinking?

You might begin this essay by examining the novella that is considered the most nonteleological of Steinbeck's books, *Of Mice and Men*. The original title of the book, *Something That Happened*, was a clear nod to the stoical "is" thinking that Steinbeck aspired to capture. A way that Steinbeck contributed to the nonteleological atmosphere of the story was through the use of an objective, nonjudgmental narrator. One approach to an essay on this topic would be to read the novella very closely to ascertain whether the narrator maintains his total objectivity. Did Steinbeck's attempt to tell a story with an objective point of view succeed? You might also consider whether the story evokes emotion in you; if it does, consider whether emotion seems antithetical to nonteleological thinking. The novels *Cannery Row* and *In Dubious Battle* are also examples of texts that attempt to exercise "is" thinking. Another approach to this topic could consider how this philosophical idea is evident in two or more works by Steinbeck.

2. **Innocence to experience:** What kind of commentary do Steinbeck's works offer on the individual's transition from innocence to experience?

Begin by selecting one or more works to focus on. Good choices include "Flight," *In Dubious Battle,* and *The Red Pony.* You will want to examine the movement that a character or characters make from innocence to experience, noting what activates the change as well as what is gained and what is lost in the process. Finally, you will want to theorize what Steinbeck is saying about the coming-of-age experience for characters.

Form and Genre

Steinbeck believed that writers are, or should be, storytellers first and foremost. Steinbeck ceaselessly experimented with the way he told his stories, and he said about his own work that he had "not written two books alike" (Shillinglaw and Hearle 3). Paying attention to the form of Steinbeck's fiction is important because it is so often related to the ideas in the work. Consider, for example, the form of *The Grapes of Wrath.* Steinbeck interspersed the chronological, novelistic story of the Joad family with "interchapters" that tell of the people, the land, the animals, the larger experiential context of the Joads' journey west. It is worthwhile to reflect on how the interchapters influence the ideas in *The Grapes of Wrath,* how they expand the novel's scope and insert a different, often more lyrical voice into the highly realistic saga of the Joad family.

The wide range of forms that Steinbeck worked within is impressive. He wrote short stories, story cycles, novels, playable novels, novels with intercalary or interchapters, family sagas, parables, and novellas. He wrote plays, screenplays, and documentary films. He wrote journalistic pieces and political speeches. He wrote voluminous letters; he usually, in fact, began each day by writing a letter to a friend or editor or editor-friend. These letters have been collected and published. He also wrote journals that documented the creation of his most famous novels:

These experiences are documented in *Journal of a Novel: The* East of Eden *Letters* (1969) and *Working Days: The Journals of* The Grapes of Wrath (1989). Steinbeck was fascinated by the formal properties of stories, and his desire to find the right form for his stories is evident in the many forms he used.

Sample Topics:

1. **Medievalism:** Some of Steinbeck's works use medieval styles, voices, and forms to tell their stories. How does the atmosphere of medievalism affect this stories?

   Steinbeck was raised on the medieval tales of King Arthur and others, and traces of this influence are seen in many of his stories. To address this topic, you might choose to examine the medieval forms in *The Red Pony, The Pastures of Heaven, Tortilla Flat, The Pearl,* or "Flight." The last three titles noted use a medieval speaking style. How does this style of voice affect our understanding of these stories? Most would say that this style lends a mythical atmosphere and formality to the characters and their situations. Critics of this style might argue that it makes the stories seem unrealistic and alienating for readers. It would be worthwhile to make your own argument for the effect that this variety of dialogue has on the stories. *The Red Pony, The Pastures of Heaven,* and *Tortilla Flat* all use an archaic story form that is often associated with medievalism: the story cycle. Another approach to this topic would be to examine how Steinbeck's use of these linked episodes or stories affects the novels. How are the episodes cohesive?

2. **Narration:** Examine the narration of Steinbeck's works and consider how narration affects the presentation of a selection of works.

   Looking closely at narration is an interesting and worthwhile approach to any work of literature. You want to consider who is telling the story and for what reasons, and you want to evaluate the values and reliability of the narrator. You should ask yourself how the narrator perceives the characters and events in his or her story. How do the narrator's opinions influence the reader's experience of a story? While any analysis of narration is invariably interesting, some particularly good texts to focus on are *The Grapes of Wrath, Cannery Row,* and *The Red Pony.*

3. **Form:** How does the form of one of Steinbeck's works affect its meaning?

Steinbeck experimented with a number of forms for his stories. These forms include short stories, story cycles, novels, novellas, playable novels, family sagas, and parables. Consider one or more works and how the form affects the story. You might imagine a different form for a given story and speculate on why you think Steinbeck opted for the form he did. In the case of *Of Mice and Men,* for example, how might the meaning of the novella have been different if Steinbeck had used a first-person narration for the novella? Which character, do you think, would have been given the narrative point of view? Ultimately, you will want to show how your analysis of the form of your chosen text(s) enables you to arrive at a new understanding of the piece's meaning.

Language, Symbols, and Imagery

Steinbeck, like all good writers of fiction, artfully used language, symbols, and imagery to convey his ideas and engage his readers. One of his most distinguishing contributions to American letters is his use of vernacular symbols and language. An example of a vernacular symbol that Steinbeck recognized as resonating in the American consciousness was that of the automobile. Both *The Grapes of Wrath* and *Cannery Row* meditate on the car, and the latter novel contains a humorous and thought-provoking passage that emphasizes how important to Americans the car had become:

Someone should write an erudite essay on the moral, physical, and esthetic effect of the Model T Ford on the American nation. Two generations of Americans knew more about the Ford coil than the clitoris, about the planetary system of gears than the solar system of stars. With the Model T, part of the concept of private property disappeared. Pliers ceased to be privately owned and a tire pump belonged to the last man who had picked it up. Most of the babies of the period were conceived in Model T Fords and not a few were born in them. (67–68)

Steinbeck identified the symbols that spoke to his readers, and he also spoke to his readers in the way they spoke to each other.

His use of vernacular language, with all its evolving novelty and natural vulgarity, is another legacy of Steinbeck's and one that had him in hot water during his lifetime. Some of his books—notably *Of Mice and Men* and *The Grapes of Wrath*—were banned because of the oaths and epithets with which his characters communicated and in which they spoke. Steinbeck wrote to his godmother about the controversial language in his books: "For too long, the language of books was different from the language of men. To the men I write about profanity is adornment and ornament and is never vulgar and I try to write it so" (Shillinglaw, "Introduction" xxv).

Along with the vernacular, Steinbeck employed other voices, such as the mythic voice that is operating in this section of *Cannery Row*, which describes the mysterious Chinese man who walks at dusk:

It had been happening for years but no one ever got used to him. Some people thought he was God and very old people thought he was Death and children thought he was a very funny old Chinaman, as children always think anything old and strange is funny. But the children did not taunt him or shout at him as they should for he carried a little cloud of fear about with him. (23)

The characters themselves take on voices appropriate to their idiom, sometimes at the deliberate expense of realism. Pepé in "Flight" for instance, proclaims his readiness for adulthood by repeatedly asserting, "I am a man." Pepé is, in essence, reassuring his mother of the rightness of his adulthood. In the story, Pepé grows from a boy to a man, and his final act, standing up straight to die, suggests that he was indeed ready for the mythic moment of his adulthood/death.

Sample Topics:

1. **Pop culture:** What is the effect of popular culture references in Steinbeck's works?

Peruse Steinbeck's works for examples of popular culture. These could include references to automobiles, to pulp magazines, to foods, or even to vernacular language. You might wish to look especially at *Of Mice and Men, The Grapes of Wrath,* and *Cannery Row.* Some conservative critics of the 1930s assailed Steinbeck for his use of "low" language and culture; are there other reasons he might have used popular culture references? In *Of Mice and Men* there is a moment when a character reading a western magazine sees in the letters section the name of a man he once worked with. Studying a scene such as this can yield fruitful analysis for the effects of popular culture on, in this case, itinerant workers. Is the excitement the character demonstrates a pathetic display of emotion, or is it a poignant demonstration of a desire to connect with the larger world? Consider what Steinbeck is saying about American society through his use of references to popular culture.

2. **Animal imagery:** What does Steinbeck's work have to say about the animal aspects of humans?

Select the work or works that seem to have the richest examples of humans acting in ways conventionally considered animal, such as the stories "Flight," "The Chrysanthemums," and/or "Johnny Bear." You could also consider how this idea and imagery operates in *Cannery Row, The Grapes of Wrath,* or *The Red Pony.* Does a character's acting like an animal suggest that humans are uncivilized or, instead, creatures of nature? Theorize why Steinbeck might so frequently describe humans in terms of animal behavior.

Comparison and Contrast Essays

It is both worthwhile and illuminating to assess two elements of literature in order to determine their similarities and differences. You might choose to look at two similar elements and spend some time focusing on their distinguishing characteristics, or you might select two dissimilar elements and examine them closely for underlying similarities. You can choose elements from within a single work, elements in two or more works by the same author, or even elements in works by different authors. Instructors assign comparison and contrast essay topics to guide you toward not only identifying differences and similarities but selecting meaningful elements and interpreting them. If you pay special attention to the significance of similarities and differences, your essay will amount to much more than a catalog. Readers appreciate seeing your analytical syntheses of the similarities and differences between and among literary elements and texts.

Sample Topics:

1. **Steinbeck's early work versus his later work:** How did Steinbeck's work change during the course of his career? What elements are consistent over the course of his career?

Compare and contrast the work that Steinbeck produced in his early days of the 1930s against the work of his later days (from the 1940s on). What differences and similarities do you find? Consider not only the writing style but also the themes that he explored. Are there themes that are consistent throughout his work, even if the form that they took is different? You might focus on a single text from his earlier and later period. Specifically, you could look at his two epics, *The Grapes of Wrath* (1939) and *East of Eden* (1952). In these two works, what similarities and differences do you see in his themes and his style?

2. **Steinbeck's work with that of another author:** Compare and contrast Steinbeck's work with that of another author to note and analyze differences.

You might choose to compare and contrast Steinbeck with one of his contemporaries, such as Ernest Hemingway, William Faulkner, or F. Scott Fitzgerald, analyzing the significance of the similarities and differences you find. For a more focused essay, you would need to narrow your scope, identifying an element to compare and contrast in the two authors' works. For example, you might select a story or two by Steinbeck and Faulkner and write an essay that compares and contrasts these two authors' treatment of family, love, poverty, narration, or history.

3. Elements across Steinbeck's works: Compare and contrast an element such as a theme or type of character across two or more of Steinbeck's works.

Begin by selecting two or more works that have an element in common. You might, for instance, have noticed that *Tortilla Flat* and *Cannery Row* deal with groups of male friends, or that *The Grapes of Wrath* and *Of Mice and Men* showcase similar shortcomings in the American Dream. Comparing and contrasting these elements across works will help you identify meaningful patterns and distinguishing characteristics. Similarly, you might analyze characters across novels. You might, for instance, compare and contrast storytellers in *The Grapes of Wrath* and *The Red Pony,* again looking for meaningful patterns or significant differences in these portrayals. You can, of course, also choose to compare and contrast elements within a single work. The novels especially offer abundant opportunities for single-work comparison and contrast: *The Grapes of Wrath's* male versus female characters, for example, or versions of success in *Cannery Row.*

Bibliography and Online Resources

Benson, Jackson J. *John Steinbeck, Writer.* New York: Penguin, 1984.

French, Warren. *John Steinbeck.* 2nd ed. Boston: Twayne Publishing, 1975.

The Martha Heasley Cox Center for Steinbeck Studies. "Works." 27 February 2007. <http://www.steinbeck.sjsu.edu/works/index.jsp>.

Schultz, Jeffrey, and Luchen Li. *Critical Companion to John Steinbeck: A Literary Reference to His Life and Work.* New York: Checkmark Books, 2005.

Shillinglaw, Susan. Introd. to *Of Mice and Men.* By John Steinbeck, New York: Penguin, 1994, vii–xxv.

———. "John Steinbeck." *Encyclopedia of American Literature.* Ed. Steven R. Serafin. New York: The Continuum Publishing Company, 1999. 1083–87.

Shillinglaw, Susan, and Kevin Hearle, eds. *Beyond Boundaries: Rereading John Steinbeck.* Tuscaloosa: U of Alabama P, 2002.

Steinbeck, John. *Journal of a Novel: The* East of Eden *Letters.* New York: Penguin, 1990.

———. "Nobel Prize Speech—1962." The Martha Heasley Cox Center for Steinbeck Studies. Retrieved 27 February 2007. <http://www.steinbeck.sjsu.edu/works/NobleSpeech.jsp>.

———. *Working Days: The Journals of* The Grapes of Wrath. New York: Penguin, 1990.

"THE CHRYSANTHEMUMS"

READING TO WRITE

JOHN STEINBECK's best work deals with individuals at odds with an unjust society. This dynamic in his literature is one that you will recognize in "The Chrysanthemums," which many consider Steinbeck's most accomplished short story.

Short stories are, by nature and by name, short; they are painstakingly and tightly crafted throughout. It follows, then, that for full understanding, stories require careful and multiple close readings. For instance, a close reading of the beginning of the story reveals the significant role of setting in "The Chrysanthemums." In fact, in only the first two sentences, the nature of the story's setting is established, and some of the more general significances of the story are anticipated. The first two sentences of the story contain many suggestive implications about the setting's role in this story:

> The high grey-flannel fog of winter closed off the Salinas Valley from the sky and from all the rest of the world. On every side it sat like a lid on the mountains and made of the great valley a closed pot.

The first sentence describes a world that is separated by the fog from both the sky and the "rest of the world." This story, then, is going to take place in a world that is all its own, so we should be prepared for a place that feels limited to itself. We have to assume that the characters we are going to meet will themselves sense, either consciously or subconsciously, the limitations of their world. The second sentence extends the idea of limitations and containment by the use of a simile and a metaphor: These two devices work in concert, describing the same image. The fog sits "like a lid [simile] on the mountains and made of the great valley a closed pot [metaphor]." Because this is a story about a woman whose domestic life leaves her unsatisfied, the narrator's use of a decidedly domestic image, a cooking pot, emphasizes and anticipates one of the central notions in the story: a woman who finds in her domestic responsibilities (cooking being one of those) an insufficient outlet for her creative drive. In fact, her actions show that she longs for a lifestyle beyond the "closed pot" of her married life. This conflict between her imaginings of the world beyond her own and the reality of her situation would make a good essay topic. To write such an essay, you would have to look for places where the setting checks her passions.

Those first two sentences, along with the remainder of that first paragraph, initiate a number of meaningful patterns that are repeated throughout the story:

> The high grey-flannel fog of winter closed off the Salinas Valley from the sky and from all the rest of the world. On every side it sat like a lid on the mountains and made of the great valley a closed pot. On the broad, level land floor the gang plows bit deep and left the black earth shining like metal where the shares had cut. On the foothill ranches across the Salinas River, the yellow stubble fields seemed to be bathed in pale cold sunshine, but there was no sunshine in the valley now in December. The thick willow scrub along the river flamed with sharp and positive yellow leaves.

The remainder of the paragraph completes the landscape's aspects. We deduce, from the mention of "plows" and "ranches," that it is an agricultural locale, and the diction conveys the harshness of this environment ("sharp," "cold," "bit," "cut"). You might ask why the setting warrants such a primary role in the beginning of the story. A good topic for an essay could focus on the role that setting plays in the story's central action. Is the environment depicted as a force conducive to growth or stagnation for its characters? Is it in the background or are the characters? How might the emptiness and solitude of the landscape set in motion the longings of the protagonist?

As you carefully read and question the story, also consider what elements of the story truly interest you. You will eventually want to limit your essay's task to a narrow field of inquiry. All good essays concentrate on a single aspect of a text; all great essays will convey the author's enthusiasm for the subject.

TOPICS AND STRATEGIES

This section of the chapter discusses various possible topics for essays on "The Chrysanthemums" and general approaches to those topics. Be advised that the material below is only a place to start from, not some kind of exhaustive master key. Use this material to generate your own analysis. Every topic discussed here could generate a wide variety of good papers.

Themes:

"The Chrysanthemums" deals with many themes, ideas, and concepts that fuel the action in the story. The plot of the story concerns the effect the arrival of a strange man has on a rural housewife, but the story is about much more than the plot. Some of the story's larger concerns are gender roles, desire, identity, and the imagination. Successful writers look to one of a story's central ideas and then consider how a story builds and treats that idea. This story uses repetition of language, action, and image and thereby establishes patterns of meaning. Tracking details such as the eponymous symbol, the chrysanthemums themselves, is crucial to an understanding of Elisa Allen, the protagonist, who so clearly values both the flowers and her talent for growing such monumental specimens. Considering how important her garden is to her will lead you to larger questions about her identity and, further, the acceptable outlets for her prodigious energy. Why does the tinker (or itinerant craftsman) pay so much attention to those flowers? Why is it so devastating to her that the tinker later throws away the sprouts? This story is very much Elisa's, so the ideas and themes of the text are refracted through her perspective.

Sample Topics:

1. **Gender:** How does the story illuminate and assess how gender expectations affect Elisa Allen?

To write an essay such as this, begin by identifying where the story highlights gender roles and then examine how the characters, particularly Elisa, heed to or undermine those roles. It would be especially important to isolate those moments where Elisa acts in ways that are considered conventionally masculine or feminine. From these meditations, a thesis can be developed about the effect that gender roles have on Elisa and on the story in general.

2. **Passion/desire:** In what ways is Elisa's passion for her garden redirected toward her sexual desire for the tinker? Does the story suggest that the garden is her substitute for sex?

This topic would require that you focus on scenes where the energies Elisa invests in the garden are described in ways synonymous with erotic energy. You would need to locate diction and action that would be appropriate for descriptions of sexual action. Furthermore, you would need to venture good analytical reasons for this overlap. Why, for instance, might there be so many sexual overtones in her hobby (another word for which is "passion")?

3. **Repression/liberation:** A great deal of Elisa's energy goes into containing nature: She mercilessly prunes flowers, banishes dirt from her house, and, later, pumices clean her own skin. But it is the antithesis of this containment of nature that she imagines she really wants: She covets the hardscrabble lifestyle of the peripatetic tinker. Is this a paradoxical desire?

This topic would force you to consider the drives that fuel Elisa's character. You would need to study those sections where she speaks passionately about what she really wants. The tinker says that his "ain't the right kind of life for a woman," and he is functioning as the voice of social expectations here. Your essay would need to evaluate what the story suggests happens to human drives deemed inappropriate by society.

Character

Good essays can focus on specific characters and their character development. Character development describes the techniques by which a character is created and made distinctive from other characters. We learn about characters through a variety of means: their physical descriptions (is he built like a linebacker or a jockey?), the way their voices are described (like a foghorn or a summer breeze through aspen leaves?), how they move in the world (like a robot? like a ferret?), how they interact with others (are they self-effacing or aggressive?), and what they think (in their heart of hearts, do they want to dominate the world or just get through life without harming anyone?). To write an essay on character, you would need to look to the cues and patterns of meaning that characterization provides. "The Chrysanthemums" gives more information about Elisa Allen than the other characters: The narrator's attention stays focused on her (though even he does not seem to fully understand her). Through character development, we come to know more fully the characters in stories. Elisa is a housewife, but the descriptions of her "terrier fingers," her "planter's hands," her "over-powerful" work in the garden tell us that she is not a stereotypical housewife and is, in fact, only reining in her profound energy and passion. Writing an essay on character development also necessitates close reading; here, you want to focus your close reading on the techniques of characterization.

Sample Topics:

1. **Elisa Allen's character development:** What does Elisa Allen learn from her interaction with the tinker? Does the interaction change her character?

An essay on this topic would need to track the characterization of Elisa: Does she change in her speech, actions, or comportment after she meets the tinker? The final scene would be especially important to an essay on this topic. What commentary is being made about her sense of her own identity when she entertains the idea of attending a boxing match and then cries "like an old woman"?

2. **Henry Allen as a character:** What kind of a figure is Henry? How do his interactions with his wife help us understand him? Understand Elisa?

The challenge of this topic would be to fully examine the clues with which Henry's brief but significant appearances in the story provide us. His fundamental confusion at his wife's behavior is important because it both demonstrates his inability to understand her (which could be either the origin or symptom of their mutual frustration) and provides us with another view of her.

3. **Character development in general:** How does the story present character to the reader? What techniques does it use? Are characters transparent and fully self-revelatory or not?

A paper on this topic would track how it is that Steinbeck gives insight into character. A possible technique would be to look carefully at a pair of characters and examine how they oppose, align with, or complement each other and how together they affect the story. For instance, an essay could talk about the way that dialogue works. What does it tell us about characterization in the story? What does it reveal about the characters themselves?

4. **The tinker as a character:** What kind of a figure is the tinker? What are the means by which we understand him?

This is an evaluative topic requiring you to analyze what information the story offers about this important but elusive character. You would need to examine his descriptions, dialogue, and actions since the narrator does not have access to the tinker's thoughts. The tinker's dumping of the chrysanthemums is, to Elisa, terribly revealing about him and about her too. A strong essay on this topic would consider his role in her life. In other words, what does his character reveal about Elisa, and what significance does the tinker represent for her?

Philosophy and Ideas

Another approach to analyzing "The Chrysanthemums" is to examine concepts that run through the story. This approach is related to the thematic approach in that it would track an idea in the story, but the result of this kind of an essay would demonstrate how you see the story as commenting on an idea in its more general form. For instance, what does this story say happens to individuals whose true natures are disapproved of by society? To answer this question you would need to locate places where Elisa's desires (for instance, to be independent and free) are deemed socially inappropriate. Then you would need to show how psychically harmful and perverting this repudiation is to her character.

Sample Topics:

1. **Nature and civilization:** Elisa's apparent civility slips on a number of occasions to reveal her more natural, indeed animal, drives. Is the story presenting the bestial drives in humans in a way that is critical of this drive, or is the story instead acknowledging the naturalness of this drive?

   This topic would enable you to look at the canine references in the story (of which there are many, such as when Elisa bares her teeth at the tinker). You would need to evaluate where you see nature superseding or overpowering civility and then draw some conclusions about how the story presents the tensions between those seemingly polarized behaviors.

2. **The nature of selfhood:** What is the story saying about the strength of our true selves? What happens to our true natures and desires when they are deemed inappropriate?

   This essay would require you to trace the trajectory of the energy that Elisa has so much of and that the story frequently mentions. You would need to analyze what you see as the origin of her energy (what it really seems to spring from) and the directions toward which her energy is focused. Why are her endeavors so often described in ways that suggest excess? The psychological notion of displacement (a human coping mechanism that directs desire for the taboo onto something considered appropriate) might be a useful concept to incorporate into this essay topic.

3. **Affinity:** How is affinity, or human connection, presented as important for Elisa? How do we see her responsive to, and vulnerable to, the suggestion of even a nascent affinity with the tinker? Is this feeling demonstrated to be a motivating force for individuals in this story overall?

To address this topic, you would need to demonstrate that Elisa is isolated and feels a lack of connection to her husband before the tinker's appearance at her ranch. You might postulate how her lack of connection to Henry results in a surplus of attention elsewhere—to her garden, for instance. You would need to identify those actions that suggest a desire for connection or affinity that Elisa demonstrates toward the tinker. In what ways does she show this, and how does the tinker capitalize on this desire of hers? From this discussion you could deduce what the story is saying about the power of affinity for individuals.

Form and Genre

In the case of "The Chrysanthemums," the genre is fiction and, more specifically, the short story. This assessing classification is more than a simple matter of defining the work; in its very categorization there is the opportunity for analysis and commentary. The 19th-century writer Edgar Allan Poe theorized about the determining characteristics of the short story form, and he claimed that stories should be singular in their "effects" on the reader. One worthwhile approach, then, to a discussion on "The Chrysanthemums" is to consider what "effect" or response in the reader the story evokes. Of course, different readers will respond in different ways to a story, but you could theorize that the effect of "The

Chrysanthemums" is, for example, isolation. If you theorized this, then your essay could build a case for how the story's different elements come together to construct this effect. The same fundamental approach could be used if you deemed the story's effect to be something other than isolation. The question of form in this story is another good approach to writing an essay. Form considers the techniques by which a story is shaped or structured, and an essay on this story could include discussions of point of view, dialogue, or style.

Sample Topics:

1. **"The Chrysanthemums" as short story:** "The Chrysanthemums" is a short story. This fact of form, seemingly obvious, is worthy of analysis. Discuss the story's fictive techniques. How does the story achieve its dramatic effects? In what ways are the "truths" of the story revealed or produced?

   This topic asks you to pay attention to how the story operates as a short story, and one approach would be to look specifically at how the story is constructed. How does the story render feeling and opinion? How do we know, for instance, that Elisa is unhappy in her marriage? Another way to look at this topic would be to consider how tension—one of the dramatic bedrocks of this story—is built. There is tension, for instance, in the diametrical oppositions of Elisa and the tinker (e.g., in their physical selves and social roles), though Elisa attempts to bridge this seemingly insurmountable social chasm by identifying with the tinker's life and values. An essay on this topic could look to the ways in which the story constructs and presents their differences as a means to establish the dramatic effect of tension.

2. **Point of view in "The Chrysanthemums":** The narrator in "The Chrysanthemums" describes what he (or she) sees, but he is not omniscient, or all-knowing. What effect does his limited perception have on the story? Is this limitation a means by which an idea in the story is emphasized?

This topic asks you to assess the impact of the narrative point of view on the story. Elisa Allen is the focus of the narrator's attention, but does he ever describe her thoughts or feelings (either of which would show omniscience)? If the narrator is more simply a disembodied and baffled observer, what effect does this stylistic choice have on the story? Furthermore, how might the narrator's uncertainty further the aims of the story? Answering this last question would synthesize your opinion about the significant effect of the story's form.

3. **The role of setting in "The Chrysanthemums":** Setting performs an important function in this story. In what ways does setting provide conflict for the characters? How is the setting rendered and, more broadly, what details of setting are emphasized to both further the goals of the story and lend verisimilitude to the story's events?

Though setting can be a simple physical backdrop, this topic asks you to consider how the setting is a force in its own right. This discussion should take into account the beginning paragraphs of the story (discussed above in "Reading to Write") and its descriptions of the landscape. You would need to isolate the details by which setting is created, notice which details the narrator selects, and evaluate the reasons those details are focused on. The question of authenticity or verisimilitude (a literary term defined as the appearance, in art, of truth or reality) can be a means by which to investigate the particular details of place in this story. How does Steinbeck's story attempt to seem real? Verisimilitude is a goal for a realistic text (such as "The Chrysanthemums") and is an aspect of form well worth an essay.

Language, Symbols, and Imagery

Language, symbols, and imagery are some of the creative means by which an author conveys certain feelings or ideas that would, if simply announced, be undermined in their imaginative and evocative power.

Consider the figurative (nonliteral) examples of when, for instance, a female character *barks* a greeting and another one *purrs* a greeting. The narrator is using animal imagery—here, verbs customarily associated with animals canine and feline, respectively. By using this language, the story could be suggesting that these particular females are like animals in the way they behave. Another possibility is that the language is suggesting a broader philosophy, and that the women are, like all humans, animal at the core. Without the framework or context of a longer narrative, we cannot know the exact nuance of these suggestive descriptions, but we do know that something animal is afoot because the language choices, or diction, of "barks" and "purrs" indicates this.

All writers, but those of imaginative fiction especially, use language deliberately and choose words based on their connotative, or suggestive, meanings. As you read fiction in preparation for writing about it, you should be alert to the connotative meanings of language, even as you understand the surface meaning of language in order to follow the plot itself. In the case of Steinbeck's "The Chrysanthemums," the language is tightly controlled and relies on the declarative assertions provided by metaphors (e.g., "her terrier fingers") and active verbs (e.g., "her eyes sharpened"). Steinbeck's language is boiled down in the sense that it feels shorn of superfluous descriptions. This writing style is itself an interesting topic for an essay on this story because the prose is as constrained as Elisa and Henry Allen themselves. In this sense, the writing style echoes its characters. Writers deliberately use language and imagery, or figurative language that represents objects, actions, or ideas, to make significances clearer and more evocative.

Symbols, usually used in conjunction with imagery, are objects, either animate or inanimate, that writers also use to convey ideas. A dove, for instance, has come to be a symbol of peace. Most literature would not, however, use a dove in art in such a transparent, straightforward way—doing so would not pack much imaginative punch because a dove is, at this point, a cliché (a hazard writers avoid) and would inspire nothing in the reader but the automatic assumption that it is a stand-in for the idea of peace. Ideally, imaginative writers will use symbols in more nuanced ways and you, as a scholar of literature, should treat symbols in the same way. In "The Chrysanthemums," the flowers themselves are a potent symbol, though what they represent shifts during the story. They are rather tragic symbols in that they signify, in turn, Elisa's triumph, her pride, and her defeat. It is important, when writing about symbolism, that you do not oversimplify the symbol itself. Oversimplification, for this story, could be a reading that claimed that the flowers symbolize the children Elisa does not have. While there might be some validity to that interpretation, such a reading would overlook the larger implications of what the flowers represent. The best essays on symbolism will look at the symbol and, perhaps, its affiliated imagery and consider these subjects in relation to the story's larger ideas. When you are asked to discuss symbolism, you are being asked to discuss what something signifies, means, and represents in light of the entire work.

Sample Topics:

1. **The symbolism of the flowers in "The Chrysanthemums":** The flowers carry considerable dramatic and symbolic weight in this story. Analyze what they signify to Elisa and, more broadly, what they might symbolize about her.

   To answer this topic you would need to look at the symbolic import of the flowers from two angles. The first angle is from Elisa's point of view, which we can glean from the opinions she delivers to her husband and the tinker. The second angle is more general, from the point of view of the overall story. A successful essay on this topic will look at the flowers in their integrated context and will not reductively claim that the flowers stand for one simple thing. You might note how she treats them, by turns savagely and lovingly. Elisa's declarations about the flowers suggest the considerable meaning she applies to those chrysanthemums. That the story begins and ends with her and the flowers tells us they are gauges, in a sense, of her feelings.

2. **Images of physicality:** Though they never really touch, Elisa and the tinker interact with each other through very physical

means. Analyze the importance of physical gestures and cues and theorize what the story is saying about physicality.

To respond to this topic would require reading for the descriptions of physical gesture that Elisa and the tinker make during their interaction. These gestures (facial expressions, near touches, even breathing) are patterned so deliberately that they supersede action or plot and become a set of images. A good essay on this topic would assess the role of physical expression in the meaning of this story. What does physicality reveal that words conceal? A further question to consider in light of this topic on physicality: Why do you think Elisa is interested in the highly physical sport of boxing?

3. **Clothing:** When the narrator announces that the dress Elisa wears toward the end of the story is "the symbol of her prettiness," he is calling our attention to the larger meanings of the dress. In fact, the clothing Elisa wears, takes off, and dons is foregrounded in the descriptions of her. Analyze the significances of her garb. Consider what we learn about her based on her clothes and how her clothes reflect her evolution in the story.

To address this topic, you would need to look closely at those scenes that highlight what Elisa wears. What does it mean, for instance, that she wears such concealing and masculine clothing at the beginning of the story and such feminine clothing at the end? This topic calls also for analysis of the bathing scene; it functions as both a toilette and a baptism, and is a significant transition point for her character. The final moments of the story see Elisa concealing her crying from her husband by pulling up the collar of her coat (hiding, in effect, within her clothing). Overall, what is the story saying about the symbolic power of clothing?

4. **Spatial imagery:** Consider how space is parceled out, protected, and divided in this story. Analyze the boundaries described

and the reasons the tinker crosses borders that Henry does not. What might these spaces reveal about the characters?

This topic asks you to analyze the markers of space (choose from among gates, the driveway, gardens, doors, doorways, walls, etc.) in the story and to consider their symbolic significance for the story and the characters. Elisa is a character who seems very aware of, even vigilant about, space; despite her vigilance, she invites the tinker into her garden (while her husband stays outside the garden fence). Another approach to this topic would be to consider how space seems gendered (that is, masculine or feminine) in this story. How do we see Henry and Elisa protecting their own gendered spheres? Do they repel incursions into their spheres, or are they more inviting to outsiders? What might their policies on space tell us about their characters and their situations?

Comparison and Contrast

Comparing components of a story in order to explain and analyze the similarities or differences between them is a useful approach to writing an essay. It is important to avoid the pitfall of merely creating a catalog or list of such similarities or differences in a work; instead, you must take the necessary step of commenting on these observations. Essays that do not study the significance of points of comparison are ineffective because they show only the writer's ability to identify, not analyze. To begin a comparison/contrast essay you might compare characters with each other: How does the tinker compare to Henry Allen? How does Henry Allen compare to Elisa, his wife? You could also compare characters (or other elements of the story like patterns of imagery or action) across different stories. For example, how do the depictions of nature compare in "The Chrysanthemums" and *The Red Pony?* The challenge of this kind of essay is deciding what the similarities or differences you identify might mean. These are the questions that make essays interesting and the ones that will have different answers for each writer. To get to these questions, it is helpful to think about what kinds of effects Steinbeck achieves by producing either similarities or differences between the elements of his stories. What, for example, do the differences between the Allens' dogs and the tinker's dog do for our understanding of these characters and their position in the world? It is not sufficient to identify a pattern and to point to the existence of similarities or differences; you must also consider what purpose those similarities or differences might serve in the story overall.

Sample Topics:

1. **Contrasting the domiciles of Elisa and the tinker:** Though the tinker does not have a house, he does have a home in his wagon. Compare the distinctive qualities of the tinker's wagon and Elisa's home. What do their homes suggest about their social position, their characterization? Because the homes are such opposites, consider finding the ways in which these domiciles share similarities. What kind of commentary on "home" can be drawn from this kind of comparison?

   Because the respective domiciles of Elisa and the tinker are drawn as such clear opposites, it would be worthwhile to look instead at how they share certain qualities. How, for instance, are the homes extensions of their inhabitants? Another approach to this topic could answer this question: What is the relationship between work and home for these two characters? A question that might be useful to consider in formulating your ideas about this topic: What does it signify that the tinker's wagon—described as so different from Elisa's Allen's house—becomes the object of her envy and the source of her fantasies of independence?

2. **Comparing communication styles:** The stilted and defensive way that Elisa reacts to her husband's attempts at communication is very suggestive of how she feels about him: She "start[s] at the sound of her husband's voice" and "sets" herself in anticipation of his arrival. Her interactions with the tinker are, by contrast, characterized by informality, ease, and even some humor. Compare the styles of communication in this story and evaluate the significance of communication styles overall.

This topic asks you to look carefully at the ways in which communication is presented in the story and to evaluate what communication, in a more general sense, tells us. Does Elisa's ease of communication with the tinker suggest that these two individuals are soul mates in a way that Elisa and her husband are not? Is the story presenting communication styles as indicative of some truth or only a ruse? Or are the styles perhaps fundamentally irrelevant?

3. **Compare women and gardens in "The Chrysanthemums" and "The White Quail":** Steinbeck wrote two short stories in which female characters are deeply invested in their gardens. Compare elements of these gardening women and consider in what ways, if any, their passions for gardening function differently and how the symbolic role of the garden functions in the stories more broadly.

This topic asks you to compare a commonality in two specific stories. A successful essay on this topic will evaluate how gardens build characterization for both Elisa Allen and Mary Teller and will theorize on the function of gardens for each character. How does a garden serve the energies of these women in a way that is different from other conventionally feminine vocations, such as a cooking or sewing? Another fruitful approach would be to consider the symbolic role of the garden in both stories. A good conclusion would then evaluate the function of the garden for the respective characters and the symbolic role of the garden in the stories.

Bibliography for "The Chrysanthemums"

Bloom, Harold, ed. *John Steinbeck*. Bloom's Major Short Story Writers. Broomall, PA: Chelsea House, 1999.

Busch, Christopher S. "Longing for the Lost Frontier: Steinbeck's Vision of Cultural Decline in 'The White Quail' and 'The Chrysanthemums.'" *Steinbeck Quarterly* 26. 3/4 (Summer–Fall 1993): 81–90.

"The Chrysanthemums." *Short Stories for Students.* Vol. 6. Farmington Hills, MI: Gale, 1999. 59–82.

Hughes, R. S., ed. *John Steinbeck: A Study of the Short Fiction.* Boston: Twayne, 1989.

Palmerino, Gregory J. "Steinbeck's 'The Chrysanthemums.'" *Explicator* 62. 3 (Spring 2004): 164–68.

THE RED PONY

READING TO WRITE

THOUGH ORIGINALLY published separately, the four stories of *The Red Pony*, "The Gift," "The Great Mountains," "The Promise," and "The Leader of the People," together constitute one story cycle and can be considered and written about as a single work of fiction. One of the common themes in the stories is that of change. Change is not limited to theme: It is also an aspect of the setting and a dynamic that can serve as a topic for a good essay. For example, a writer might examine the varieties of change in the story and assess how the constancy of change reflects the story's overall philosophy of life. No matter what topic a writer chooses to write about, he or she must first grapple with Steinbeck's language. This section of the chapter will demonstrate how to read a particular passage of *The Red Pony* in preparation for writing an essay.

The first story, "The Gift," opens with Billy Buck starting his workday on the Tiflin ranch. This beginning is an interesting aspect of the story and its interpretation: Why is it that a story about Jody Tiflin's coming of age begins not with the boy or his father but with a ranch hand? Billy Buck will prove to be a pivotal character in the story, and the reader, like Jody himself, will come to rely on Billy Buck's steadfastness, humanity, wisdom, and good sense as measures against which to gauge other characters and their actions. Billy Buck is the character that Jody looks to for guidance in his shifting world.

A full understanding of literature is gained by careful, close readings of passages. As you read closely, be aware of details of language, characterization, setting, and conflicts, and look for what these details are telling you about the story. In the first few pages of *The Red Pony*, we see that Jody is sensing the changes that he is on the verge of experiencing and, to a certain degree, understanding. The following passage is from a paragraph that describes Jody's walking around the ranch on the morning that the story begins. As you read it, mark details that will help you understand what is being established about change:

> Jody looked along at the farm buildings. He felt an uncertainty in the air, a feeling of change and of loss and of the gain of new and unfamiliar things. Over the hillside two big black buzzards sailed low to the ground and their shadows slipped smoothly and quickly ahead of them. Some animal had died in the vicinity. Jody knew it. It might be a cow or it might be the remains of a rabbit. The buzzards overlooked nothing. Jody hated them as all decent things hate them, but they could not be hurt because they made away with carrion.

This passage is laden with significance that will prove useful for an understanding of the entirety of the story. The first task in approaching this passage would be to determine what kind of information it conveys. One important fact is unequivocally stated: Jody "felt an uncertainty in the air." That this disclosure is followed by the sighting of buzzards is significant: To Jody, the buzzards signal death because they live off the remains of dead animals. Therefore, the implication being made here is that the changes ahead will be fatal or, on a more symbolic level, threatening. Furthermore, the changes, like the buzzards, "will slip smoothly and quickly." The other important fact is that the buzzards are necessary presences: "they could not be hurt because they made away with carrion." The narrator is suggesting that it is a universal truth that though repellent to "all decent things," the buzzards are necessary for the health of the ranch and, more broadly, the ecosystem on which the ranch depends. The necessity of death or change for healthy life is evident here, and even if Jody does not yet fully understand this complementary dynamic, he recognizes its fundamental truths on a subconscious level. Larger questions that arise from this section could prove worthwhile to address in an essay. For instance, how does the story depict the reciprocal relationship of a ranch and its landscape? Why, in a story about growth, is so much emphasis placed on death? Exploring these questions could lead to an essay dealing with the complicated question of what this story is really about.

A slow and careful reading of *The Red Pony* will better enable you to recognize the patterns, issues, and ideas in the stories. Reading slowly and taking notes will make for a more enriched understanding of the stories, while also enabling you to gather the evidence you need to write a strong essay.

TOPICS AND STRATEGIES

This section of the chapter discusses various possible topics for essays on *The Red Pony* and general approaches to those topics. Be advised that the material below is only a place to start from, not some kind of exhaustive master key. Use this material to generate your own analysis. Every topic discussed here could encompass a wide variety of good papers.

Themes

The stories that constitute *The Red Pony* include many themes, ideas, and concepts that propel the action. Some of these ideas include change (as discussed above) and loss, growth, nature, coming of age, the challenges of love, the legacies of the past, and the expectations of manhood. Writers approaching the story often begin by identifying a central theme they see as important and then deciding what the story is saying about that theme. You can identify a theme by noticing the ideas, symbols, or even words that recur in the story—in the beginning of *The Red Pony*, for instance, change is repeatedly alluded to, and indeed change proves to be a major concept in the story. Next, decide what you think the story is saying about the theme of change. Events such as the cessation of Jody's reign of terror on small animals (simultaneous with his receiving his beloved pony) might lead to an investigation of other shifts in the story where aggression is replaced by compassion, such as when Carl Tiflin's callousness to Gitano is palliated by Jody's subsequent overtures of compassion to Gitano. Other themes could be approached in similar ways:

You could approach the theme of heroism by looking at the story's depiction of characters' reactions to heroic stories of the past and then analyze what the role of heroism might be in the story. Thematic approaches also blend with the philosophical approaches described below.

Sample Topics:

1. **Growing up:** How does this work portray the process of growing up? What must children experience before they become independent yet empathetic adults?

   To write an essay such as this, begin by identifying where the story describes Jody Tiflin's new experiences, such as moments of new responsibility, kindness, cruelty, doubt, birth, death, and compassion. You will want to focus on only a few of these events, and then you will need to evaluate how these transforming experiences are portrayed and in what ways, if any, Jody changes as a result of them. Based on your assessment of the portrayal of these experiences, you can develop a thesis about the representation of growing up in the stories.

2. **Honor:** What does *The Red Pony* suggest about honorable ways of living in and understanding the world? Which character best embodies the work's sense of honor?

   Such an essay would need to locate scenes that remark on not only honor and dignity but also shame and pettiness. For example, in the beginning of the first story, Jody demonstrates that his impulses are alternately base and laudatory, but despite his own naturally conflicting approach to the world, he appears instinctively drawn to the humane and honorable approaches (particularly those he sees enacted by Billy Buck). Another example is seen in Gitano's return and departure, which both seem ritualistic (as does his rapier), and thus these scenes are excellent sources for discussions of honor. A thesis for this topic would need to argue for what the story is saying about the social and individual value of honor and dishonor; to that end, it would be worthwhile to consider the characters' own awareness of honor.

3. **Heroism:** What is the nature of heroism in *The Red Pony?* Is the story suggesting that heroism belongs only to the greats of the past, or is it attainable regardless of the era?

This topic invites you to read closely those sections that reference tales of knights and chivalry (in "The Gift") and western pioneering (in "The Leader of the People") and to consider what purposes these stories serve for the larger story cycle and for the characters themselves. For Jody specifically, it would be useful to consider the particulars of his heroic fantasies (e.g., when he imagines his horse as a "Black Demon" that would alternately rescue and terrorize the community) and assess the effect these stories have on Jody. Are these fantasies preparing him for the adult world he is entering or providing him with an escape from the tensions of growing up? Jody's grandfather believes that the era of greatness (which also happens to be the grandfather's glory years) is long gone, and Jody worries that that heroism is indeed lost. How might the story be arguing against the grandfather and instead suggesting that heroism is alive and well? What valiant traits does Jody display? A good thesis will demonstrate the conclusions you reach about these questions.

4. **Loss:** How does the story represent and evaluate the force of loss? Does it judge loss?

To write an essay such as this, begin by identifying the major loss that occurs in each of the four stories, and then look at how each loss benefits or damages one character. If loss is represented as inescapable, it would be worthwhile to consider whether there is a redemptive component to loss. Does growth follow loss in these stories?

Character

Papers can focus on questions of character development (such as how Steinbeck distinguishes Billy Buck from Carl Tiflin by their distinctive manner with vulnerable individuals), means of characterization (like the way Jody's sensitivity to his father's criticisms so clearly signals Carl

Tiflin's carping behavior), or interpretations of changes in a character as the story proceeds (such as the transformation of Jody from a shy, yielding boy in "The Gift" to a more forthright, self-directed youth in "The Leader of the People"). To write an essay on character, you would need to approach the story by way of questions about how readers come to know various characters. An essay could center on the means by which Steinbeck constructs the distinctive natures of his characters. How, for instance, does Steinbeck distinguish a character's manner? In the case of *The Red Pony*, Billy Buck's ease with and care for the young, the elderly, and the animal demonstrates to the reader that he is a sensitive and humane individual. Billy Buck's foil, or illuminating opposing character, Carl Tiflin, is uncomfortable with, dismissive of, and impatient with vulnerable beings, and that trait tells the reader that he is not humane (and, furthermore, is perhaps prevented from his humanity because of his responsibility as a patriarch and landowner). In a story such as *The Red Pony*, one that is shorn of the insight that an interior monologue might provide, it is that much more important when examining character development to assess the actions and reactions of the characters. To answer questions of character development, look closely for examples of language, action, or interactions with other characters. The ways in which characters behave with one another helps the reader understand who the characters are. Essays on character development not only assess the means by which characters are created but also explain what characters signify and represent for the story as a whole.

Sample Topics:

1. **Jody Tiflin's character development:** How does Jody change over the course of the stories? Why might these changes occur?

   An essay on this topic would force you to decide what kinds of changes happen in Jody's character. A successful approach to this topic would limit the scope of inquiry to a manageable one: You might consider, for instance, how Jody's awareness of love and empathy develops and then argue the reasons for this change. Another narrow scope could be Jody's growing sense of mortality in the face of the losses he experiences.

Evidence for these topics (or other approaches to changes in Jody's behavior) can be drawn from noting scenes where Jody's behavior toward other characters or toward animals has demonstrated change. Finally, assess whether the changes you identified represent growth for Jody.

2. **Character development in general:** How does the story present character to the reader? What techniques does the story use?

A paper on this topic would observe how Steinbeck gives insight into character. A possible approach to this essay would be to look at the actions of a pair of characters and attempt to show what effects they have on events and on other characters. For instance, an essay could study how and why the characters within the story tell stories. What does the content of the stories of the old men (Gitano and grandfather) tells us about their characters? Another paired approach could look at the stories narrated by Carl Tiflin and Billy Buck. These last two characters tell stories to Jody for different reasons: Your analysis of these reasons would provide the substance of a good essay.

3. **Billy Buck as a character:** What kind of figure is Billy Buck? What is his role in the story? In Jody's life?

This is an evaluative topic that requires you to analyze the descriptions of the largely sympathetic and very important character of Billy Buck. An essay on this topic would require you to consider his distinguishing aspects, including those that demonstrate how different he is from Jody's father in terms of social standing, vocation, actions, and level of empathy. In what ways is the model of male adulthood that Billy embodies an antidote to the model Carl Tiflin provides? You would need to examine Billy's reactions to Jody's anxiety and ultimate rage at the end of "The Gift." The gruesome birth scene in "The Promise" also offers insights into Billy's character. Based on this evidence, the essay can present opinions about the kind of character Billy Buck is.

4. **Carl Tiflin as a character:** In what ways is Carl Tiflin a flawed character? In what ways do his character flaws, in action and speech, for instance, contribute to a greater understanding of the story?

This is a topic that asks you to reach some conclusions about an evaluative statement. Carl Tiflin is a character who is initially introduced to the reader as "stern" and inhibiting to those around him, and these character traits are reiterated in different descriptions and in different actions throughout the story. Carl Tiflin's discomfort with emotion, with the unusual, and with the natural are instructive. If Carl Tiflin is, indeed, an antagonizing force in the story, which of his opposing qualities do we see the story valuing? To take this topic to the next level of sophistication, you might consider a couple of ways in which Carl Tiflin is a sympathetic character. Could he, in fact, be the voice of reason in *The Red Pony?*

History and Context

History and context provide another productive approach to the story; they take into account the rural central California setting of the early 1900s (the story is given an indeterminate era). In this story's timeframe, California would have been a era for approximately 70 years, and this historical fact would, of course, have an impact on California identity. Not only was California's first-generation frontier identity disappearing as survivors of initial migrations had mostly died, but the demographics of the state were changing too: This was a time that saw increasing urbanization as more Californians were living in the cities than in the country. Indeed, California was coming to see itself as a stabilized American state with sizable metropoles, though it was still subject to an economy made manic by speculation. The chaotic boom times of the Gold Rush (1849 to 1852, at its height) were over, but California's ongoing real estate booms and busts were (and remain) prone to the mythic image that the country at large had about what California represented. Though no longer thought of as an easy source of quick riches in gold, California was still imagined as a place of new beginnings, sunny skies, oranges, and healthful living. In short, it was a Promised Land for the rest of the country. Since Steinbeck was a native son, he knew firsthand what living in California was like, but that fact did not prevent his perceiving in the landscape the same Eden that California boosters advocated.

After doing some historical research into 1920s California and perhaps looking into primary sources such as newspapers, magazines, or even real-estate brochures, you could explore in an essay how *The Red Pony* supports or undermines more popular expectations of the state. The story cycle describes individuals who once fell under the spell of California. The Tiflin family, at least through the maternal line, was a pioneer family, and Grandfather himself led a party of settlers to California. Now, two generations into California, it is implied that the Tiflins worry that they have lost all vestiges of their once-adventuresome pioneering nature. The story also poses questions about the legacy of settling in California: What, for instance, was the impact on the people the U.S. settlers displaced? In its broadest historical sense, *The Red Pony* depicts a number of moments and tensions: the identity crises of rural California residents; the historical legacy of displaced Mexican Californians; the physical end of the continent's U.S. western frontier; and the more symbolic but nonetheless palpable coming to terms with California's Edenic reputation. Papers can productively explore what the story is saying about these questions of history and context.

Sample Topics:

1. **The American frontier and *The Red Pony*:** The story refers explicitly to the migration of Yankee settlers to the West and, more specifically, California. How does the story treat the legacy of the frontier? What is the significance of the frontier for this story's characters?

   A paper on *The Red Pony* and the American frontier would need to include an examination of the ideas surrounding and the facts concerning the frontier at the beginning of the 20th century. In 1893 historian Frederick Turner wrote an influential essay in which he argued that the United States's westward expansion was the source of America's character and spirit, and the physical end of the continent was a source of crisis for the American identity. An essay on this topic might explore how Turner's thesis is enacted in this story. How do the characters demonstrate anxiety about the end of the frontier? How does the frontier pique Jody's fantasies for heroism and adventure? You would want to examine Jody's fantasies for any undercurrents of dread, a feeling that would clearly signal anxiety.

2. **The legacy of Mexican California:** The story "The Great Mountains," the second tale in *The Red Pony*, features the arrival of Gitano, the elderly Mexican man who has returned to the Tiflin ranch (his childhood home) "to die." How is the presentation of Gitano related to the American present and the Mexican past of California?

For Gitano's family, Mexico's loss of California meant an enforced homelessness. Whether Gitano's family owned the land or worked it is irrelevant; in either case, he seems to have been wandering ever since, and his name, Gitano ("gypsy" in Spanish), underscores his peripatetic life. You could research the history of Mexican land rights in California around the time of the cession (when under intense pressure Mexico sold California and New Mexico to the United States and officially recognized the annexation of Texas). A broader approach could be the ideas of Mexican legacies, or, broader still, the pull of home. Another approach is somewhat related to a thematic one: In what ways does Jody Tiflin perceive romance in Gitano's Mexican past and how is that perception contrasted with the American present with which Jody is familiar?

3. **California history in *The Red Pony:*** *The Red Pony* is a story deeply engaged with the history of California. It concerns itself with questions of historical traditions, legacies, and cultures.

What kind of commentary on history is the story presenting? In other words, how does the notion of history function in this story?

This is a broad topic, and you would need to focus on a few elements and evaluate the story's position on them. Techniques might include close readings of characters talking about pioneering, or community, for example. In your opinion, what does it signify that Jody Tiflin is so fascinated by the stories of the past narrated by Billy Buck, Gitano, and Grandfather?

Philosophy and Ideas

Another approach to forming an argument about *The Red Pony* is to identify and then analyze the philosophical ideas that circulate in the story. This approach is related to the thematic approach in that it tracks an idea in the story, but this kind of an essay would demonstrate how you see the story as commenting on an idea in its more general form. Many critics have noted how pivotal the dynamic of coming-of-age, or growing up, is in *The Red Pony*, for both the story's plot and the characters, but also as a more general notion. Observing the innocence-to-experience dynamic that so pervades *The Red Pony* and concentrating on those areas of the story that do not directly involve Jody would allow the writer to explore how the idea of gaining experience functions in the story. Evidence would arise from the way the story presents families, communities, and regions as going through much the same arc of innocence to experience. Consider, for example, how the settler community (represented by the Tiflins) looks back on its past as innocent and as a better, more idealistic version of itself. Other broad ideas deal with the past, the communal, and adulthood.

Sample Topics:

1. **The Fall of Man:** One of the more specific variations of loss in this story is analogous to the biblical idea of humanity's first loss: the Fall of Man from God's grace. With that in mind, consider how Jody's experiences in *The Red Pony* effectively allow him to gain knowledge and experience but remove him from a state of innocence and grace.

This topic presents loss in its specifically Old Testament variation. You would need to be familiar with the story in Genesis
about Adam and Eve and how the notions of knowledge and
experience, in their abstract forms, are identical concepts.
What does Jody Tiflin learn (knowledge) that eliminates his
innocence (ignorance)? You should also do close readings of
those scenes that mention his seemingly innate senses of guilt
and shame.

2. **Phalanx:** John Steinbeck was interested in the notion of a
phalanx, which is defined as an ancient Greek style of warfare
where troops move shoulder to shoulder into battle. To Steinbeck, there was a certain degree of heroism in the subsuming
of the self into a greater unit. How is the related idea that a collectivity is stronger than an individual presented in this story?

For this kind of essay you would need to read closely those
sections where the characters discuss the advantages of working together toward common goals. "The Leader of the People"
merits special attention because in that story the grandfather
is so pained at the individualism he sees around him and
longs for the collectivity he experienced during the overland
migrations.

3. **Adulthood:** As discussed previously, much of this story is
about Jody Tiflin's growing up, or becoming a full-fledged adult
human, and one of the ways we see this is in his increasing
understanding of the joy and sadness that is a natural part of
life. In this story, what does it mean to be an adult? A human?

An essay on the question of adulthood in this story should
include some larger discussion of the human condition. What
elements of conventionally universal experience (e.g., love) is
Jody made aware of in this story? For this topic you would
want to look to those scenes where Jody Tiflin experiences
exaltation or, alternatively, deep despair and demonstrate how
the story underscores the adult nature of these feelings.

4. **Nostalgia:** Nostalgia, or longing for the past, is demonstrated by a number of characters in *The Red Pony*. Consider what the effect of nostalgia is on a given set of characters in the present.

This is a somewhat broad topic about the past as a source of desire and longing. To see nostalgia in action, you need only read those wistful stories of days gone by that are narrated by Billy Buck and Grandfather. The challenge of this topic is to examine how nostalgia, or a longing for the past, can be a more general state of being and a potentially complicating mindset. To address this topic, you might note those stories of the past that captivate Jody and analyze why you think they do. A possible further question: What does it mean that Carl Tiflin is not nostalgic for California's past?

Form and Genre

Form and genre provide illuminating ways of analyzing literary works. Form is defined as the shape and structure of a literary work; genre is defined as the kind, or classification, of a literary work. Though technically independent of the content of literature, form and genre are used deliberately by authors to help cultivate the ideas in, strengthen the dramatic impact of, and generally refine their stories. In the case of *The Red Pony*, the genre is fiction and, more specifically, it is a bildungsroman. The form of *The Red Pony* is an unusual one, a story cycle, which is composed of related but autonomous works of fiction that are together concerned with a single idea, theme, or event. Story cycles are more often associated with much older texts, such as Homer's *Iliad* or Chaucer's *Canterbury Tales*, and the fact that a 20th-century American writer would use this form is itself a choice worthy of an essay. What does this somewhat archaic story form contribute to Jody Tiflin's story? More specifically, does the use of a story cycle lend a mythic gravity or universality to Jody's story that would not be present in a more straightforward novella?

Jody's story is a bildungsroman, which is the technical literary term for a coming-of-age story. There are customarily two important aspects of the coming-of-age process for a protagonist in a bildungsroman: preparation for adult life and a search for an existence that is fitting for the protagonist. This bildungsroman definition itself provides a worthwhile topic, and a writer who is considering this question would want to consider whether Jody's coming-of-age is complete. Does the story end with Jody's full initiation into manhood? Questions of form and genre can be considered in tandem as well. For example, in what ways do the form (story cycle) and the genre (bildungsroman) work together?

Sample Topics:

1. *The Red Pony* as bildungsroman: How is *The Red Pony* a bildungsroman? In what ways does Jody grow and develop as an individual? Are there ways in which his development seems truncated or incomplete?

   This topic requires some understanding of the bildungsroman genre (as discussed above). Ways to approach this topic can include examinations of Jody Tiflin's development from child to adult. Scenes to consider would be those that demonstrate the most dramatic contrasts (e.g., his breaking away from his family's values). The final question of the topic should point you toward any places that indicate that Jody is not yet an adult. One missing step of development is that he demonstrates no interest in romantic love, though he does see love in action. What does he learn about what he has not yet experienced, and is this good preparation for his adulthood?

2. *The Red Pony* as elegiac: When Grandfather describes his arrival in California, he laments, "[t]hen we came down to the sea, and it was done" (225). He is speaking in an elegiac way, one that celebrates or laments something that is dead and gone. In what ways does *The Red Pony* utilize the manners of an elegy and for what purpose?

   Elegy is a term that describes a Greek poem that was written in a certain form and that celebrated a dead person or past time. Though not a poem, *The Red Pony* does use some of the same mannerisms of an elegy or lament. This topic asks you to think about how this story is an ode to the past. If it is a celebration of the past, what in the past is worth celebrating or lamenting? Could the story be lamenting a culture, a time, an individual, or even something as abstract as a feeling? To further a discussion of genre, you could consider how the elegiac mode interacts with the bildungsroman: For instance, how does a story of development also become a story about a lost time?

3. **Form of *The Red Pony*:** How do the autonomous stories of *The Red Pony* connect and form a cohesive unit? How does the overall story achieve its progressive drama and singularity of effect, despite the interruptions of time and action? And how do the titles of the stories contribute form to *The Red Pony?*

This topic asks you to study how the overall story is constructed and to look specifically at how the individual stories cohere. You would need to look at the beginnings and endings of the individual stories for moments of connection: Do these beginnings and endings of stories present an evolving protagonist? Another question to consider with this topic of overall form is that of the organization of stories within stories: They are arranged alternately with a story of a horse and a story of an old man. Why? You would also need to analyze how the story titles contribute formal organization to the stories and theorize why the stories were collected under the title *The Red Pony*, though only the first story features the red pony. What does this arrangement say about the meaning of the red pony for this overall story?

Comparison and Contrast

Comparing components of a story in order to explain and analyze the similarities or differences between them is a useful approach to writing an essay. It is important to avoid the pitfall of merely creating a list of such similarities or differences in a work; instead, you must take the necessary step of commenting on these observations. Essays that do not study the significance of points of comparison are ineffective because they only show the writer's ability to identify, not analyze. To begin a comparison/contrast essay you might compare characters with each other: How does

Billy Buck compare to Carl Tiflin? How does Gitano compare to Grand-father? How does Carl Tiflin compare to Grandfather? You could also compare characters (or other elements of the story like patterns of imag-ery or action) across different stories. For example, how do the depictions of nature compare in "The Chrysanthemums" and *The Red Pony?* The challenge of this kind of essay is deciding what the similarities or differ-ences you identify might mean. These are the questions that make essays interesting and the ones that will have different answers for each writer. To get to these questions, it is often helpful to think about what kinds of effects Steinbeck achieves by producing either similarities or differences between elements of his stories. What, for example, does the difference between Billy Buck's and Carl Tiflin's attitudes toward the elderly do for our understanding of each character and his views of the world? It is not sufficient to identify a pattern and to point to the existence of similarities or differences; you must also consider what purpose those similarities or differences might serve in the story overall.

Sample Topics:

1. **Comparing attitudes to parenting:** Jody Tiflin has two men in his life who are father figures: his father and Billy Buck. Com-pare how these characters attempt to teach Jody how to be in the world and make an evaluative assessment of the story's atti-tudes to these father figures.

   The focus here would be on looking specifically at the meth-ods these father figures use to guide Jody. Do they cite rules or explain reasons or give parables? The content of their lessons is another interesting point of comparison. A strong essay on this topic would draw some conclusions about what it is, spe-cifically, in Billy Buck's approach that Jody so clearly responds to. Furthermore, is the story supporting one form of teaching over another? Look for commentary from the narrator to sup-port your interpretation.

2. **Comparing attitudes toward storytelling:** The notion of story-telling pervades each of the four stories that comprise *The Red Pony* and gives dimension to each of the principal characters. Select three characters and compare how they approach story-

telling and what the act means to them. Assess what *The Red Pony* is saying about storytelling.

This topic would require you to examine closely the stories within the stories of *The Red Pony*. You would need to concentrate on a limited number of characters, ascertain the motivations behind their stories, and assess what their stories contribute to the overall story. Why, do you think, does Steinbeck have all the characters telling stories? You could consider the form of *The Red Pony* and how stories to some degree replace the narrator's limited access to the characters' interior lives.

3. **Compare the idea of the "unknown" in "The Chrysanthemums" and *The Red Pony*:** The protagonists of both "The Chrysanthemums" and *The Red Pony* are preoccupied by imagining life beyond their known worlds. Compare how these two protagonists imagine the unknown and consider what their fantasies about the unknown imply about their known worlds and about themselves.

This topic asks you to examine closely the fantasies of Elisa Allen and Jody Tiflin and to consider why these two characters spend so much time imagining a life beyond their known worlds. It would be worthwhile to demonstrate how similar are the characterizations of their respective homes (known world) and also to demonstrate any similarities or differences in their individual imaginings of the unknown world. A strong essay on this topic would include evaluative assessments of what Elisa's and Jody's homes (known worlds) deny them that they imagine the world beyond would satisfy. An outstanding essay will also take into account these two characters' social roles and how those roles affect their respective senses of independence.

Bibliography and Online Resources for *The Red Pony*

Hart, Joyce. "Critical Essay on *The Red Pony*." *Novels for Students*. Vol. 17. Detroit: Gale, 2003. 129–42.

Hayashi, Tetsumano. *Steinbeck's Short Stories in* The Long Valley: *Essays in Criticism.* Muncie, IN: Steinbeck Research Institute, 1991.

Hughes, R. S., ed. *John Steinbeck: A Study of the Short Fiction.* Boston: Twayne, 1989.

The Martha Heasley Cox Center for Steinbeck Studies. "The Red Pony (1937)." Retrieved 27 February 2007. <http://www.steinbeck.sjsu.edu/works/The%20 Red%20Pony.jsp>.

Satyanarayana, M. R. "And Then the Child Becomes a Man: Three Initiation Stories of John Steinbeck." *Contemporary Literary Criticism.* Vol. 124. Detroit: Gale, 2000. 393–96. Originally published in *John Steinbeck: A Study of the Short Fiction,* by R. S. Hughes. Boston: Twayne, 1989.

Shaw, Patrick W. "Steinbeck's *The Red Pony.*" *A New Study Guide to Steinbeck's Major Works, with Critical Explications.* Ed. Tetsumano Hayashi. Metuchen, NJ: Scarecrow Press, 1993. 186–205.

"FLIGHT"

READING TO WRITE

R EADERS OF John Steinbeck's "Flight" (1938) often comment on the richness of imagery in the story's descriptions of the natural world of Pepé Torres, the story's protagonist. "Flight" tells the story of a young man leaving home for the first time, going to the city, being insulted, instinctively killing the offending party, and then escaping into the mountains. In effect, it is the story of a boy becoming a man, but the progressive development that a coming-of-age story typically signifies is complicated by the current of doom that runs through the story. Much of the doom is due to the fierceness of the natural setting in which the story takes place.

The complexity and personality of the setting could be the subject of a very good essay. For example, you might examine how inhospitable this rugged California coastline is to human life and, further, how this hostile setting highlights the perilousness of the protagonist's travails. No matter what topic you choose to write about, you must first grapple with Steinbeck's language. This section of the chapter will demonstrate how to do a close reading of a passage of "Flight" in order to prepare for writing an essay.

The primary significance of the setting is demonstrated by the fact that it is the setting, not individuals, that the narrator first describes. In fact, the setting proves to be the final entity described as well (when an avalanche buries Pepé). This authorial decision is an interesting aspect of the story's construction, and it brings up one clear question: Why, in a coming-of-age story, is the human drama secondary to the natural drama? This hierarchy of emphasis could be explored in an essay. You could, for example, interpret the overall philosophy of the story: Is the emphasis on nature a comment on how humans are subjected to the whims of nature? And, if so, how is nature's role in human life shown?

Nature's threatening power is highlighted in the story's opening sentence: "About fifteen miles below Monterey, on the wild coast, the Torres family had their farm, a few sloping acres above a cliff that dropped to the brown reeds and to the hissing white waters of the ocean." The tenuousness of the family home and farm is emphasized in this sentence. Both their lives (home) and their livelihood (farm) sit on a "*wild* coast," atop a cliff that "*drop[s]* to the brown reefs and to the *hissing* white waters of the ocean" (emphases added). The Torres farm, this sentence strongly suggests, is vulnerable to the destructive and hostile power of nature. The verb "hissing" is one that will be repeated in the story many times, and the attentive reader will note that the onomatopoeia (a word that mimics a sound) of "hiss" approximates the sound that an aggressive animal makes. Furthermore, hissing is a sound associated with snakes, an animal associated with evil in Judeo-Christian mythology. The hissing ocean highlights the vulnerability of the family; the precariousness of their situation is amplified in the remainder of the first paragraph:

> Behind the farm the stone mountains stood up against the sky. The farm buildings huddled like little clinging aphids on the mountain skirts, couched low to the ground as though the wind might blow them into the sea. The little shack, the rattling, rotting barn were grey-bitten with sea salt, beaten by the damp wind until they had taken on the color of the granite hills. Two horses, a red cow and a red calf, half a dozen pigs and a flock of lean, multicolored chickens stocked the place. A little corn was raised on the sterile slope, and it grew short and thick under the wind, and all the cobs formed on the landward sides of the stalks.

This paragraph is filled with portentous symbolism and imagery. The diction in the paragraph extends the first sentence's sense of human vulnerability. The "shack" they live in is "little," and their barn (symbolic center of a farm) "huddle[s]," "crouche[s]," is "rotting," "grey-bitten by sea salt," and "beaten by the damp wind." The crops are visibly suffering from the harshness of the landscape: The corn is raised on a "sterile slope" and the cobs are stunted, only forming on the "landward sides of the stalks." Humans are noticeably absent from this tableau, but the marks of human habitation show us, by their embattled descriptions, that the human will to survive is challenged at all sides by the forces of nature.

A successful writer will always look for the small details (in diction, image, etc.) that point toward the larger truths in a story. After carefully reading the story and then reflecting on this first paragraph, you might consider how the small details in this paragraph connect to the larger ideas in the story. For instance, you might notice how the circumstances of setting heighten the tension in Pepé's coming-of-age. You might also study how tension and suspense are created and sustained through the use of literary devices (such as diction). Or you might see the global, thematic resonances of Pepé's situation. For instance, his struggle to survive in a harsh world might be interpreted as having broader implications for a commentary on the human condition; in this analysis, Pepé's flight is a parable for all individuals trying to beat the poor odds that fate has meted out.

Reading slowly and carefully will make for a more nuanced understanding of the story, while also enabling you to gather the evidence you need to write a strong essay.

TOPICS AND STRATEGIES

This section of the chapter discusses various possible topics for essays on "Flight" and general approaches to those topics. Remember that these are only starting points for your own analysis, not a comprehensive code to the novel. Every topic discussed here could encompass a wide variety of good papers.

Themes

"Flight" deals with many themes, ideas, and concepts that organize the action in the short story. Some of these ideas include nature (as discussed above), pride, knowledge, coming-of-age, and the expectations of adult manhood. Writers approaching the story often begin by identifying a central theme they see as important and then deciding what it is that the story is saying about that theme. You can identify a theme by noticing the ideas, symbols, or even words that recur in the story—in the beginning of "Flight," for instance, expectations of manhood are repeatedly voiced by the characters. Next, decide what you think the story is saying about the theme of manhood. Studying events such Mama Torres's sending Pepé on a journey to town raises the possibility that this signals his becoming an adult; this might lead to an investigation of other places in the story where manhood is discussed or acted out. After analyzing these scenes, you would be able to reach thoughtful conclusions about this idea in the story. Other themes could be approached in similar ways: The theme of understanding could be explored by studying how Pepé learns to deal with the treachery around him. Thematic approaches also blend with the philosophical approaches described below.

Sample Topics:

1. **Growing up:** How does this story characterize the process of growing up?

The narrator describes Pepé as being physically and emotionally "changed" by his time in Monterey. One approach to this topic would be to explore what elements of his experience constitute change or growing up. After you assess the aspects of growing up that this story presents as crucial, you will want to identify how the story characterizes the process. Another approach to this topic would be to explore how Pepé's growing up is representative of a more general human experience. This interpretation of the story would see in Pepé's experience an analogue for that of all humans. One way to tackle this approach would be to look at how the natural world Pepé passes through on his "flight" is characterized as symptomatic of the human life cycle: It begins lush and full of life, becomes dark and complicated, and finally is desiccated and bereft of life. This is an allegorical approach, in which scenes in the story correlate to an exterior story; to do a strong essay with an allegorical bent, you will need to reach some conclusions about the significance of the allegorical interpretation you are making. For instance, what purpose is served by Pepé's story's having more general applications? Does this make Pepé a kind of everyman? Would that, then, increase the reader's identification with his character or perhaps serve another significant function?

2. **Instinct/knowledge:** How does the story portray the forces of instinct and knowlege? Does the story present humans as driven more by knowledge or by instinct?

To write an essay on instinct and knowledge, begin by identifying scenes that portray Pepé's being motivated by natural drives versus knowledge. This topic assumes that there is a difference between those two motivations, and that distinction would have to be defined in your argument. The most basic natural drive demonstrated in "Flight" would be the survival instinct. You could approach this topic by analyzing scenes where Pepé's instinct for survival is supplemented by his learned understanding of how to survive. The scene where he decides against shooting the mountain lion (which would draw unwanted attention to his location), for instance, is a moment where his knowledge (that the men pursuing him pose the greater threat) supersedes his instinct (to protect himself from the lion). Based on your assessment of the portrayal of these scenes, you can develop a thesis about the representations of instinct and knowledge in this story. Ultimately, you will want to assess whether the story suggests that an adult is distinguished from a child by the predominance of either instinct or knowledge.

3. **Pride:** How does the story represent and evaluate pride? Is it characterized as a positive quality, in the sense of honor, or is it a negative quality, in the sense of ego?

This topic asks you to focus on the quality of pride in this story. You would need to locate the places where pride is mentioned (in the beginning, for instance, when Pepé grins "with pride" as he leaves for Monterey), but also where it is implied (such as the cause for his killing the man who insults him). Based on your analysis of pride in this story, do you think it is characterized as an honorable quality or a petty one? You will need to reach an opinion on its overall role in this story. You could broaden the focus to include pride as a marker (good or bad) of identity and adulthood.

Character

Papers can focus on questions of character development (such as how Steinbeck distinguishes Rosy from Emilio by their distinctive levels of insight), means of characterization (like the way we learn about Mama Torres from the differences between how she acts toward Pepé and how she really feels about him), or interpretations of changes in a character as the novella proceeds (the changes in Pepé from a lazy and literally recumbent boy to a literally upright man before his death). For a work such as "Flight," which has a limited number of characters but many presences, you might need to broaden the scope of inquiry to include actors such as the Dark Watchers or even nature itself.

To write an essay on questions of character, you would need to approach the story by way of questions about how the readers come to know the various characters. Steinbeck creates the illusion that his characters are individuals, and an essay could center on the techniques by which that illusion is produced. How does Steinbeck distinguish one character from another? In the case of Pepé, he is initially described for us as he is observed by his mother; we watch him for a time (throwing his father's knife for the entertainment of his siblings), and we learn a great deal about his character simply by noticing how he is depicted at play. He is portrayed as grinning, "lazy," and gangly: all adjectives that emphasize his boyishness. We also learn that he is 19, old enough to be a man, and there are signs that he has within him the power, and perhaps capacity for danger, of a man. For example, the knife that he is throwing—expertly—functions as an extension of his own body: "Pepé's wrist flicked like the head of a snake. The blade seemed to fly open in mid-air, and with a thump the point dug into the redwood post, and the black handle quivered." This knife later proves to be a means of revealing important character traits of Pepé: It is the knife, after all, that he uses to kill a man, and the wrist's action being compared to a snake's suggests the savagery within him. Pepé's facility with the knife but seeming lack of awareness about its deadly potential are two aspects of his characterization that propel the conflicts he later initiates and suffers from.

To answer questions of character development, look closely at the details of language, action, or interactions with outside forces (such as other characters). The ways characters behave with one another help the reader understand who the characters are. Essays on character development assess not only the means by which characters are created but also what characters signify and represent for the story as a whole.

Sample Topics:

1. **Pepé's character development:** How does Pepé change over the course of this story? What causes these changes to occur?

To argue a thesis on a topic such as this, you must first decide what kinds of changes happen in Pepé's character: Are they defining changes in persona and outlook or are they smaller changes, such as in physical appearance? One way to tackle this topic would be to find causes for the changes you identify. How, for instance, does the loss of his knife (called his "inheritance" because it belonged to his dead father) affect or change Pepé? Might it liberate him while also making him more vulnerable? How about the loss of the use of his arm? Finally, you will want to theorize in what specific ways, overall, Pepé's character changes.

2. **Mama Torres as a character:** What kind of character is Mama Torres? In what ways does she attempt to teach Pepé valuable lessons about adulthood and manhood? What kind of figure is she, independent of her motherhood?

This is an evaluative topic that requires you to analyze Mama Torres, and you could approach the topic in one of two ways. One approach would be to explore how her character affects Pepé's character: For example, what lessons does he learn from her (e.g., about how to survive the Dark Watchers)? Is there a way that her withholding of praise has a practical function for the creation of his masculine identity? The second way to approach this topic would be to analyze Mama Torres as a character in her own right. The narrator characterizes her as a figure of wisdom and strength, but are her laudatory qualities of any consequence in this hostile environment? You would certainly want to discuss her ritualistic mourning scene (the last time she is in the story). What does her formal approach to grief say about both her role as a purveyor of civilization and her own ability to persevere?

3. **Dark Watchers:** Among the parting instructions Mama Torres gives Pepé are these: "When thou comest to the high mountains, if thou seest any of the dark watching men, go not near to them nor try to speak to them." What are we to make of these dark figures? Are they real characters or supernatural ones? Finally, are they there?

The Dark Watchers are strong presences in this story. To address this topic, you should study closely the commentary on these figures and the behavior of the unidentified beings that Pepé encounters on his "flight." Arguments could be made for their being Native Americans, ghostly menaces, or perhaps members of the posse that is presumably pursuing Pepé. Your conclusions about what these figures are will be rooted in the close readings of passages where they are mentioned. You will certainly want to discuss whether it is the Dark Watchers or another entity altogether that shoots Pepé at the end.

Philosophy and Ideas

Another approach to forming an argument about "Flight" is to identify and then analyze the philosophical ideas that circulate in the story. This approach is related to the thematic approach discussed above in that it tracks an idea in the story, but the result of this kind of an essay would demonstrate how you see the story as commenting on the idea in its more general form. The idea of masculinity, for instance, is one that not only is integral to the action in the story but also underlies the philosophical underpinnings of the story. In the early scenes, Pepé and his mother debate whether he is a man. He asserts that he is, and she responds, "Thou? A man? Thou art a peanut." The question of what constitutes manhood is an interesting one in this story: Is it congenital, earned, or born out of necessity? Mama Torres argues for the last reason. She claims that Pepé is being sent on this errand to Monterey only because the family needs the medicine that he will fetch (this implies that Pepé is not yet a man). She later tells her other son that manhood arises out of necessity: "A boy gets to be a man when he is needed" (this implies that Pepé is a man because of the family's need for one). An essay could fruitfully explore how and when Pepé becomes a man and the means by which his manhood is achieved (need? inheritance?). "Flight" is a story that is abundant in ideas and that makes this approach a promising one for an essay. Other ideas to consider include free will or the relationship between nature and humans.

Sample Topics:

1. **Notions of masculinity:** Pepé asserts three times that he is "a man." How is the idea of "a man" represented in this story? At what point does Pepé become a man?

   To write an essay such as this, begin by analyzing those sections where what it means to be a man is discussed by the characters. One approach to this topic would focus on how Mama Torres seeks to instill in her son his masculinity. You may notice that her teasing of him has an educative aspect to it. Based on what she says to him and to her other children, what does Mama Torres believe is the nature of manhood? Furthermore, why is it that when she acknowledges that he is a man, she pities him ("my poor, little Pepé")? Another approach to this topic could focus on Pepé's embodying the traits of masculinity in which he has been instructed. In the beginning of the story he seems to be acting the masculine role (he plays a form of dress-up by asking for his father's hat and coat), but at some point in the story (perhaps after he loses the symbols of masculinity: hat, gun, knife, etc.) he becomes a man. Is it when he leaves home the second time? Is it at the moment of his death? Your argument will need supporting evidence.

2. **Humans and nature:** The tension between nature and humans is a constant here; we see the power of nature threatening human life throughout the story. But despite nature's authority, Pepé works to maintain his separation from raw nature. Does he?

This topic enables you to look at the animal references in the story (of which there are many, such as when Pepé crawls, hisses, and howls). You would need to evaluate where you see nature superseding or overpowering civility and then draw some conclusions about how the story presents the tensions between those two entities. You will want to discuss whether Pepé's final act is a human or animal one. How is his burial by avalanche a commentary on the conflicts between humans and nature?

3. **Free will or determinism?:** How does the story represent the possibility of free will? Does Pepé act out of his wishes and desires, or is some other force determining his actions?

The philosophical notion of determinism declares that free will is an illusion and that human action is generated out of accountable and explainable phenomena. One approach to writing on this topic would be to focus on the ways that the story represents the origins of Pepé's actions. You would want to explain why he felt like an unwitting accomplice in the man's death ("the knife went almost by itself").

Form and Genre

Form and genre provide illuminating ways of analyzing many literary works. Form is defined as the shape and structure of a literary work; genre is defined as the kind, or classification, of a literary work. Though technically independent of the content of literature, form and genre are used deliberately by authors to help further the ideas in, strengthen the dramatic impact of, and generally refine their stories. In "Flight," the genre is fiction and the form is that of a short story. A short story is a very tightly constructed work of art; because of its tight construction "Flight" should be read a number of times before being analyzed. The way a literary device is used in a story can form the basis for a good essay on form. In "Flight" one literary device that is skillfully employed is foreshadowing, or the use of clues about the eventual outcome of a story. An example of this is when Pepé's facility with a knife is demonstrated at the beginning of the story; this facility suggests to the reader that the outcome of the story will be determined in some measure by this skill. Beyond form, a good essay could also consider genre; in the case of "Flight," you could explore how the bildungsroman, or coming-of-age, genre plays out. Bildungsroman is a technical term for a work of literature that features the coming-of-age (transition from adolescence to adulthood) of an individual. An effective essay could explore how the bildungsroman genre is implemented in this story and should also reach a conclusion about the significance of Pepé's coming-of-age experience. Does it, for example, culminate in his becoming an adult?

Sample Topics:

1. **Foreshadowing in "Flight":** Discuss the use of foreshadowing in this story. How might its prevalence be suggestive of a philosophy in the story?

This topic is asking you to analyze and track the use of a literary device (foreshadowing) and then assess how that device emphasizes an idea in the story. One example of suggestive foreshadowing includes Pepé's becoming transparent as he leaves the land he knows for the canyons into which he will try to escape; another example of foreshadowing occurs when Pepé's horse walks the trail into the canyon and the earth "giv[es] up a hollow sound under the walking hoofbeats." Both of these examples are suggestive of death, and they heighten the sense of doom that pervades this story. Does this device also contribute to the building of suspense? Ultimately, you will want to discuss how foreshadowing highlights an idea in the story. You might, for instance, explore how foreshadowing speaks to the idea of determinism (defined above under "Philosophy and Ideas"). To that end, in what ways does foreshadowing suggest a contained, already determined outcome (in a way that is in keeping with determinism)?

2. **"Flight" as bildungsroman:** A bildungsroman is typically a story in which the protagonist learns how to be a full-fledged adult. In what ways does "Flight" embody the fundamental demands of a bildungsroman? Are there ways in which the bildungsroman genre breaks down?

This topic asks you to consider the ways in which "Flight" is and is not a bildungsroman. One approach would be to discuss what Pepé learns as the story progresses. You might, for instance, look for places where Pepé's autonomy increases (because of either choice or circumstance) and note how that changes his comportment, his actions, or any other gauges of maturation. Examples of change are seen after he loses physical symbols of family or inheritance (such as his gun and his hat). The end of the story sees Pepé standing and facing his certain death (in a posture of pride and bravery): Does this suggest that he has fulfilled the demands of the bildungsroman?

Language, Symbols, and Imagery

Language, symbol, and imagery are some of the creative means by which an author conveys certain feelings or ideas that would, if simply announced, be undermined in their imaginative and evocative power. All writers, and those of imaginative fiction especially, use language deliberately and choose words based on their connotative, or suggestive, meanings. As you read fiction in preparation for writing about it, you need to be alert to the connotative meanings of language even as you register the surface meaning of language in order to follow the plot itself.

Symbols, usually used in conjunction with imagery, are objects, either animate or inanimate, that writers also use to convey ideas. In "Flight," repetitions of objects (such as weapons), of ideas (such as the animal aspects of people), and of settings (canyons, pools, forests, the sea) are significant. Each of these things has meaning beyond its denotative definition; by the very nature of their repetition and careful presentation, these objects serve symbolic functions in the story. The best essays on symbolism will look at the symbol and, perhaps, its affiliated imagery and consider these subjects in relation to the story's larger ideas. When you are asked to discuss symbolism, you are being asked to discuss what something signifies, means, and represents in light of the entire work.

Sample Topics:

1. **Animal and human imagery:** What is the animal imagery in "Flight" signifying about the events in this story? About the characters?

This is a broad topic, and your first task would be to focus your approach to it. One way to approach this topic would be to note the many instances of Pepé's being described in ways conventionally thought of as animal. After identifying instances of this, consider what this imagery is saying about Pepé's situation. Are animal qualities, for instance, a sign of Pepé's backsliding into primitivism, or do they instead signal that he is acquiring the brutal skills necessary for survival in a hostile world? Another way to approach this topic would be to examine how animals and other manifestations of nature seem to act with more humanity than the humans do. Consider, for instance, what it means that while the "oak trees whispered softly in the night breeze," Pepé is moving with "the instinctive care of an animal" and "worm[ing]" and wriggl[ing]" his way around the mountaintops. Your essay should include discussion of Pepé's death and how it symbolically connects him to either the human or the animal sphere.

2. **Light/dark imagery:** In what ways are images of light and dark important to the action in and significance of this story?

This topic asks you to analyze the lighting of characters and things (these could include Pepé, the forest, the farmstead, the mountains, etc.) in the story and to consider their symbolic significance for the story. Pepé is an especially interesting figure in this regard because the light imagery connected to him changes so profoundly. He is initially described as reflecting light (e.g., teeth "glisten[ing]") and later as losing light and coloring (e.g., before he disappears from the horizon, he is described as a "grey, indefinite shadow"), and in his final moments he is described as "black against the morning sky." An analysis of light and dark could include a discussion of the "Dark Watchers" and what they might signify in this story. Do you think that Steinbeck uses light and dark here as a means to emphasize the significance of the story's events, or might these gradations of illumination be telling the reader a different story beneath the surface?

Comparison and Contrast

Comparing components of a story in order to explain and analyze the similarities or differences between them is a useful approach to writing an essay. Remember to avoid the mistake of merely creating a catalog or list of such similarities or differences in a work; instead, you must take the necessary step of commenting on these observations. To begin a comparison/contrast essay you might compare characters with each other: How does Mama Torres compare to Pepé? How do the male characters compare with the female characters? You could also compare characters (or other elements of the story like patterns of imagery or action) across different stories. For example, how do the depictions of place compare in "Flight" and *Tortilla Flat?* How is the experience of growing up depicted differently in *The Red Pony* and "Flight"? The challenge of this kind of essay is to decide what the similarities or differences you identify might mean. These are the questions that make essays interesting and the ones that will have different answers for each writer. To get to these questions, it is often helpful to think about what kinds of effects Steinbeck achieves by producing either similarities or differences between elements of his stories. How, for example, does community isolation affect our understanding of Pepé's characterization and motivation? It is not sufficient to identify a pattern and to point to the existence of similarities or differences; you must also consider what purpose those similarities or differences might serve in the story overall.

Sample Topics:

1. **Comparing depictions of nature:** As shown in the beginning of this chapter, the story spends a great deal of time talking about nature and its presence in the world in which the Torres family lives. Compare the depictions of nature from the beginning of the story to the end and comment on what the similarities and/or differences might be suggesting about the story's portrayal of nature.

This topic asks you to look carefully at the ways in which nature is presented in the story and to evaluate what these mean. Is nature depicted in a more or less hostile way? Does nature make a kind of peace with Pepé at the end of the story? Based on the conclusions you reach after doing your close readings, you can assess whether depictions of nature are constant or change in this story.

2. **Comparing male and female characters:** How are male and female characters characterized in this story? Does this story argue for feminine and masculine "types"? What are they?

This topic asks you to compare the masculine and feminine characters in this story. The only ones you can speak about with any authority are the members of the Torres family. One approach would be to assess whether the story presents men and women as having essential character types, or fundamental traits. What, in this story, does it mean to be a woman or a man? You will want discuss how Rosy seems to be aware of things that Emilio is not. A good essay will pay special attention to the gender roles of Mama Torres, since she has had to be both mother and father to her children. You might consider also discussing how Pepé is initially described in the story as having some feminine traits: His mouth, for instance, is as "sweet and shapely as a girl's mouth." His mouth becomes more "masculine" after his trip to Monterey. Does Pepé's switching of gender markers suggest that his gender is in flux or that all humans' are?

3. **Constrasting the comings-of-age of Pepé and Jody Tiflin:** Both "Flight" and *The Red Pony* describe the coming-of-age experiences of male protagonists. Compare the circumstances of their development and comment on what the similarities and differences signify for these characters.

This kind of essay would need to apply the kinds of questions posed in the bildungsroman topic above (under "Form and

Genre") with the goal of observing how these two characters experience the coming-of-age transition. Consider, for example, Pepé's utter isolation during the moments of challenge, compared with Jody's modicum of family company during his moments of challenge. There are many differences between these characters' circumstances, and it would be useful to identify some points of similarity, such as what mountains represent to them or their desire for adulthood.

Bibliography for "Flight"

"Flight." *John Steinbeck*. Ed. Harold Bloom. Bloom's Major Short Story Writers. Broomall, PA: Chelsea House, 1999. 78–89.

Gladstein, Mimi Reisel. "Female Characters in Steinbeck: Minor Characters of Major Importance?" *Steinbeck's Women: Essays in Criticism*. Ed. Tetsumaro Hayashi. Muncie, IN: The Steinbeck Society of America, 1979. 22–23.

Hayashi, Tetsumano. *Steinbeck's Short Stories in* The Long Valley: *Essays in Criticism*. Muncie, IN: Steinbeck Research Institute, 1991.

Hughes, R. S. *Beyond* The Red Pony. Metuchen, NJ: Scarecrow Press, 1987.

———, ed. *John Steinbeck: A Study of the Short Fiction*. Boston: Twayne, 1989.

Satyanarayana, M. R. "And Then the Child Becomes a Man: Three Initiation Stories of John Steinbeck." *Contemporary Literary Criticism*. Vol. 124. Detroit: Gale, 2000. 393–96. Originally published in *John Steinbeck: A Study of the Short Fiction*. By R. S. Hughes. Boston: Twayne, 1989.

TORTILLA FLAT

READING TO WRITE

*T*ORTILLA *FLAT,* published in 1936, marked Steinbeck's first commercial success as a writer, and the timing of its publication must have had a hand in its success. Readers certainly responded to what they perceived as the quaint community of Tortilla Flat, near Monterey, California, a community that valued camaraderie, vitality, honor, a story, and a good time over the dull, bourgeois values of ambition, respectability, and careerism. In fact, the *paisanos* (people from the same country or, in California at this time, people of mixed European and Mexican backgrounds) featured in this novel perceive in prosperity an impediment to character; when opportunities for wealth materialize, the *paisanos* do their best to sabotage the potentially ruinous effects that money could bring to their friends and on their friendships. American readers, for the most part, took *Tortilla Flat* to be an opportunity for imaginative escape from the social unrest and uncertainties of the depression.

American readers today, however, generally have a very different sensibility and consequent reaction to the characterization of the *paisanos.* While we still respond to escapist fictions, it is sometimes challenging to read and blithely enjoy this novel that many people now interpret as featuring caricatures and stereotypes of Mexican-American characters. Steinbeck's letters and some critics explain that Steinbeck wrote about the *paisanos* with genuine admiration, and they contend that he was trying to capture affectionately a world he knew by association and to offer, through his use of medieval romanticism, a method for gilding and elevating (in the American public's mind) the *paisano* culture. Futhermore, these critics explain that Steinbeck was a product of his era, and all things considered, his depiction could have been much more offensive. This is a line of reasoning that does have merit; works of literature (e.g., *The Merchant of Venice, Heart of Darkness,* the Bible) do not always, after all, conform in their totality to the values of succeeding generations, but they still may have profound spiritual, intellectual, aesthetic, and historical merit. Other critics have strong objections to Steinbeck's appropriation of a culture about which he was not a true authority (since he was not Mexican American) and see in his depiction of the residents of Tortilla Flat a misguided and offensive rendering of a socially marginalized group by a member of a socially dominant group. In short, these critics (and some of today's readers) often interpret Steinbeck's *Tortilla Flat* as patronizing the very group he sought to glorify.

Controversial art often provides fertile ground for analysis, and that is certainly true in this case. After reading and considering the merits of the novel, it would be a fair scholarly proposition to investigate aspects of the novel that seem troubling to you. It is not, of course, a valuable stance to take that a work of art is bad because it offends you; it is, however, intellectually worthwhile to investigate those aspects of a work about which you have the most interest or strongest feelings. One topic that could be usefully explored would be to investigate the way ethnicity and race are represented in the novel; you could, for instance, assess how the characters themselves perceive of ethnic and racial difference. Are they highly conscious of ethnicity, or is ethnicity inconsequential? A broader approach to a topic like this would be to assess how identity is constructed and understood in the *paisano* community; ethnicity could, in this example, be a part of a topic on identity instead of an entire topic in itself.

To talk only about this story's representations of difference—such as ethnic difference—overlooks the spirit of a book that is so much about the connection of individuals through the bonds of friendship and community. Either friendship or community could serve as excellent topics for this novel, and you could gather evidence for your analysis as you examine the characters acting on their impulses for human companionship (or, in the case of Pirate, canine companionship).

The first sentence of the novel announces straightforwardly the importance of friendship as an idea: "This is the story of Danny and of Danny's friends and of Danny's house." Doing a close reading of this sentence reveals a great deal more about the literary significances that could lead a writer to an insightful analysis of the novel. A close reading registers the plot of the action while also noting the smaller meanings in diction, image, and characterization. The repetition of Danny's name in the first sentence is one detail that stands out: "This is the story of *Danny* and of *Danny's* friends and of *Danny's* house" (italics added). This repetition certainly implies the centrality of Danny to the story as a whole. This avowal could serve as a source for discussion in an essay. An essay could, for instance, explore whether Danny is, in fact, what this novel is about. An argument could be made that Danny is not nearly as pivotal to the story as the narrator contends at the beginning. You could also explore how the form does or does not support the importance of Danny as a character.

This question of how the form of the novel reflects the narrator's pronouncements could be extended beyond the question of Danny's centrality. The remainder of the first paragraph elaborates on the goals of this book; as you read the entirety of this paragraph, consider what else about the story is being established:

> This is the story of Danny and of Danny's friends and of Danny's house. It is a story of how these three became one thing, so that in Tortilla Flat if you speak of Danny's house you do not mean a structure of wood flaked with old whitewash, overgrown with an ancient untrimmed rose of Castile. No, when you speak of Danny's house you are understood to mean a unit of which the parts are men, from which came sweetness and joy, philanthropy and, in the end, a mystic sorrow. For Danny's house was not unlike the Round Table, and Danny's friends were not unlike the knights of it. And this is the story of how that group came into being, of how it flourished and grew to be an organization beautiful and wise. This story deals with the adventuring of Danny's friends, with the good they did, with their thoughts and their endeavors. In the end, this story tells how the talisman was lost and how the group disintegrated.

There are a great many significant details to notice in this unusual, lyrical first paragraph, which functions like an overture for the entire novel. The paragraph contains details of setting, characterization, philosophy, and the basic facts of the plot (a group that comes together and then "disintegrate[s]"). A romantic atmosphere is established by references to "an ancient untrimmed rose of Castile," "the Round Table," "knights," and "mystic sorrow." The narrator's invocation of the knights of King Arthur's Round Table invites a consideration that would be worth exploring in an essay. How, for instance, does a chivalric code materialize in *Tortilla Flat?* Furthermore, if Danny and his friends are knightly in their behavior, what kind of commentary is being implied about the nature of chivalry? Other important details here connect to characterization and how the individuals are presented. Danny and his friends are associated with "sweetness and joy" and "philanthropy," and the group as a whole is described as "beautiful and wise." The narrator clearly approves of these characters and their efforts, and as readers we are being urged to adopt the same favorable expectations of Danny and company. An essay could explore whether this narrative approval is maintained throughout the novel; evidence for support of your ideas could be gathered through your close readings of passages.

Reading slowly and carefully will make for a more nuanced understanding of the novel while also enabling you to gather the evidence you need to write a strong essay.

TOPICS AND STRATEGIES

This section of the chapter discusses various possible topics for essays on *Tortilla Flat* and general approaches to those topics. Remember that these are only starting points for your own analysis, not a comprehensive code to the novel. Every topic discussed here could encompass a wide variety of good papers.

Themes

Tortilla Flat is composed of many themes, ideas, and concepts that generate the action in the story. Some of these ideas include friendship (as briefly discussed above), ethnicity, and gender. Writers approaching a novel often begin by identifying a central theme they see as important and then deciding what the novel is saying about that theme. You can identify a theme by noticing the ideas, symbols, or even words that recur in the story. In the initial passages of *Tortilla Flat*, for example, the pronouncements of the narrator suggest that the story to be told will valorize the notions of friendship and human connection. Next, when you write an essay, you have to decide what the novel is saying about the theme of friendship. The narrator's adoption of romantic language to describe the moments of human connection suggests that friendship is the most exalted state of human existence. Furthermore, the narrator's use of an archaic rhetorical style (e.g., "Where goest thou so fast?") implies the heroism of friendship (whether or not this is mock heroism can only be determined with greater analysis). Looking closely at the language surrounding an idea enables you to gain an understanding of how the novel is presenting a theme; in this case, the romantic and the medieval language contributes to a feeling that friendship is a valuable entity. Other themes could be approached in similar ways: You could approach the theme of reason through the novel's depiction of how characters make sense of their motivations and goals and then assess what the role of reason might be in the novel (or what the novel might be saying about humans and the way they make sense of their actions). Thematic approaches also blend with the philosophical approaches described below.

Sample Topics:

1. **Friendship:** How is friendship presented in this novel? What does the disintegration of the group at the end of the story suggest about the nature of friendship?

To write an essay on friendship, begin by identifying scenes that portray characters being motivated by a desire to establish a companionable human connection. Pirate's impassioned feelings about human friendship, once sparked, become a benevolent force in their own right. One approach to this essay could be to track in a selection of episodes how friendship is threatened and eventually emerges triumphant because of the actions of the characters. Ultimately, you will want to consider what the group's eventual disintegration suggests about the nature of friendship: Is it fragile, durable, unique, ineffable? Considering the ending of this novel will help you reach an overall conclusion about how the novel presents friendship.

2. **Ethnicity/race:** What is the role of ethnicity or race in the community of Tortilla Flat? Is ethnicity/race a means by which residents understand one another's behaviors or actions, or are these inherited markers relatively inconsequential on a practical level?

The narrator's definition of *paisanos* in the novel's preface highlights the term's fundamental ethnic mixture, but understandings of characters' race and ethnicity persist in a way that suggests that these are recognized and potentially contentious differences (so, even if mixed, ethnic difference still carries weight). Consider, for example, Tia Ignacia, who has in her "veins more Indian blood than is considered decent in Tortilla Flat" (chapter 11). This topic guides you toward an analysis of difference as it is practiced and lived in the fictional world of *Tortilla Flat*. What is the effect of ethnic or racial difference for the characters? Another approach to this topic would consider the use of racial epithets by characters. When Danny returns from the war (World War I), for instance, he goes on a drunken rampage, is "overc[ome]" by "race antipathy," and calls some fishermen "Sicilian bastards" (chapter 11). The fishermen respond with a friendly, "Hello, Danny. When'd you get home?" In this example, the hostility of the phrase "race antipathy" is proved comically hyperbolic, and the racial epithet ("Sicilian bastards") is not, in itself, understood by its objects (the fishermen) to be consequential. Other examples of epithets seem more loaded with aggression. You will want to reach a conclusion about what these epithets suggest about the cultural values of these characters.

3. **Gender:** How does the story illuminate and assess how gender expectations determine the behavior of characters?

To write an essay such as this, begin by identifying where the story highlights gender roles and then examine how the characters, particularly the female characters, cede to or work around those roles. You might, for instance, consider how Sweets Ramirez can pursue Danny only by staying at home and waiting for him to pass by. Consider too how the rules of chivalry resonate in terms of gender. In what ways are gender roles here determined by the chivalric code of knights and ladies? One example of this is seen in chapter 14 in the stories about Petey Ravanno and Gracie Montez: His unrequited affection for her results in his pining for her and physically wasting away (stories of chivalric love often featured physical illness as a symptom of true love, especially for men). These meditations on chivalry can lead to an insightful discussion of gender in this novel.

Character

Papers can focus on questions of character development (such as how Steinbeck distinguishes Sweets Ramirez from Tia Ignacia by their distinctive manners with love and men), means of characterization (such as the way we learn of Jesus Maria's altruism through the instances of his helping the corporal and others), or interpretations of changes in a character as the story proceeds (such as the transformations that homeownership brings to Danny). To write an essay on character, you would need to approach the story by investigating how readers come to know various characters. An essay could center on the means by which Steinbeck constructs the distinctive natures of his characters. How, for instance, does Steinbeck distinguish a character's manner? In the case of *Tortilla Flat,* Pilon's ability to rationalize his actions will raise questions about how sympathetic a character he is. We come to be reassured of the rightness of this behavior, however, when we observe how his rationalization customarily leads to conventionally moral ends. To answer questions of character development, look closely for characteristics of language, action, or interactions with other characters. The ways characters behave with one another help the reader understand who the characters are. Essays on character development not only assess the means by which characters are created but also analyze what characters signify and represent for the story as a whole.

Sample Topics:

1. **Danny's character development:** How does Danny change over the course of the novel? Why might these changes occur?

   An essay on this topic would force the writer to decide what kinds of specific changes happen in Danny's character. You might consider, for instance, how Danny is changed by the inheritance of two houses and the responsibility that this property signifies to him. In this case, it would be worthwhile to examine how the loss of one house is, to Danny, a relief. Another approach to the topic could be to examine Danny's depression at the end of the novel. He is said to have experienced an "amok" (chapter 16), which is a term that describes an inexplicable and often suicidal madness (we now tend to use *amok* as an adjective or adverb, but it was originally a noun and so Steinbeck employs it here). Consider tracking how Danny's madness is, in fact, explicable and what it means for a character who is presented as a kind of Arthurian hero. To that end, what is the significance of Danny's final run into the woods to find and fight an enemy?

2. **Character development in general:** How does the story present character to the reader? What techniques does the story use?

   A paper on this topic would observe how Steinbeck gives insight into character. A possible approach to this essay would be to look at the ways in which different characters respond to love. What does it signify that Danny is customarily open to love but that Pilon sees only the pitfalls of romantic entanglements? Looking at the actions of a pair of characters (such as Danny and Pilon) reveals the effects they have on events and on other characters. Another pair of characters to examine could be Jesus Maria and Pirate; they demonstrate a kindred fascination with God and miracles that galvanizes the larger group.

3. **Pilon as a character:** The narrator describes Pilon in ways that emphasize his intelligence, cunning, and fundamental goodness, and yet we see him acting in ways that are decidedly dodgy.

What is Pilon's true nature, and what role does he serve in the group?

A writer would need to think about Pilon's behavior overall and come to a conclusion about what his behavior suggests about his nature. He is characterized as the brains of the group, and he has a role of importance since he is, in effect, Danny's first appointed knight. Beyond his position of second in command, what does he contribute to the group? Is his intelligence beneficial or divisive? Is he always a force for good? Another question to consider is why he does not replace Danny as leader of the group when Danny dies. Is this a comment on Pilon, Danny, or the particulars of this group?

Philosophy and Ideas

Another approach to forming an argument about *Tortilla Flat* is to identify and then analyze the philosophical ideas that circulate in the novel. This approach is related to the thematic approach discussed above in that it tracks an idea in the story, but the result of this kind of an essay would demonstrate how you see the story as commenting on the idea in its more general form. This approach is made a bit more challenging by the often ironic tone of this novel, but a close reader will have little difficulty assessing the values and philosophy of the book. One idea that circulates in the story is that of economies of exchange and how materialism in particular negatively affects characters. Danny, for instance, bristles at the responsibility of homeownership and sees in this seeming boon only spiritual, social, and psychological danger. Other characters in the novel are likewise sensitive to the negative changes brought about by material wealth, and they prefer instead the value of nonmaterial things. Observing how the characters react to money (even as they ostensibly seek it for the purposes of wine acquisition) can lead to a worthwhile discussion of their principles. You could locate evidence for the importance of this idea by looking at how the action presents sympathetic characters as expressing awareness about materialism's risks. Materialism is clearly parodied when Sweets Ramirez receives the gift of a vacuum cleaner and, despite the lack of electricity in the house or a motor in the appliance, her status in the neighborhood is comically elevated and envied. Other broad ideas in the novel include the divine, reason/logic, and chivalry.

Sample Topics:

1. **Value:** What is valued by Danny and his friends? How does this novel present the connection between money and value?

This is a topic that you could approach in various ways. One approach would be to discuss the idea of value in an economic way: How, for instance, are economic values made anathema to this community? You might note that actual cash does not generally exist in Tortilla Flat: Pilon, in one episode, works to acquire money in order to pay Danny rent, but the closer Pilon gets to home, the more vulgar the money seems. He opts instead to bring a gift (wine) to Danny (chapter 3). Another approach to this topic would assess how the book represents value, in the sense of merit. You might, in an essay such as this, consider the qualities of a person that are presented as the most important, what actions demonstrate merit, and so on. A third approach to the topic on value could assess what it is about the world itself that seems valuable. Through close readings, consider how the natural world is presented, such as in this description about the beauty of dew: "It is a time of quiet joy, the sunny morning. When the glittery dew is on the mallow weeds, each leaf holds a jewel which is beautiful, if not valuable" (chapter 4). An ambitious essay could consider the meaning of the money-free world of Tortilla Flat in the context of its depression-era publication date.

2. **The Divine:** How is the experience of the divine represented in this novel? To whom is it available and by what means is it attainable?

This topic asks you to track the existence of the divine, a quality that the characters of *Tortilla Flat* hold in high regard. One approach to this topic would be to assess how a number of characters respond to the notion of the divine; one example of this is when Pirate explains that his plan for his hoarded money is to buy a golden candlestick for Saint Francis of Assisi (referred to as "San Francisco" here) in thanks for a favor (the sparing of a sick dog's life) the saint had extended to him. You could analyze the effect of this revelation on the other characters' behaviors. Another approach to this topic could be to explore which characters have access to the divine and theorize about the reasons for this. You could also broaden the topic to consider more generally the notion of reverence and analyze what institutions and ideas the characters demonstrate reverence for. One example of reverence worth discussing is the time the characters decide that they cannot attend Danny's funeral because their clothing is too shabby for the reverence they feel.

3. **Reason/logic:** How is the process of human reason and logic represented as a work of art in this novel? Consider the fluidity of categories such as truth and fiction for characters such as Pilon. What, ultimately, do you think the novel is saying about the ways in which humans create morality?

This topic makes an assertion about the novel and asks you to elaborate on the assertion. To respond to the topic you would need to identify those scenes where individuals make sense of their actions or goals through creative reasoning. You might, for instance, examine how Pilon makes sense of his fleecing of Pirate (though Pilon later changes his goal): The logic of this episode is a tour de force of convolution and rationalization. Ultimately, you will want to reach a conclusion about how reason—or the broader category of morality—is represented in this novel. Is morality, for example, represented as having a reality outside of human creativity?

4. **Chivalry:** The novel makes repeated and overt allusions to medieval notions of chivalry. Analyze how chivalry is practiced in this novel.

To address this topic you would need to do some research into the history of chivalry and the chivalric code (which is characterized by loyalty, courage, and courtesy). The next steps would be to examine how the customs of knighthood are practiced by the characters and to discuss whether the novel's actions are in accord with or show deviations from the chivalric code. It would be worthwhile to consider discussing Danny's and his friends' understandings of (and discussions about) the Torellis, the corporal, or any of Tortilla Flat's female characters. In what ways do rules of protocol determine their actions? Ultimately, you will want to assess if the narrator's comparisons between these men and the chivalrous knights of yore are in jest or in earnest.

Form and Genre

Form and genre provide illuminating ways of analyzing many literary works, especially a modern novel such as *Tortilla Flat* that uses so many archaic forms. Form is defined as the shape and structure of a literary work; genre is defined as the kind, or classification, of a literary work. Though technically independent of the content of literature, form and genre are used deliberately by authors to help further the ideas in, strengthen the dramatic effect of, and generally refine their stories. In the case of *Tortilla Flat*, the genre is fiction and the form is that of an episodic story cycle that reads like a novel (with rising action, conflict, climax, falling action, chronological unity, etc.). This episodic style is an homage to the romances surrounding King Arthur that were collected in Thomas Malory's *Le Morte d'Arthur* (1485), and the fact that a 20th-century American writer would choose this form is itself worthy of an essay. How does this somewhat archaic story form contribute to an understanding of the characters of Tortilla Flat? You could consider, for instance, the use of the archaic convention of descriptive titles for each of the episodes: In what ways do these episode titles contribute to or change the meaning of the episodes themselves? Another question one could pose about the episode titles is how they make the novel cohere. More traditional essay topics are also useful for *Tortilla Flat*. Consider, for example, the techniques by which the story is shaped or structured through discussions of narrative point of view, tone, dialogue, or style.

Sample Topics:

1. ***Tortilla Flat* as medieval romance:** Consider the elements of medieval romance that *Tortilla Flat* utilizes. Be sure to discuss technique, form, atmosphere, and dramatic action.

This topic is asking you to consider what elements of medieval romance *Tortilla Flat* utilizes in the construction of its story. You would want to discuss form (such as the episode titles and style of dialogue), atmosphere (such as the atmospherics that are in keeping with the misty and foggy England of King Arthur), and dramatic action (such as the occurrence of miracles or the conflict that temptation presents). You will want to do some research into medieval romances such as the stories about King Arthur and Robin Hood (these were very popular when Steinbeck was growing up) and consider how *Tortilla Flat* uses these elements to create its own story. Another approach would be to concentrate on one aspect of the medieval romance; you might focus, for instance, on the medieval style of dialogue. A wholly different approach to this topic would analyze the novel's use not of medieval romance but of medieval hagiography, or the stories of saints. How, for instance, is the story of Danny told in the same kind of legendary, myth-making form as a saint's story is told? You could research the stories of Saint Francis of Assisi for an example of a saint (since he is so important to Pirate and known to the rest of the characters).

2. **Irony:** There is so much irony in this work that it can be challenging to ascertain when it is not teasing. Based on your close reading of the novel, what does *Tortilla Flat* want us to take seriously and what does it suggest we dismiss?

Irony is a notoriously slippery notion, but it can provide a worthwhile direction for an essay. Irony is loosely defined in literature as a device where something contains two simultaneous meanings, such as those found in innuendo, puns, Freudian slips, satire, and parody. In dramatic irony, for instance, the audience is aware of a fact that a character onstage is ignorant of; the irony, here, is that an open window, for example, has two meanings: the one for the character (who thinks, "The window is open") and the one for the audience (which thinks, "The villain left the window open after he came into the house"). Irony can be used in art for the simple purpose of mockery (wherein an object, person, or institution is ridiculed), but irony can also be used for instructive purposes. In this last case, irony can communicate to an audience or reader the need to rethink a commonly held belief. One approach to this topic would be to read through the ironic tone in this novel to ascertain what principles, individuals, and institutions it values. You should also theorize about what the ironic tone contributes to the meanings of its stories. You could, for instance, argue that the heroism of Danny and his friends is mock-heroism; if that were your argument, then you would be essentially arguing that Steinbeck's irony misfires (unless you think he really meant to dismissively mock Danny and his friends). Another approach to this topic would be to read closely in order to identify sections where irony, as a pervading tone, ceases. Consider, for example, the section on Pirate's beatitude in chapter 13. Yet one more approach to this topic would be to examine how the ironic tone is achieved. To that end, you would need to research the literary devices associated with irony such as litotes, hyperbole, and understatement, all of which Steinbeck uses in this narrative. Examples of litotes (a rhetorical device where exaggerated understatement is used to emphasize a quality) are found in the preface: "Danny's house was not unlike the Round Table." Hyperbole and understatement are liberally sprinkled throughout the novel.

3. **Narration:** Characterize the narrator. In what ways does the narration change forms during the course of the novel?

This question asks you to consider the narrator and the narration. One approach to this topic would be to identify the persona of the narrator and decide what he likes and dislikes. To gain an understanding of the narrator, you should examine the preface of the book where the narrator speaks directly to the reader. What is the effect of this choice? Are there other places where the narrator is as direct and revealing? To address the second half of the topic (about changes in the narration), you will need to track the narrative style as the novel goes on.

You might discuss, for instance, how the narrator takes a more active, even participatory role in the story in the last three chapters (e.g., when he addresses characters such as Mr. Torrelli: "Oh, beware, Torrelli, when Pilon moves smiling upon you!" [chapter 15]). Finally, you will want to theorize about the role of the narrator in this novel overall. How does the narration contribute to the story itself?

4. **Setting:** In what ways is setting important to the novel? Consider setting as both an atmosphere and a powerful force in its own right.

This topic asks you to consider in what ways the setting (time and place) is important to the story. You could consider discussing either the time or the place. In what ways, for instance, does the post–World War I time period contribute to the conflicts in the novel? What about the existence of Prohibition? You could also consider in what ways the natural setting of the Monterey Peninsula is a force in this story. You would want to reach a conclusion about the role of the forest for Danny at the end of his life: What does it mean that he goes into the forest to search for his "Enemy"? Consider discussing as well whether the regional population constitutes setting: Are people an element of place? Whether you concentrate on time or place, you will want to read passages closely to gather evidence for your analytical claims.

Comparison and Contrast

Comparing components of a story in order to explain and analyze the similarities or differences between them is a useful approach to writing an essay. Remember to avoid the mistake of merely creating a list of such similarities or differences in a work; instead, you must take the necessary step of commenting on these observations. To begin a comparison/contrast essay you might compare characters with each other: How does Danny compare to Pilon? How does Jesus Maria compare to Big Joe Portagee? You could also compare characters (or other elements of the story like patterns of imagery or action) across different stories. For example, how do the depictions of place compare in *Tortilla Flat* and *Cannery Row?* How is the experience of economic poverty depicted differently in *The Grapes of Wrath* and *Tortilla Flat?* The challenge of this kind of essay is to decide what the similarities or differences you identify might mean. These are the questions that make essays interesting and the ones that will have different answers for each writer. To get to these questions, it is often helpful to think about what kinds of effects Steinbeck achieves by producing either similarities or differences between elements of his stories. How, for example, does the fact of home ownership affect our understanding of Danny's and Pilon's characterization and motivation? It is not sufficient to identify a pattern and to point to the existence of similarities or differences; you must also consider what purpose those similarities or differences might serve in the story overall.

Sample Topics:

1. **Contrast two of the knights:** Contrast two of Danny's friends and consider what they respectively contribute to both the group and the novel.

   This topic asks you to choose two characters and evaluate how they are different in terms of personality and action. You could, for example, look at Jesus Maria and Big Joe and analyze what we learn about the group through the behaviors of these two characters. For example, what do we learn about the customs of this group from the fact that Big Joe steals from Pirate and then is brutally punished by the group for this transgression? What does Jesus Maria demonstrate about the group's sense of mercy and comradeship when he offers Big Joe wine after the beating? You might also consider building a comparative essay around Pilon and Pablo.

2. **Compare the idea of divine grace in *Tortilla Flat* and *The Grapes of Wrath*:** The notions of God and divinity are demonstrably important to the characters in both *Tortilla Flat* and *The Grapes of Wrath:* The characters in both novels take seriously their relationships with God. Though divine grace is important in both

books, it is presented differently. Compare how these two novels depict grace and consider what these theological beliefs imply about the novels' cultural worlds and about the characters.

This topic asks the writer to compare the idea of divine grace in two texts. One approach would be to think about how phenomena such as miracles warrant different atmospheres and reactions in the respective characters. While the residents of Tortilla Flat hope for divine intervention, the members of the Joad family do not seem to hold out any hope for such miracles. What impact does this difference have on these characters? Close consideration of the two books might also result in some other points of theological comparison, such as in the notions of sin.

3. **Compare Danny's demise to another heroic demise:** How is Danny's demise heroic? Choose a version of a hero's death in another literary work to ascertain whether there are connections to Danny's death.

This topic is asking you to discover whether there are heroic aspects in Danny's death. To develop the topic you would need to read closely Danny's death scene as well as another literary depiction of a hero's death; consider, for example, reading the poem "Ulysses" by Tennyson or reading the death of Arthur in Malory's *Le Morte d'Arthur.* You will want to verify whether Danny's death is indeed depicted as heroic. Consider discussing the psychology of heroism that seems to invite early death. What is heroic, to these figures, about dying young?

Bibliography for *Tortilla Flat*:

Levant, Howard. "The First Public Success, *Tortilla Flat.*" *The Novels of John Steinbeck: A Critical Study.* Columbia, MO: U of Missouri P, 1974. 52–73.

Metzger, Charles R. "John Steinbeck's Paisano Knights." *Readings on John Steinbeck.* Ed. Clarice Swisher. San Diego, CA: Greenhaven Press, 1996. 65–72.

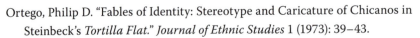

Ortego, Philip D. "Fables of Identity: Stereotype and Caricature of Chicanos in Steinbeck's *Tortilla Flat.*" *Journal of Ethnic Studies* 1 (1973): 39–43.

Prindle, Dennis. "The Pretexts of Romance: Steinbeck's Allegorical Naturalism from *Cup of Gold* to *Tortilla Flat.*" *The Steinbeck Question: New Essays in Criticism.* Ed. Donald R. Noble. Troy, NY: Whitston Publishing Company, 1993. 23–36.

IN DUBIOUS BATTLE

READING TO WRITE

JOHN STEINBECK originally conceived of *In Dubious Battle* as taking the form of a diary of an individual participating in a strike in agricultural California. This first-person approach, however, must have conflicted with Steinbeck's desire to write a nonpartisan account of a strike. The third-person point of view that Steinbeck ultimately adopted does indeed create more universal sympathy and understanding than a first-person narrative could offer, though this understanding is tempered by the pessimistic tone of the story. This sympathetic parity can be somewhat disconcerting to the reader: There are no clear heroes in this story; neither are there absolute villains. This book's form reveals that Steinbeck's sympathies were not with the ideologies being so vehemently debated at the time but with the individuals caught up in and propelling the events described in the novel.

This issue of how form emphasizes content is one that is worth treating in an essay. Consider, for instance, how the third-person narration keeps its focus on the young man, Jim Nolan, who becomes an increasingly authoritative participant in the strike in the fictional Torgas Valley. The novel's action begins with Jim on the verge of joining the labor movement and ends with a fellow activist commemorating Jim's death with a firebrand eulogy. Paying close attention to the overall form of the novel shows how *In Dubious Battle* is less the story of a strike than the story of a young man who participates in a strike. This question of narrative focus might seem like a small distinction, but it is a defining one because it reveals that the true battle at the core of this story is not between growers and workers; instead, it is within Jim Nolan and, by extension, every individual who lives in a time of political and economic upheaval. That is to say, *In Dubious Battle* is a story about the battles within all individuals. Seeking an understanding of the overall stakes in any story is crucial to assessing the broader implications of its ideas. Supporting evidence for your essay's analysis will come from recognizing these comprehensive patterns of form, as well as from scrutinizing the smaller details found in diction, image, and characterization.

Reading carefully the details of meaning in literature is called "close reading." A close reading of the beginnings of literary works is worthwhile because that is customarily where characters, setting, and dramatic conflicts are initiated, if only by suggestion. Consider, for example, the opening sentence of *In Dubious Battle:* "At last it was evening." That "at last" implies retroactive waiting; though we were not privy to the waiting period, we are here for what will shortly take place. Another detail that is suggestive is that the waiting is for "evening," or night, a time more conventionally associated with the end of the day and nocturnal, even forbidden activities. "At last it was evening" could be the beginning of a vampire story, and while there is nothing here remotely supernatural, the first sentence conjures up associations of danger. While the remainder of the first paragraph does not clarify the particulars of the dramatic situation (that is, what is about to happen), it does establish a great deal more about the character and the setting. Here is the entire first paragraph:

At last it was evening. The lights in the street outside came on, and the Neon [sic] restaurant sign on the corner jerked on and off, exploding its hard red light in the air. Into Jim Nolan's room the sign threw a soft red light. For two hours Jim had been sitting in a small, hard rocking-chair, his feet up on the white bedspread. Now that it was quite dark, he brought his feet down to the floor and slapped the sleeping legs. For a moment he sat quietly while waves of itching rolled up and down his calves; then he stood up and reached for the unshaded light. The furnished room lighted up—the big white bed with its chalk-white spread, the golden-oak bureau, the clean red carpet worn through to a brown warp.

Jim Nolan's character traits are established in this first paragraph by his actions. His focus, determination, and ability to tolerate physical discomfort are all made clear by the fact that for two hours he had been sitting "in a small, hard rocking-chair." That he has been immobile for that long also suggests that he is serious about whatever it is he is waiting for. The small physical actions in this scene are symbolically significant and imply that Jim is transitioning from a kind of death (darkness) to life: He rubs his sleeping legs awake and turns on a lamp. The act of illumination is particularly evocative because light in literature so often represents understanding, epiphany, and vitality. Overall, this scene's suggestions of rebirth anticipate Jim's pursuit of the life force that he sees in political activism.

Reading closely for the details in the physical setting is likewise revealing: the refracted neon light, the hard red light (clearly signaling a red-light district), the "worn" carpet, the "unshaded" light. The harsh anonymity of the room helps explain the life that Jim is leaving behind; such harsh anonymity (in the form of his grisly death) will later prove to be, ironically, exactly what he is fated for.

A good topic for an essay could focus on the details at the beginning and end of this novel. You might consider, for example, if Jim attains his goals of a meaningful life and a sense of belonging. Does the book imply, instead, that his political activism was an exercise in futility?

Reading slowly and carefully will make for a more nuanced understanding of the novel while also enabling you to gather the evidence you need to write a strong essay.

TOPICS AND STRATEGIES

This section of the chapter discusses various possible topics for essays on *In Dubious Battle* and general approaches to those topics. Remember that these are only starting points for your own analysis, not a comprehensive code to the novel. Every topic discussed here could encompass a wide variety of good papers.

Themes

In Dubious Battle is composed of many themes, ideas, and concepts that fuel the action. Some of these ideas include rebirth (as discussed above), instinct, belonging, the individual, faith, and work. Writers approaching the novel often begin by identifying a central theme they see as important and then deciding what it is that the novel is saying about that theme. You can identify a theme by noticing the ideas, symbols, or even words that recur in the story—in the initial discussion of *In Dubious Battle*, for example, the actions of the protagonist suggest that he is undergoing a personal rebirth, and indeed this is both discussed and demonstrated throughout the novel. Next, when you write an essay, you have to decide what the novel is saying about the theme of Jim's rebirth. Qualities such as his bourgeoning absolutism suggest that while he has become formidable, he has also become less humane, so his rebirth is also a kind of death. Other themes could be approached in similar ways: You could approach the theme of instinct through the novel's depiction of how instinct motivates and controls characters and then assess what the role of instinct might be in the novel. Thematic approaches also overlap with the philosophical approach described below.

Sample Topics:

1. **Instinct:** How does the novel portray the force of instinct? What does the power of instinct suggest about humanity?

   To write an essay on instinct, begin by identifying scenes that portray characters being motivated by drives they cannot rationally explain. The scenes of mob violence, for instance, depict groups of individuals whose instinctive desires supersede their more customary modes of conduct. There are scenes, especially with Mac and Jim, where individuals wonder why they do what they do. Based on your assessment of the portrayal of these scenes, you can develop a thesis about the representations of instinct in this novel. Ultimately, you will want to assess whether the novel is portraying instinct as a backsliding into barbarism or as a natural and human phenomenon. Do our instincts prove us human or inhuman?

2. **Belonging:** What is the novel saying about the human desire to be part of a group? Why are so many individuals portrayed

as wanting to lose themselves to a larger body? What do these individuals hope to gain or change about themselves?

This topic invites you to reflect on how the desire to belong to a social group motivates characters in this novel. Jim, for instance, remarks on wanting to be part of something "bigger than [him]self." That he is otherwise without family might make him more prone to this desire, but he is not the only character who experiences this longing. You might consider how characters express a desire for meaning that they do not feel they can have without the social ties a group endeavor provides. You might also consider how belonging contributes to adversarial enmity toward other groups (the growers and the police, for example, clearly feel connected to one another in ways that are identical to the strikers' connections, and they too identify themselves against others, such as the strikers). Based on your close reading of what characters express about belonging, you will be able to reach a thesis on the role of belonging in this novel.

3. **The individual:** There is considerable discussion of both radical and status quo ideas, strategies, and other theoretical abstractions in this novel, but time and again we see that individuals, not ideologies, precipitate change. How does the novel evaluate the influence of single individuals? Furthermore, do individuals redeem the actions of the mobs?

This topic makes an assertion about the novel and asks you to elaborate on the assertion. To respond to the topic you would need to identify those scenes where single individuals change the course of events, for better or worse. Mac, for instance, instigates the strike itself. Ultimately, you will want to assess the qualities of individuality (e.g., self-sufficiency, charisma, vision) of which the novel seems to approve and disapprove. Decide whether the novel sets us up to see the power of the individual as glorious or threatening.

4. **Faith:** This novel suggests that there is considerable overlap between political and religious faiths: Both types of belief systems generate fanaticism and ecstasy. How does the story represent and evaluate the role of faith for individuals?

To write an essay on this topic, you might find it useful to focus on a narrow collection of examples or even a single character. Jim would be a good character to study in conjunction with this topic as he evinces a zealotry that both Doc Burton and Mac remark upon. For his part, Mac is a character who demonstrates a facility for generating a religious ecstasy in crowds and individuals both. What is the novel saying about faith and the euphoria it can generate? Are political ideologies tantamount to religious ones, or, more simply, are people unable to be motivated without the promise of ecstasy?

5. **Work ethic and the American Dream:** How is the role of work represented in this novel? How does the strikers' desire for work imply a critique of the American Dream?

To answer these questions, a writer needs to keep in mind the fact that the American Dream (e.g., property ownership, economic self-sufficiency, independence) is supposed to be attainable by any hardworking person. There are numerous illustrations in the novel of the strikers' desire to work hard. Consider, for example, the pride old Dan takes in his industriousness and his reluctance to accept charity. There are also examples of the important role hard work plays in the psyches and egos of men. Ultimately, you will need to assess whether the novel is charging the American Dream with speciousness.

Character

Papers can focus on questions of character development (such as how Steinbeck distinguishes Dick from Joy by their distinctive manner with police and other authority figures), means of characterization (such as the way we learn of Lisa's combined pride and modesty through the way she breast-feeds her baby), or interpretations of changes in a character as the story proceeds (the transformation of Jim from an eager neophyte at the beginning of the novel to a merciless zealot at the end). To write an essay on character, you would need to approach the story by investigating how readers come to know various characters. An essay could center on the means by which Steinbeck constructs the distinctive natures of his characters. How, for instance, does Steinbeck distinguish a character's manner? In the case of *In Dubious Battle,* Mac's ability to adopt the speech, manners, and comportment of the people he is with demonstrates that he is malleable and, perhaps, not wholly authentic. We come to understand the practical applications of this behavior, however, when we observe the unproductive aggressive behavior of Joy, who is unable to check his hatred for authority and so suffers the physical consequences of calling police officers "sons-of-bitches." We understand more readily these two characters when we see them together. To answer questions of character development, look closely for characteristics of language, action, or interactions with other characters. The ways characters behave with one another help the reader understand who the characters are. Essays on character development not only assess the means by which characters are created but also analyze what characters signify and represent for the story as a whole.

Sample Topics:

1. **Jim Nolan's character development:** How does Jim Nolan change over the course of the novel? Why might these changes occur?

An essay on this topic guides the writer to decide what kinds of specific changes happen in Jim's character. You might consider, for instance, how Jim's desire for belonging is fulfilled and why he later disregards, to a degree, this strong desire. Another approach to the topic could be to examine Jim's growing sense of purpose: What experiences contribute to this change in his personality? Jim is very much a searching innocent at the beginning of the novel and a found man at the end: Does the novel represent Jim's profound character changes as monstrous or elevating?

2. **Character development in general:** How does the story present character to the reader? What techniques does the story use?

A paper on this topic would observe how Steinbeck gives insight into character. A possible approach to this essay would be to look at the ways in which different characters respond to conflict. What does it signify that Joy is always poised to fight and that Dick is so apt to avoid conflict? Looking at the actions of a pair of characters (such as Joy and Dick) reveals the effects they have on events and on other characters. Another pair of characters to examine could be Jim and Mac; they provide analytically interesting oppositions at different points in the novel. A particularly instructive scene for a topic on this pair would be the one featuring the interrogation and beating of the high school vigilante. What do Jim's ruthlessness and Mac's misgivings in this scene tell us about the switched positions of this pair?

3. **Mac as a character:** Doc describes Mac as a mixture of sentimentality and brutality, and we see him acting, by turns, exploitative and caring. What is Mac's true nature, and what role does he serve in Jim's life?

You would need to think about Mac's behavior overall and come to a conclusion about what his behavior suggests about his nature. His role for Jim in the strike is to mentor the younger man, but that role undergoes significant change when Jim proves to be adept at organizing and enforcing. The scenes where Jim seems to supersede Mac in his opportunism also offer insight into Mac's character as we thereby recognize Mac's sense of morality. It would be worthwhile to consider in what ways Mac generates conflict in his world: Since he searches it out and exacerbates fractious situations, does that make him both Jim's antagonist and teacher?

4. **Dan and Lisa:** Dan and Lisa, an old man and a young woman, are opposites in many ways, and as such they broaden our

understanding of the effect of labor conditions and unrest. How are these characters presented in the novel? How do they contribute to a fuller understanding of the strike and of the novel's protagonist?

This essay would need to describe and evaluate both characters and their respective roles in the novel. What qualities do these individuals embody? What qualities of Jim's do they enable us to perceive? This essay would need to bring in some discussion about Jim's growing interest in Lisa as well as Lisa's growing fondness for the ailing Dan.

History and Context

Considering *In Dubious Battle*'s historical context offers another productive approach to analysis since the novel utilizes so much history to ground its story. Historical references include those to actual labor groups, particular strikes, growers' associations, and publications of the era. References to specific individuals and places are veiled, and this conscientious censoring on Steinbeck's part is itself worthy of further consideration and could make for an interesting essay. Economic conditions during the depression era in which this novel was published generated conflicts between owners and laborers. Sympathy for the workers was a celebrated cause among many in the arts, and sometimes critics themselves judged art by what they believed was the art's political, instead of aesthetic, value. This kind of criticism could form an interesting subject for an essay. Consider, for example, how the novel's approach to its subject was received by Steinbeck's contemporaries. Do you think that its reception would be different today? Answering questions such as these would demonstrate your understanding not only of the political stakes of this novel but also of the political climates of then and now. Another approach to studying history and context would be to examine how historical events function in the novel. San Francisco's general strike of 1934 and its violent conflagration, Bloody Thursday, are both referred to in the novel. Doing some research into Bloody Thursday (which the longshoreman's union still celebrates every year) would enable you to assess how the event resonates in the story. The same approach would be worth taking for an analysis of the history of violence (used by and on strikers) in the labor movement at that time. To address this last topic or any other historical topic, you would need to do some research to be able to consider knowledgeably what the novel is asserting about the world it describes.

Sample Topics:

1. ***In Dubious Battle* as a political novel:** *In Dubious Battle* is a novel that concerns itself with politics, but is it a political novel? How did Steinbeck's contemporaries interpret the novel's political stance? How do you think today's audiences would interpret the book's political stance?

   While Steinbeck sought to write a nonpartisan novel about a labor strike, the reception of the novel was not nonpartisan; in fact, some reviewers took umbrage with what they believed to be the book's implicit political ideology. This topic requires you to research reviews of the novel from the time of its publication and to both discuss and analyze your findings. Consider how the reviews assess the the novel's politics. Also consider discussing what, based on your research's findings, the most controversial aspect of the novel was. Finally, consider speculating on how you think today's audiences would interpret the book's politics. Give explanations for your conclusions.

2. **Bloody Thursday and the novel:** The characters make explicit reference to Bloody Thursday, a day of violence that took place during a 1934 San Francisco strike. How does Steinbeck use this contemporary event in the story? What purposes are served by this kind of historical reference?

   A paper on *In Dubious Battle* and Bloody Thursday would need to offer a thorough examination of the historical events of the San Francisco dockworkers strike as well as its political aftermath. This consideration would lead to an analysis of how Steinbeck uses the event in his novel. How does Bloody Thursday resonate with the characters? Does Bloody Thursday serve as an inspiring reference or a cautionary tale?

3. **Violence and the labor movement:** Strikes in this novel are understood by the characters as likely to culminate in violence.

Is this in keeping with actual strikes of the time? In what ways does Steinbeck use the acts of violence for aesthetic or symbolic reasons?

This topic requires you to study 1930s labor movements and the prevalence and variety of violent acts that are connected with them. You will need to study the practices of police, "citizen's committees," government troops, and the strikers themselves. For the benefit of focus, consider limiting your study to California labor unrest. Using your research as a point of comparison, consider how *In Dubious Battle* crafts the violence for its storytelling potential. You will want to pay special attention to scenes where violence serves a symbolic or aesthetic function in the story.

Philosophy and Ideas

Another approach to forming an argument about *In Dubious Battle* is to identify and then analyze the philosophical ideas that circulate in the story. This approach is related to the thematic approach previously discussed in that it tracks an idea in the story, but the result of this kind of essay would demonstrate how you see the story as commenting on an idea in its more general form. In *In Dubious Battle*, the characters themselves discuss and debate their philosophical points of view. Of the ideas debated, the most prominent example is the idea of group-man, as distinct from individual man. Doc Burton asserts in chapter 8 that a man in a group and a man alone are two entirely different entities: "A man in a group isn't himself at all: he's a cell in an organism that isn't like him any more than the cells in your body are like you." Doc's understanding of group-man assigns an amorality to phenomena such as mobs. Jim, though he never endorses mobs, expresses a desire to give himself to a group; he sees in group-man an opportunity for individual meaning and redemption. In addition to being an idea that the characters discuss, the notion of group-man is a useful way to think about the events in the novel; doing so helps clarify the group psychology and the dynamics of both formal group actions (such as Joy's funeral) and more impromptu group actions (such as the strikers attacking the pickers in the orchard). Observing the ways that the characters—especially Mac, Doc, and Jim—discuss the group-man idea also reveals aspects of these characters that would otherwise be difficult to discern. Other broad ideas in the novel include utilitarianism and historical progress. To write on these or other ideas, you should look for philosophical ideas in their theoretical, abstract forms, as well as for practiced examples of them.

Sample Topics:

1. **Group-man:** How do the novel's main characters define the group-man idea? Which definition of group-man seems to be supported by the novel's events?

This topic would require that you study carefully the discussions of group-man conducted by Mac, Doc, and Jim. After closely reading these sections, you will need to show how the three characters' theories are distinct. Then, based on your assessment of events in the story, you can argue which of the characters' theories are validated by the events in the novel.

2. **Utilitarianism:** That Mac sometimes balks at "using" others suggests that he has ambivalent feelings about utilitarianism as a practical mode of conduct (though he is simultaneously a proponent of using any means necessary to fight for justice). What other examples of utilitarianism are shown in this novel? Does the story present utilitarianism as morally tenable or as troubling? Are its costs worth its benefits?

Utilitarianism understands that the morality of an action is determined by its doing the greatest good for the greatest number of people. This philosophy is very much in evidence in Mac's stated point of view (especially at the beginning of the novel), but there are places where he is reluctant to "use" individuals. You will want to analyze the examples of this hesitation and note when and why Mac is reluctant to "use" Jim. Pay special attention to the end of the novel, when Jim's corpse becomes a kind of prop to illustrate a point about injustice. Ultimately, you should reach a conclusion about whether the book presents utilitarianism as an acceptable philosophy.

3. **Historical progress?:** The incidents of violence in the novel are brutal. While Jim is convinced that this brutality is necessary for achieving political justice, Doc Burton argues that the notion of progress is an illusion; he sees the violence as simply repeating an endless cycle of human-on-human violence. Whose point of view of history do you think the novel supports?

This topic asks you to concentrate on characters' understandings of history and of their individual place in the historical continuum. To answer this question, you would need to study how these two characters look to history for clues to the present: Jim, for instance, is an enthusiastic reader of history and sees in it valuable information for the present (e.g., when he shares a story of ancient warfare for a lesson about how to combat the ebbing enthusiasm of the strikers). Doc, in contrast, sees humankind as wretched and as perversely and ceaselessly dedicated to making itself miserable. You will want to read closely the discussions on this topic in chapter 13. To answer the final part of this topic, you will need to gauge whether either understanding of history is reflected in the overall action of the novel. Does *In Dubious Battle* show patterns of progress and change, or of repetition and stagnation?

Form and Genre

Form and genre provide illuminating ways of analyzing many literary works. Form is defined as the shape and structure of a literary work; genre is defined as the kind, or classification, of a literary work. Though technically independent of the content of literature, form and genre are used deliberately by authors to help further the ideas in, strengthen the dramatic effect of, and generally refine their stories. The genre of *In Dubious Battle* is fiction and the form is the novel. The form that the narrative point of view takes is an interesting one, because Steinbeck, after all, sought to make his narration unbiased. The viability of complete impartiality is an interesting question and one worth exploring in an essay. Beyond form, a good paper could also contemplate the literary ramifications of genre, such as the bildungsroman. Jim experiences a rapid coming-of-age in this novel, but the customary conclusion of a bildungsroman, personal understanding and inclusion in the adult world, is replaced with the protagonist's death; that modification to the coming-of-age story trajectory is significant and would be interesting to analyze in an essay. Another good essay might consider the different varieties of writing that constitute this novel.

Sample Topics:

1. ***In Dubious Battle* as bildungsroman:** How is this novel a bildungsroman? In what ways does Jim grow and develop as an individual? Is his development checked or accelerated by his involvement with the strike?

   This topic requires some understanding of the bildungsroman genre. You can approach this topic by assessing how Jim changes from the beginning to the end of the novel. You will want to pay particular attention to his characterization at the book's inception, because so much of the story comments on Jim's increasing vitality and newfound sense of purpose and belonging. You will also want to identify places where his senses of autonomy and authority (two conventional signs of maturation) transform. Ultimately, you will want to address what the novel is saying about what happens to individuals caught up in this kind of group movement. Another important element to discuss is Jim's death: In what ways is Jim's literal facelessness a symbolic commentary on his individuality and, more broadly, on this bildungsroman?

2. **Proletarian literature:** Some critics have decreed *In Dubious Battle* an example of proletarian literature, but there are fundamental elements of this story that refute such a categorization. Analyze the genre and consider whether this novel is an example of proletarian literature.

   We know that Steinbeck himself did not consider this novel an example of proletarian literature, but that fact does not put the question to rest. This topic requires you to do some research into proletarian literature and to consider the ways in which this novel satisfies (or does not) the qualities of a proletarian novel. One approach to this essay would be to assess in what way the proletariat is characterized and represented in this novel. Is it wholly sympathetic? You will want to offer an analysis of what you think this novel is saying about the working poor and their situation.

3. **Impartial narration:** Steinbeck wanted this novel to have an unbiased narration, a "recording consciousness." Examine the rhetorical strategies he uses in this novel and reach a conclusion about whether Steinbeck's approach is successful. If you find fundamental biases in the novel, consider how he might have erased them and what costs to the story that erasure might have incurred.

This is a topic that asks you to examine closely the way that form (rhetorical strategies) performs function (unbiased narration). One approach would be to examine how the narrator steps aside to allow the characters to build the story through narration and action. To that end, are there places where we hear the narrator's opinion (in word choice, for instance)? Another approach would be to examine whose stories are told in this novel and why you think some characters are given a voice while others are not. What are we to conclude about the fact that we do not hear the growers, for instance, discussing the labor strike? It would be interesting to consider the effect on form that different media—newspaper articles, protest songs, letters—have on the novel. This topic ultimately moves you toward thinking about the form that this story takes and the consequences of the form that Steinbeck adopts.

Language, Symbols, and Imagery

Language, symbol, and imagery are some of the creative means by which an author conveys certain feelings or ideas that would, if simply announced, be undermined in their imaginative and evocative power. All writers, but those of imaginative fiction especially, use language deliberately, and they choose words based on their connotative, or suggestive, meanings. As you read fiction in preparation for writing about it, you need to be alert to the connotative meanings of language even as you register the surface meaning of language in order to follow the plot itself. In *In Dubious Battle,* the form of the narration limits the imagistic language because the story relies on a contained narrative voice and very heavily on dialogue and action. Steinbeck's language here is boiled down in the sense that it feels shorn of superfluous descriptions. This writing style is itself an interesting topic for an essay on this novel because the prose's understatement emphasizes the sense of an impartial narrator. In this way, the language parallels the approach to the subject.

Symbols, usually used in conjunction with imagery, are objects, either animate or inanimate, that writers also use to convey ideas. In *In Dubious Battle,* the narration does not rely very much on symbols, but the characters within the story do. Both the strikers and the growers use symbols to express their respective points of view. You could explore this aspect of the novel in an essay on how the groups (or even individuals) deploy and employ symbols and, further, what it means that they communicate in this manner. The best essays on symbolism will look at the symbol and, perhaps, its affiliated imagery and consider these subjects in relation to the story's larger ideas. When you are asked to discuss symbolism, you are being asked to discuss what something signifies, means, and represents in light of the entire work.

Sample Topics:

1. **Characters' use of symbolism:** In what ways do the characters utilize symbols in this novel? What are we to draw from their heavy reliance on symbolism?

This novel is somewhat unusual in that it showcases how individual characters rely on the power of symbols. One approach to this topic would be to focus on how a character (Mac would be a good choice) demonstrates an understanding of, facility with, and fluency in symbols. His orchestration of Joy's funeral, for instance, shows Mac's awareness of the figurative powers of the dead body, the tattered American flag on the casket, and the eulogy. All three of these elements operate as symbols to Mac and, as the scene shows, to the audience as well. Another character to discuss in this context could be Jim. Jim becomes so attuned to symbols that they become the only meaning that he sees; for example, Jim understands Mac's interrogation and assault of the high school student not as a brutal action but as a cautionary "example" to others who might play at being vigilantes (in this case, the boy symbolizes, or stands in for, "example"). Yet one more approach would be to examine how the growers and civic authorities themselves use symbols. Consider, for this approach, examining their utilization of newspaper headlines and stories, the public and private use of violence and vandalism (of Anderson's lunch wagon, for example), and the calculated public demonstrations of tolerance. To adequately examine your subject, you should limit your focus to one character or one group.

2. **Religious imagery:** Consider how the narrator and the characters describe experience in religious terms. What significance are we to draw from these comparisons?

This topic is a variation on the discussion of faith as discussed in the section on theme. To write an essay on this topic, you would want to show how political passion is described in terms customarily associated with religious experiences. Consider discussing how the characters and narrator utilize specific religious language, postures, and symbols such as ecstasy, genuflection, suffering, and martyrdom. What conclusions are we to draw from the symbolism of religion in this very secular drama?

Comparison and Contrast

Comparing components of a story in order to explain and analyze the similarities or differences between them is a useful approach to writing an essay. Remember to avoid the pitfall of merely creating a catalog or list of such similarities or differences in a work; instead, you must take the necessary step of commenting on these observations. To begin a comparison/contrast essay, you might compare characters with each other: How does Dakin compare to London? How does Joy compare to

Jim Nolan's father, Roy? You could also compare characters (or other elements of the story like patterns of imagery or action) across different stories. For example, how do the depictions of labor compare in *In Dubious Battle* and *The Grapes of Wrath?* In *Of Mice and Men* and *In Dubious Battle?* The challenge of this kind of essay is deciding what the similarities or differences you identify might mean. These are the questions that make essays interesting and the ones that will have different answers for each writer. To get to these questions, you might think about what kinds of effects Steinbeck achieves by producing either similarities or differences between elements of his stories. How, for example, does the fact of ownership affect our understanding of London's and Dakin's characterization and motivation? It is not sufficient to identify a pattern and to point to the existence of similarities or differences; you must also consider what purpose those similarities or differences might serve in the story overall.

Sample Topics:

1. **Comparing Roy Nolan and Joy:** What are the roles of these two pugnacious men to the cause, to the novel, and to Jim?

   This topic asks you to consider two characters as performing similar functions. You would need to assess the connections between these figures and measure their significance in terms of what they reveal to us about the political cause, the novel, and Jim. Ultimately, you will want to offer a theory that explains their overall roles: What does it mean that they both suffer and die in support of the fight for justice? How do their different temperaments affect their contributions to the cause?

2. **Comparing the mob experience:** *In Dubious Battle* and "The Vigilante" both depict the social and psychological experience of being a part of a mob. How are they mutually informative?

   This topic asks you to examine the experience of being a part of a mob as described in a short story and a novel. In what ways are these experiences described similarly? One intriguing point of comparison for mob activity is the fused sex and violence drives. These are more overtly articulated in "The Vigilante," but you could analyze how this connection to primal drives resonates with the mob experiences described by Jim, Mac, or Sam in *In Dubious Battle*. You will want to reach an assessment about how being part of a mob is described in these texts: What does the mob experience tell us about man in a group context? And what does that tell us about humans?

Bibliography and Online Resources for *In Dubious Battle*:

Benson, Jackson, and Anne Loftis. "John Steinbeck and Farm Labor Unionization: The Background of *In Dubious Battle*." *American Literature* 52 (1980): 194–222.

"*In Dubious Battle*." *John Steinbeck*. Bloom's Major Novelists. Broomall, PA: Chelea House, 2000. 33–52.

Levant, Howard. "Panorama and Drama Unified: *In Dubious Battle*." *The Novels of John Steinbeck: A Critical Study*. Columbia, MO: U of Missouri P, 1974. 74–92.

Owens, Louis. "Writing 'In Costume': The Missing Voices of *In Dubious Battle*." *John Steinbeck: The Years of Greatness, 1936–1939*. Ed. Tetsumaro Hayashi. Tuscaloosa, AL: U of Alabama P, 1993. 77–94.

The Martha Heasley Cox Center for Steinbeck Studies. "*In Dubious Battle* (1936)." Retrieved 27 February 2007. <http://www.steinbeck.sjsu.edu/works/In%20Dubious%20Battle.jsp>.

OF MICE AND MEN

READING TO WRITE

*O*F *MICE and Men* remains for many readers John Steinbeck's most memorable work. Steinbeck experimented with the form of this story, which he described as a "playable novel," a novel that could be read as a play and even staged without making changes to the narrative. We will here refer to *Of Mice and Men* as a novella, but discussion of Steinbeck's radical method of fusing drama and fiction will be explored below under "Form and Genre." Steinbeck's experiments in form here promote the themes that the story contains: themes of friendship, dreams, humanity, injustice, cruelty, and the vicissitudes of fate. It is a story that demonstrates the dignity and courage of humble people battling difficult circumstances. George, Lennie, and the other characters in the book, though they live on society's margins, are assailed by the forces of nature's and society's whims, goals, and ethos.

The fraught relationship between large forces (such as nature and society) and small objects (such as animals and individuals) is an idea that is initiated by sly suggestion in the first paragraphs of the novella, where the natural setting is described. There, small creatures demonstrate instinctive awareness of the threatening power of larger creatures, despite the idyllic tranquility of the setting. To fully understand this novella and any other example of literature, you must pay attention to the meanings found in connotative and figurative language. As you read the following section of the first paragraph, look for details that will help you understand what is being established about this natural place:

A few miles south of Soledad, the Salinas River drops in close to the hillside band and runs deep and green. The water is warm too, for it has slipped twinkling over the yellow sands in the sunlight before reaching the narrow pool. On one side of the river the golden foothill slopes curve up to the strong and rocky Galiban mountains, but on the valley side the water is lined with trees— willows fresh and green with every spring, carrying in their lower leaf junctures the debris of the winter's flooding; and sycamores with mottled, white, recumbent limbs and branches that arch over the pool.

Here the large and small elements of society have a harmonious relationship. The river, the mountains, the pools, and the trees are all described as living in enviable accord. While the distant mountains are dauntingly large and "rocky," notice how the valley and river are described using peaceful diction: "warm," "twinkling," "fresh and green," "golden," and "recumbent." Notice too that the atmosphere is so docile that even floods are unthreatening: The previous winter's floodwaters, for instance, leave behind debris that the trees "carr[y]" in their lower branches, in a manner suggestive of parental cradling. This idyllic riparian scene provides sustenance and shelter to the small animals—lizards, deer, rabbits, dogs—that frequent the pool. The vitality of the scene takes place in the absence of humans. The notion of humans' negative influence on nature could be an interesting topic for an essay. To gather evidence for such a discussion, you could assess how nature responds to the presence of humans and, furthermore, how nature conducts itself in its depopulated state (such as the one described in this first paragraph). You could even consider nature in its biblical sense—that is, how is nature like the Eden that humans were banished from when God discovered the disobedience of Adam and Eve?

The tranquility of the pool is disrupted by the arrival of George and Lennie, our two heroes, who, like the fauna, are attracted to the sanctuary that the pool seems to be. The birds and animals flee the pool, and though the men display no aggressive behavior toward the animals (and we will be shortly acquainted with Lennie's fervent affection for aminals), it is clear that the animals interpret the men as fundamentally threatening. Though the men mean no harm, they nevertheless negatively affect the wildlife. The hierarchy of power, of predator and prey, is presented as neither a positive nor a negative fact of life in this novella: Like a food chain, it simply is.

This dynamic of the powerful threatening the powerless is one that is observed by the characters and demonstrated in their actions and their experiences; the indifferent way in which the stronger force consistently affects the weaker one is therefore both a theme (idea) and a motif (pattern of repeated imagery). The prevalence of this dynamic is a deliberate inclusion on Steinbeck's part. He was interested in what he called "is" thinking: in short, a belief in the way things are in the present—not how they came to be and not what they might become, but what they are. This "is" philosophy could be another source for an essay, and to gather evidence for it you would need to identify those places where events transpire with little or no editorial comment or judgment. One example of this nonjudgmental narration is found in the tragedies that take place at the end of this book. Lennie's killing of Curley's wife, for instance, is not the result of a malevolent force but the inevitable result of unfortunate circumstances. Even deeming this death a tragedy might run counter to the spirit of "is" thinking, which is, after all, a way of looking at things not as they should be (morally), but as they are.

Considering the tragic elements of this novella could become the source for another topic. What is the effect of an impassive narration on a tragic story? This is an interpretation of form and readership: If things in the world exist in ways that are neither good nor bad, then why is this novella almost universally considered tragic? Is "is" thinking at odds with the tragic form or is it, by its sense of inevitability, akin to tragedy?

A slow and careful reading of *Of Mice and Men* will better allow you to identify and analyze the patterns, issues, and ideas in the story. Reading slowly and taking notes will make for a richer understanding of the novella, while also enabling you to gather the evidence you need to write a strong essay.

TOPICS AND STRATEGIES

This section of the chapter discusses various possible topics for essays on *Of Mice and Men* and general approaches to those topics. Remember that these are only starting points for your own analysis, not a comprehensive code to the novel. Every topic discussed here could encompass a wide variety of good papers.

Themes

Of Mice and Men includes many themes, ideas, and concepts that fuel the action. Some of these ideas include power, fellowship, dreams, isolation, and nature. Writers approaching the story often begin by identifying a central theme they see as important and then arguing what the story is saying about that theme. You can identify a theme by noticing the ideas, symbols, or even words that recur in the story. In the beginning of this novella, for instance, the particulars of George and Lennie's shared dream are spoken aloud, discussed, and meditated on: Dreams prove to be a common preoccupation for all the sympathetic characters in the novella. Next, decide what you think the story is saying about the theme of dreams. That our heroes, as well as Candy, Crooks, and Curley's wife, dream of a different kind of life reveals their dissatisfaction. Reading closely their dreams could lead to an understanding about the role of dreams for the have-nots, or, perhaps, all people. Other themes could be approached in similar ways: You could approach the theme of isolation or alienation through a character's pronouncements on solitude, and then you could analyze the effect of that condition on characters, or what you interpret the novella saying about isolation. Thematic approaches also blend with the philosophical approach described below.

Sample Topics

1. **Dreams:** How does the story characterize and evaluate the force of dreams? Based on the dreams we see represented here, what basic human needs do the dreams reveal?

   To write an essay such as this, begin by identifying the aspects of dreams that the characters describe and then look at what functions dreams perform for a select number of characters. For Lennie and George, dreams are a means by which they distinguish themselves from other men. Their ritualistic speaking of the dream (wherein they will "live off the fatta the lan'") functions as a means by which they identify themselves (as men with a future) and reassure themselves about the choices they are making. The stalwart power of dreaming for these men provides comfort and a means of identification. The second question in this topic could become the source for a different approach to this essay, one that looks for similarities across the dreams of different characters. In this approach, you would need to assess what the dreams have in common. Security and companionship, for instance, are two qualities common to all the dreams in this novella. What might these dreams suggest about universal human desires?

2. **Power:** How do we see power at work in this novella? Is it always represented impassively, or are there sections where the book criticizes it?

This is a broad topic, and the first step would be to select which examples of power you think are good ones to analyze. One approach could be to look at power dynamics in terms of their social manifestations. The dynamic between Crooks and Curley's wife, for instance, demonstrates the power that social hierarchies assign to some people over others. Instead of looking at social power, you could look at how power materializes in its more naturalistic manifestations. When Curley first meets Lennie, for instance, he demonstrates an instinctive drive for dominance and control; his circling of Lennie is a good example of this because the descriptions of that scene convey how primitive and instinctive are Curley's impulses. There are other examples where people (or animals) instinctively acknowledge the threat that a more powerful individual poses. The last part of the topic asks you to consider whether the novella judges the wielding of power; both Curley and his wife could be characters to discuss for this part of the topic.

3. **Isolation/alienation:** Feeling isolated is a lament that nearly all the characters express. How does the novella depict the effects of isolation on individuals?

An essay on this topic might begin by describing the prevalence of characters who express feelings of loneliness or social isolation. Next, you will want to analyze the effect this condition has on individual characters or on the population of the ranch. You might also want to discuss any reasons you see that individuals are unable to overcome their alienated state. Crooks would be an interesting character to discuss in this context; he believes strongly in the futility of social connections, yet he is attracted to the idea of becoming a part of George and Lennie's farm. Another way to approach this topic would be to assess what qualities this novella presents as contributing to an individual's isolated state. In this context, you could discuss race, age, and gender.

4. **Friendship:** George is both driven by his friendship with Lennie and deeply conflicted about it. How does the story depict friendship, and why is it such an unusual phenomenon in this society?

This topic begins with an assertion about George's friendship with Lennie; you will want to assess that statement's veracity before you reflect more generally on friendship in the book overall. Once you decide what George's fundamental feeling is about the role of friendship in his life (worthwhile? pointless?), you will be able to analyze the story's overall depiction of friendship. George and Lennie's friendship is so singular that no fewer than four people query George about the reason behind the friendship. What does its uniqueness say about friendship in this society? For what reasons does the story present friendship as so unusual?

Character

Papers can focus on questions of character development (such as how Steinbeck distinguishes Carlson from Slim by their distinctive senses of compassion), means of characterization (like the way we learn about Lennie's background from what he says and what George says about him), or interpretations of changes in a character as the novella proceeds (the rapid gain and loss of Crooks's hope for a better life in chapter 4). To write an essay on character, you would need to approach the story by way of questions about how readers come to know various characters. An essay could center on the means by which Steinbeck constructs the distinctive natures of his characters. How, for instance, does Steinbeck distinguish a character's manner? In the case of *Of Mice and Men*, Slim's natural grace and kind manner distinguish him as a naturally evolved individual. Slim's foil, or illuminating opposing character, Carlson, is impatient, crude, and thoughtless. The reader recognizes the differences between these men when Candy's dog is killed: Though both characters think it time for the dog to be euthanized, Slim realizes how difficult the loss of the dog's companionship will be for Candy, while Carlson has no sense of the gravity of this circumstance. In terms of the way it constructs character, *Of Mice and Men* is more like a play than a novel: Characters are established by what they do and say and how they interact with other characters. To answer questions of character development, look closely at the details of language, action, or interactions with other characters. The ways characters behave with one another helps the reader understand who the characters are. Essays on character development assess not only the means by which characters are created but also what characters signify and represent for the story as a whole.

Sample Topics:

1. **George's character development:** How does George change over the course of the novella? Why do these changes take place?

   This topic guides the writer to decide what kinds of changes happen in George's character. One way to approach a topic on George's character development would be to examine what having Lennie in his life gives to George; these effects include the importance of having goals and the need to be steadfast and responsible. Next, you would want to examine how George changes once he knows that Lennie is going to be out of his life. How is it significant that George anticipates that he could, from now on, spend all his time and money in brothels? You will certainly want to examine the final scene of this book: Do the changes that take place in George's character include his feelings about Lennie, or are those always the same?

2. **Character development in general:** How does the story present character to the reader? What techniques does the story use?

A paper on this topic would observe how Steinbeck gives insight into character. A possible approach to this essay would be to look at the actions of a pair of characters and attempt to show what effects they have on events and on other characters. For instance, an essay could study how and why characters react to loss in distinctive ways. What do Slim and Carlson's reactions to the death of Candy's dog tell us about their characters? Another paired approach could look at how Crooks and Curley's wife react to Lennie's guilelessness. These last two characters seek solace in and, to some extent, exploit Lennie's friendly obtuseness. An analysis of their interactions with Lennie could provide the substance of a good essay.

3. **Curley's wife as a character:** What kind of figure is Curley's wife? How do her final revelations change our perception of her?

This is an evaluative topic that requires the writer to analyze Curley's wife. An essay on this topic would require you to consider her distinguishing characteristics, such as her social situation, her dashed dreams, and her loneliness. What does her namelessness say, for instance, about her social standing? Her final revelations to Lennie disclose a much more sympathetic character than the vamp she had presented herself as in the story up to that point. One approach to this topic would be to explain her earlier behavior using her later revelations. A question to consider is her role in the story overall. Do you think that she is a figure of temptation and destruction (in the mode of the biblical Eve) or a figure of fallibility and sympathy (perhaps also in the mode of Eve)?

4. **Crooks and Candy:** How are these characters presented in the story? Are they complementary figures, or do they represent

significantly different types? In what ways is their shared out-cast status a commentary on the society in which they live?

This essay would need to describe and evaluate both charac-ters and their limited relationship to each other. What circum-stances do they share? On what issues do they conflict? This essay should bring in some questions about social hierarchies and divisions as well, since both men are pushed to the mar-gins of society (though for different reasons). Finally, it would be worthwhile to theorize why neither character looks to the other for a possible partnership: Is this fact a commentary on these men or on this society?

History and Context

Though not fixed in a specific time, the historical context of *Of Mice and Men* provides a worthwhile opportunity for analysis of the novella. The novella describes a world that existed in California and other states during their post-frontier eras. Though situated near the city of Soledad, the circumstances of the novella could have taken place in any number of farms or ranches in California. One approach to writing about history in this work would be to consider the social and psychological results of an itinerant workforce, one that is subject to the vagaries of the agricul-tural season, and a specifically single male population. Popular cultures of California and the United States have fostered a romantic impression of a man's life that is free of the responsibilities of a wife and family; we still imagine (in movies and books that feature cowboys, for instance) what it would be like to take to the road, to ride off into the sunset, and to answer to no one but ourselves. The dark side of this dream is actual-ized in *Of Mice and Men,* and one approach to this subject could be to investigate the social and psychological impact of this historical fact. For instance, in what ways does this novella represent the social freedom of itinerancy as a slow, lonely death of an individual's humanity? Another analytical question to pose would be how individuals seek to construct a variety of domesticity into their peripatetic lives. Another interest-ing essay on history would look at the ongoing reception of this novella. While it is one of the most taught books by Steinbeck, it is also one of the most frequently banned. This intriguing paradox could be explored in an essay that would include primary sources and interpretations of the still-controversial elements of this book.

Sample Topics:

1. **Itinerancy in *Of Mice and Men:*** Analyze the psychological and social impact of California's itinerant laboring class in this novella. Compare some historical antecedents to the circumstances experienced by George and Lennie.

This is a broad topic, and you would need to focus on a few key elements of the novella to assess how it presents the effects of itinerancy. You might, for instance, focus on attempts to make domestic a transient, homeless life; these are demonstrated most clearly by George and Lennie, though Candy and Crooks also show a desire for a steady, domestic life. You will need to do some research into the social lives of farm laborers from the early part of the 20th century and then assess how the novella speaks to their experience.

2. **The dark side of the frontier's freedom:** Analyze how *Of Mice and Men* dismantles the romantic fantasy of the unfettered individual.

To answer this topic, you would need to offer an example of how the American imagination reveres the idea of an individual (actually, it is men and not women who star in this imagined life) unfettered by domestic responsibilities. You might, for instance, discuss the cowboy. Then you will want to assess how the solitary individual's existence is portrayed in this novella. In what ways is the individual in *Of Mice and Men* more vulnerable than an individual in a group? You will want to be specific about how the individual has less power, and you can gather evidence for this by identifying how the working man's goals and individuality are incidental to the needs of the farm or ranch owner (here, his sustenance is at the will of the owner). Overall, how does the very notion of individuality prove to be a liability in this novella?

3. **The historical reputation of** *Of Mice and Men:* Why has this popular and frequently taught novel been so deplored and sometimes even banned? Analyze what cultural values are revealed about the societies or regions that have banned this novel.

This topic would require you to research the reception of this novella; you would need to track down reviews from the time of its 1937 publication and any other information you can get on the many places that have, at one time or another, banned the book. Next, you will need to analyze the excoriating reviews and rationalizations for banning so that you will be able to answer the second part of this topic, which asks you to analyze the cultural values of the societies that ban this book. This requires a kind of assertion by inference: What can we infer, for instance, about a society that calls this novella morbid and degenerate? It could prove interesting to argue against the objections of censors and to offer a theory explaining in what ways *Of Mice and Men* is a valuable book for students to read.

Philosophy and Ideas

Another approach to forming an argument about *Of Mice and Men* is to identify and then analyze the philosophical ideas that circulate in the novel. This approach is related to the thematic approach discussed above in that it tracks an idea in the story, but this kind of essay would demonstrate how you see the story as commenting on the idea in its more general form. For instance, Sigmund Freud's theory of the id and ego provides a compelling way to analyze the two main characters of the novella. Lennie's behavior resembles the anarchy of the id drive, which does not recognize checks or limitations: About Lennie, George observes, "he don't know no rules" (chapter 2). George's own acute sense of social checks and barriers is a contrast to Lennie's lack thereof: George, in fact, works tirelessly to protect Lennie from Lennie and the world at large. Even if Steinbeck was not intentionally using Freud's ideas here, Freud's ideas (indeed, many outside ideas) can provide useful ways to interpret this or other works. One philosophical idea that we know Steinbeck had in mind while writing this book can also be a useful way to interpret *Of*

Mice and Men. As discussed in "Reading to Write" above, Steinbeck was fascinated by what he and his friend Ed Ricketts called "nonteleological" or "is" thinking. The idea was to look at the world as it is, not as it should or could be. "Is" thinking shows itself many times in the novella and would be an excellent source for the material of an essay. You could analyze whether the novella registers culpability or responsibility for the unfortunate events that befall Lennie and George. Based on an analysis of this, you should be able to ascertain whether or not the story simply "is." Other broad ideas in the novel include chance and mercy.

Sample Topics:

1. **Ego and id:** In some ways, George and Lennie demonstrate such mutual interdependence that they seem like two halves of a single unit. While Lennie is a being of impulse, George is a being of caution. Consider, in this regard, how Freud's theory of the human psyche—as encompassed in his separating of the id, ego, and superego—helps us understand the connection between these two characters.

   This topic asks you to consider how, in view of Freud's theory, George and Lennie are two parts of a single being. Freud theorized that each of us comprises three parts: the id (primitive impulses), the ego (a force that mediates between social law and primitive desires), and the superego (the assimilated awareness of the rules of society or another powerful force). One way to approach this topic would be to examine how George functions for the pair as the mediating force of Lennie's anarchic impulses. In what ways, for example, does George seek to prevent Lennie's being punished by the forces of society? Taken from the opposite angle, how do Lennie's primitive impulses help George define himself? You might, for example, analyze those places where George purposely contrasts himself with Lennie. Furthermore, it would be interesting to study how Lennie's simple desires for shelter, hunger, pleasure, and security benefit George's own life. Finally, you will want to examine closely the final scene, where George terminates Lennie's life, and think about this as a kind of suicide.

In that light, what does it mean that George intends to spend his post-Lennie days in a brothel? Might he be replicating the drives of the id he had to kill?

2. **Nonteleological thinking:** In what ways does *Of Mice and Men* embody the ideas promoted by nonteleological, or "is," thinking? Are there places where the impassivity of "is" thinking is replaced by pathos?

This topic asks you to track the notion of "is" thinking (for Steinbeck this described the philosophical outlook that examined the world as it is, instead of how it should be or could be) demonstrated in *Of Mice and Men*. How, for instance, do the novella's events take place without editorial commentary? You can amass evidence for the existence of narrative commentary or stoicism in the most dramatic scenes (such as the euthanizing of Candy's dog or the death of Curley's wife). In those scenes, it would be instructive to note whether the narrative impartialness slips and reveals itself to be sensitive to feelings of pity or tragedy. Ultimately, you will want to decide whether you believe *Of Mice and Men* is a successful and effective exercise in "is" thinking.

3. **Chance:** How is the notion of chance represented in this novella? How does it operate in the dramatic events of this novel? Is it chance or fate or some other force that creates the tragedies in this story?

This topic asks you to consider how chance is represented in this work and to consider how chance contributes to the events in the novella. One representation of chance is associated with games and, specifically, the solitaire that George frequently plays. What does his frequent playing of solitaire suggest about George's character? Chance can be understood to be another version of fate and, in this sense, chance can be seen as a determining force in the outcome of the story. Consider, for example, the two human deaths that take place in the story: Lennie and Curley's wife are together a volatile combination because of their backgrounds and who they are as individuals. Is there a way that the story sets up Lennie to be fated to meet his end because of someone like Curley's wife? Was she likewise fated to meet her end because of someone like Lennie? A strong essay on this topic would include in its analysis some discussion of the connection between "is" thinking and chance.

4. **Mercy:** Consider the discussions of euthanasia and determine what the story is suggesting about correlating the death of Candy's dog to the death of Lennie.

This topic asks you to examine two deaths and reach a conclusion about how the story presents those deaths. The first step would be to show the ways in which the two deaths are presented similarly, but for (perhaps) different reasons. You will want to analyze what the characters express about these deaths and consider whether they were both acts of mercy. You should also theorize why you think the last words in the book are about Carlson's inability to understand the grief following Lennie's death. Why is Carlson's callousness the last impression with which we are left?

Form and Genre

Form and genre provide illuminating ways of analyzing many literary works. Form is defined as the shape and structure of a literary work; genre is defined as the kind, or classification, of a literary work. Though technically independent of the content of literature ("love," for instance, is an idea that can be communicated in various forms), form and genre are used deliberately by authors to help further the ideas in, strengthen the dramatic impact of, and generally refine their stories. Steinbeck was always testing different ways to tell his stories, and this spirit is highlighted in *Of Mice and Men,* a work that is structured as a hybrid of novella (or novelette) and play. His belief that the conventional novelistic form had lost the interest of the readers he wanted to reach compelled him to devise this "playable novel" form. (Other critics have also called this a "play/novella" and a "playet," but we are using the more common "novella" label here.) Steinbeck described this generic hybrid as "[w]ritten in novel form but so scened [sic] and set that it can be played as it stands" (qtd. in Shillinglaw xvi); it was a form that proved so useful to him that he would return to it later in *The Moon Is Down* and other works. Steinbeck believed that this form would prove easily adapted to the theater, and indeed *Of Mice and Men* would be a celebrated play on Broadway within a year of its best-selling literary publication.

This experimental form is one well worth exploring in an essay. Identifying in what ways the story is structured like a play permits you to assess how the differences in the story's form change the experience of reading the story. You could, for instance, analyze whether the form of the work makes it more or less accessible to readers. Others interesting aspects of genre and form include the setting and the story's use of silences.

Sample Topics:

1. *Of Mice and Men* **as a drama:** Steinbeck intended this story to be as much a play as a novelistic form of literature. Discuss the story's dramaturgical technique. How does it achieve its sense of tension, drama, and character?

   This topic asks you to consider the story as a performance text and to address the specifically dramatic elements of the story. How does the dialogue work to create tension, drama, and character? Consider also how scenes operate like chapters and how the description of setting performs the same function as stage directions. Comment on the benefits of Steinbeck's hybridizing these two forms instead of having the story take solely one or the other literary form.

2. **Setting:** Analyze how setting is an organizing force in this story in terms of character, conflict, and atmosphere.

   To answer this topic, you need to gain an awareness of how setting operates in this story. As discussed in "Reading to Write" above, the beginning of the first chapter establishes the natural setting of the pool where Lennie and George take refuge for the night. Close reading of the remainder of the chapters (or scenes) will show that each one begins with a description of the setting (six chapters, three settings: pool, bunkhouse, barn). That each chapter begins with the same attention to setting establishes that setting is an organizing principle of the story's structure. One approach to this topic could discuss how setting responds to action, such as when nature reacts to human activity. Setting is a decisive means by which to study and understand this story and is an aspect of form that would be rewarding to explore in an essay.

3. **Silences/lacunae:** Consider the effect of the many silences in this story. What significances do these lacunae (lacks or gaps) in the narration have for the action?

This topic asks you to examine one technique that the story uses and to analyze how silences have dramatic or symbolic effects. Assess whether you think these silences simply lend authenticity to the realism in the story or serve a more specific storytelling function. You might, for instance, consider how the silences provide an opportunity for readers to "fill in the blanks" and in so doing become more active participants in the story. As you track this technique, you will note that silences pepper this story, but pay special attention to the silence following the death of Curley's wife.

Language, Symbols, and Imagery

Language, symbol, and imagery are some of the creative means by which an author conveys certain feelings or ideas that would, if simply announced, be undermined in their imaginative and evocative power. All writers, and those of imaginative fiction especially, use language deliberately, and they choose words based on their connotative, or suggestive, meanings. As you read fiction in preparation for writing about it, you need to be alert to the connotative meanings of language, even as you register the surface meaning of language in order to follow the plot itself. Steinbeck's *Of Mice and Men* uses a contained narrative voice and relies very heavily on dialogue and action.

Symbols, usually used in conjunction with imagery, are objects, either animate or inanimate, that writers also use to convey ideas. In *Of Mice and Men*, repetitions of objects (such as hands and eyes), of ideas (such as the animal aspects of people), and of settings (the pool, the bunkhouse, and the barn) are significant. Each of these things, by nature of its repetition and careful presentation, serves a symbolic function in the story. These things have meaning beyond their denotative definitions. The best essays on symbolism will look at the symbol and, perhaps, its affiliated imagery and consider these subjects in relation to the story's larger ideas. When you are asked to discuss symbolism, you are being asked to discuss what something signifies, means, and represents in light of the entire work.

Sample Topics:

1. **Hands:** Consider how much information we get about characters from the descriptions of their hands. Examine this symbolic appendage and pay special attention to physical descriptions, gestures, and actions.

   This topic asks you to analyze the attention paid to hands and to decide why you think hands are featured so prominently in this story. Curley's wife, for instance, shows Lennie her acting abilities by dramatically gesturing with her hands. Curley's hands are described as fists, in gloves, and crushed. Lennie takes pleasure and reassurance from what he touches with his hands. Lennie's hands are especially interesting because they show both his sympathetic intentions and violent impulses. An effective essay will reach a conclusion about what hands, overall, signify in this story.

2. **Animal imagery:** What does the animal imagery in *Of Mice and Men* signify about the events in this story? About the characters?

This is a broad topic, and your first task would be to focus your approach to it. One approach would be to limit your analysis to the representations and roles of actual animals in the story. How do the mice, dogs, horses, and wildlife contribute meaning to the overall story? Are they, for example, simply the casualties of human action? Or might they provide more substantive means by which to understand the humans in the story? Another way to approach this topic would be to observe the many instances of humans being described in ways conventionally thought of as animal. After identifying instances of this, consider what this imagery is saying about the characters. Are animal qualities a sign of primitiveness or naturalness?

Bibliography for *Of Mice and Men:*

Benson, Jackson J. *The Short Novels of John Steinbeck: Critical Essays with a Checklist to Steinbeck Criticism.* Durham, NC: Duke U P, 1990.

Johnson, Claudia D. *Understanding* Of Mice and Men, The Red Pony, *and* The Pearl: *A Student Casebook to Issues, Sources, and Historical Documents.* Literature in Context. Westport, CT: Greenwood Press, 1997.

Owens, Louis. "Of Mice and Men: The Dream of Commitment." *John Steinbeck's Re-Vision of America.* Athens: U of Georgia P, 1985. 100–106.

Shillinglaw, Susan. Introd. to *Of Mice and Men.* By John Steinbeck. Penguin Twentieth-Century Classics. New York: Viking Penguin, 1994. vii–xxv.

THE GRAPES
OF WRATH

READING TO WRITE

*T*HE GRAPES *of Wrath* was an immediate best-seller upon its publication in 1939, and in the following year it was awarded the Pulitzer
Prize. The novel continues to be prized and widely read—by students and
the general public—and some consider it to have attained the status of
the "Great American novel." That *The Grapes of Wrath* is so praised and
popular does not make it any less interesting and odd a book. It is a novel
with a socially conscious content and an unusual form: Its form and its
content both present intriguing challenges to readers and writers.

Readers and critics of *The Grapes of Wrath* often comment on the
symphonic variety of voices and forms that collectively compose the
book. The voice of the narrator is by turns realistic, lyrical, mythical,
folksy, and biblical. And the form that the narrative adopts is likewise
unusual: Half of the narrative follows the plot of the Joad family, the
other half is a mosaic of American voices, scenes, and situations. The
novel's complex variety of forms and focuses could be the subjects for
an essay. For example, you might analyze the ways that the complexity
of the story's narration—particularly the switching of voices—further
broadens the scope of the novel. No matter what topic you choose to
analyze, you must first contend with Steinbeck's use of language. This
section of the chapter will demonstrate how to read closely two early
passages in *The Grapes of Wrath* in preparation for writing an essay.

As you read passages, and especially those at the beginning of a story, you must locate both the literal significances and the figurative ones. In this novel, the beginning literally establishes the Oklahoma setting and the environmental and financial conflicts that are besetting the farmers. The figurative significances suggested at the beginning of the novel point to the lifelessness of the land and people and to the heartlessness of those who are capitalizing on the disasters. To ascertain the figurative meanings—the nuances and shades of intention in a narrative—you need to pay attention to the clues given by the author's diction, or word choices. Reading for both literal and figurative meanings is called "close reading" and is the method by which you will generate ideas and interpretations in preparation for writing insightfully about literature.

Read closely the first paragraph of *The Grapes of Wrath* to get not only the literal but also the figurative meanings of the story to come:

To the red country and part of the gray country of Oklahoma, the last rains came gently, and they did not cut the scarred earth. The plows crossed and recrossed the rivulet marks. The last rains lifted the corn quickly and scattered weed colonies and grass along the sides of the roads so that the gray country and the dark red country began to disappear under a green cover. In the last part of May the sky grew pale and the clouds that had hung in high puffs for so long in the spring were dissipated. The sun flared down on the growing corn day after day until a line of brown spread along the edge of each green bayonet. The clouds appeared, and went away, and in a while they did not try any more. The weeds grew darker green to protect themselves, and they did not spread any more. The surface of the earth crusted, a thin hard crust, and as the sky became pale, so the earth became pale, pink in the red country and white in the gray country.

This is a largely expository, if somewhat abstracted, narration of events, and it uses mostly declarative sentences. You have to read carefully to note the figurative language, such as "bayonet," "scarred," "protect themselves," "scattered," "day after day." You will notice that this language is suggestive of battle and siege. What it suggests here plays out in the novel, and the implication is that not only the land but the people, and farmers especially, are battling the ecological mistakes and disasters that will result in the dust bowl. We will read how the financial ruin of the Great Depression will further aggravate the farmers' livelihoods.

You may have also noticed in the paragraph the prevalence of colors mentioned: green, gray, red, white, pink, brown. The colors describe the literal appearance of the landscape, but the simplicity with which they are given is telling. The colors are described in a way that is unadorned (no regal vermilion here), and they are made specific only by their shades ("darker" and "pale"), and even these color gradations are infrequent. This description of the coloration suggests that the landscape is so depleted that adjectives are superfluities. The lifelessness of the landscape establishes in its description of the setting what will prove to be one of the primary conflicts in the novel: that between humanity and the land.

The first chapter situates the conflict between the people and the earth, and the second chapter situates the conflict among people and introduces us to our first protagonist. This second chapter begins, however, not with humans but with the description of a "huge red transport truck" that stands outside a roadside diner; that the truck is described before the people signals the principal position that machinery plays in the new economy about which the novel will soon express so much anxiety. The truck is new, the tires are new, and it had a "brass padlock [standing] straight out from the hasp on the big back doors." Against the backdrop of the desiccated, lackluster landscape of the first chapter, the newness and relative extravagance of the truck stands out. A careful reader will note details that stick out in the same way that that truck's padlock sticks "straight out" and consider the significance of those details. One interpretation of that padlock is that the truck's contents are valuable or that they are being protected from an outside threat (a thief?). Other details about the truck, though technically inanimate, also give us information about the human drama: The corporate lettering and the "No Riders" sticker on its windshield proclaim a company policy that infuriates Tom Joad, the book's ostensible protagonist. Tom's rage is rooted in his desire for a ride (he is hitchhiking and that sticker presents an obstacle to his goal), but he also bristles at the sticker because it smacks of authoritarianism. These dynamics—between people and companies and between Tom and autocratic authorities—are established quickly and will cycle throughout the novel.

The two dramatic thrusts—human and environmental—coalesce in the novel and together amplify the concurrent distresses and interdependence of humans and the land. When faced with an unusual story form such as that in *The Grapes of Wrath*, you want to question what purpose it serves: This kind of focus on form is also a variety of close reading. As a specific topic of analysis, the two strains of the narrative are discussed in the section "Form and Genre."

A slow and careful reading of *The Grapes of Wrath* will better allow you to recognize the patterns, issues, and ideas in the novel. Reading slowly and taking notes will make for a more enriched understanding of the story, while also enabling you to gather the evidence you need to write a strong essay.

TOPICS AND STRATEGIES

This section of the chapter discusses various possible topics for essays on *The Grapes of Wrath* and general approaches to those topics. Be advised that the material below is only a place to start from, not an exhaustive master key. Use this material to generate your own analysis. Every topic discussed here could encompass a wide variety of good papers.

Themes:

The Grapes of Wrath grapples with many themes, ideas, and concepts that organize and underscore the importance of the events in the novel. Some of these ideas include solidarity, anger, family, violence, technology, and compassion. Writers analyzing the novel often begin by identifying a central theme they see as important and then determining what the story is saying about that theme. You can identify a theme by noticing the ideas, symbols, or even words that recur in the story—in the initial scene of *The Grapes of Wrath*, for instance, Tom Joad lectures the truck driver on the importance of worker solidarity, of being a "good guy" despite company policies. Tom's immediate goal is to convince the driver to give him a ride, regardless of company policies, but this idea of workers standing their ground against the divisive and inhuman practices of corporations is one that courses through the novel and proves to be one of the novel's central themes. Thinking about these connections among people might lead to a consideration of other moments of solidarity that are forged among people on the road, such as the fellowship between the Joad and the Wilson families. The next step is to decide what you think the story is saying about the theme of solidarity: Does it present the notion as ludicrous or laudatory? For evidence you would need to look for examples of the results of solidarity and also to places where sympathetic characters comment on solidarity (though they might use different words to describe that concept). Other themes could be approached in similar ways: You could approach the theme of anger by examining the story's depiction of angry characters and then offering an analysis about what the role of anger might be in this story. Thematic approaches also blend with the approaches described below under "Philosophy and Ideas."

Sample Topics:

1. **Family:** Explain how the notion of what constitutes a family evolves over the course of the novel. How does the concept of family operate in this novel overall?

   This topic guides you toward a thesis-driven approach to the idea of family. To write an essay such as this, begin by identifying shifts you see in the idea of a family (the notion of a family as a collective might be useful here). It would be worthwhile to recognize how the notion of family seems to change as the members of the Joad family diminish in number. The second part of this topic asks you to consider what meaning the concept of family has to the characters or, more broadly, to the novel itself. One approach to this would be to consider why family is so important to Ma Joad. What meaning does family have for her? What does family mean to Jim Casy? A further consideration might be to consider whether the novel is presenting family as a potentially revolutionary force. For this, you would want to consider any connections the novel makes between the nuclear family and the extended family (of other migrants, for instance).

2. **Anger:** How is anger (wrath) presented as an idea in this novel? Does the story suggest that some outbursts of anger are justified and appropriate? When is anger inappropriate or misguided?

Such an essay would need to locate those scenes that feature characters expressing anger and the narrator commenting on that anger. The topic suggests that anger is represented in the book as alternately appropriate and inappropriate. The anger of the migrants at inhumane treatment, for instance, seems to be a reaction rooted in dignity and a sense of self-worth. The anger directed at the migrants by corporations and their administrators (the police, the vigilantes, etc.) is represented as inappropriate because of its misdirection. You will want to limit your focus so you can thoroughly analyze your examples. It would be worth exploring how the biblical allusion in the book's title is itself suggestive of righteous anger. Based on your assessment of the portrayal of this emotion, you can develop a thesis about the various significances of anger in this novel.

3. **Violence:** How does the story represent and evaluate the use of violence? Is violence characterized as aberrant or natural behavior?

To write an essay on this topic, it would be useful to focus on a tight collection of examples or even on a single character. Tom Joad, the novel's ostensible protagonist, would be a good choice for this topic because he is represented sympathetically while also demonstrating persistently violent tendencies. Look to the narrator and the reactions of other characters to determine how Tom's (or another character's) violent acts are judged. Ultimately, you will want to reach a conclusion about how the novel judges violence.

4. **Compassion:** How does this novel characterize the conditions that promote compassion? What does the novel's final scene of compassion suggest about the book's overall message?

This topic asks you to consider what the novel suggests are the necessary conditions for compassion. One approach to this topic would be to examine the instances of kindness or generosity that occur in the novel and then assess how they came to be. The scene in chapter 15 with the waitress and the truck drivers and Ma Joad's interaction with the company store clerk in chapter 26 are two of many examples of compassion. You would want to theorize about the conditions, the participants, and the situation that make kindness possible. The final scene of the novel—with Rose of Sharon and the starving man—is an unforgettable example of taboos suspended for the sake of compassion. Rose of Sharon has not—up until the end—been a compassionate, selfless person. What is the novel testifying to about people and compassion? An alternative approach to this topic would be to consider how the novel characterizes the conditions that promote cruelty.

Character

Good essays can focus on questions of character development (such as how Steinbeck distinguishes Granma and Granpa from each other by the content of their outbursts), means of characterization (such as the way the reader learns about Jim Casy from his monologues and the discussions about him by other characters), or interpretations of changes in a character as the novel proceeds (such as the profound shifts from selfishness to selflessness that we see in both Tom Joad and Rose of Sharon). To write an essay on character, you would need to approach the story by way of questions about how readers come to know various characters. How, for instance, does Steinbeck distinguish a character's manner? In *The Grapes of Wrath*, Granpa's lasciviousness is underscored by his literal inability to button his trousers. Ma Joad's generous heart is demonstrated by her feeding of hungry strangers, even if in doing so she herself goes hungry. To analyze questions of character development, look closely for distinguishing traits of language, action, or interactions with other characters. The ways characters behave with one another helps the reader not only understand the means by which characters are created but also assess what characters signify and represent for the story overall.

Sample Topics:

1. **Tom Joad's character development:** How does Tom Joad change over the course of the novel? Why might these changes occur?

To write an essay on this topic, you would need to decide what kinds of changes Tom Joad undergoes. Consider, for example, how his connection to the world around him shifts from limited to more expansive. To that end, it would be important to analyze the differences in the two deaths for which he is responsible: How are the reasons behind these fatal acts different from each other? Analytical evidence for the changes he undergoes can be gathered from the conversations he has with other characters (especially with Ma Joad and Jim Casy). After you assess the substance of Tom Joad's changes, consider whether the changes he experiences represent growth. A strong essay will also assess how his growth connects to the story's overall significance.

2. **Character development in general:** How does the story present characters to the reader? What techniques does the novel use?

A paper on this topic would observe how Steinbeck gives insight into character. A possible technique would be to look carefully at a pair of characters or a set of techniques and attempt to show what effects they have. A paper could discuss the way that two characters deal differently with the act of leaving home, for instance. What might these reactions tell us about the character? About the meaning of home? Other subjects could also be fruitful for this topic. Analyzing the techniques of dialogue and physical description, for instance, is another way of writing about character development.

3. **Jim Casy as a character:** Though Jim Casy insists he is no longer a man of the cloth, the characters and the narrator consistently refer to him as "the preacher." What does "the preacher" contribute to the family he becomes a part of? What does Jim Casy contribute to the novel?

This is an evaluative topic that asks you to consider the effect Jim Casy has on the family specifically and, more broadly, on the story itself. Note that from the outset, Jim Casy recognizes the larger, cosmic issues that Tom and the others are initially blind to or simply ignore. Consider how his presence figuratively enlarges the Joad family and the other people with whom he comes into contact. Consider also what Jim Casy's philosophy contributes to the novel's overall message. A word of caution about this character: Much has been speculated about the Christlike aspects of Jim Casy, and Steinbeck was certainly making suggestive connections between this character and Jesus (see, for instance, Jim Casy's last words, which paraphrase what Jesus Christ said before his own martyrdom). This is interesting and potentially rich analytically, but you should avoid simplistic assertions (such as Jim Casy *is* Jesus Christ) in essays. Such allegorical readings are too restrictive and limiting for good analysis.

4. **Eccentrics/grotesques:** Sprinkled among the Joads are a number of eccentric characters, figures who are outcast because of a condition, situation, or belief. Choose one or two characters and analyze what these eccentrics reveal about the central characters in the novel.

This is an evaluative topic requiring you to analyze what information the story offers about these important, somewhat strange, and sometimes mysterious characters. You might consider analyzing the religious woman of Weedpatch, the one-eyed man at the gas station, the company store clerk at Hooper [R]anch, or Muley Graves. In the case of Muley Graves, we learn from his life what happens to a man whose allegiance to his land is greater than that to his family. The consequences of becoming a "ghost" in Oklahoma are dire, and his experience effectively illustrates the impossibility of Tom's staying in Oklahoma to fight for his family's land. Muley also illustrates the vulnerability of a single man opposing an amorphous agricultural corporation. Muley's experience foreshadows Tom's eventual fugitive life: Both men are taking moral stands that require a severing of family ties. Whichever eccentrics you choose to analyze, be sure to discuss in your essay what they reveal about the action or the other characters.

History and Context

Another especially worthwhile approach to *The Grapes of Wrath* is through history and context. The novel sought to capture a current social crisis, and in doing this so aptly, the book became a historical event in its own right. The general population knew that human failures and natural disasters culminated in the exodus of economic refugees from the Great Plains to California. People were aware that this dust bowl migration featured starvation, dislocation, social unrest, and tremendous general misery. Steinbeck's novel put human (if fictive) faces on the dust bowl tragedy, and the book struck a nerve for readers across the country. *The Grapes of Wrath* was considered controversial, in part, for its candid portrayal of the Joads and for the negative light in which the book presented the social calamity it discussed: Some civic leaders in Oklahoma, for example, were so outraged by the novel's depiction of their state that book burnings were held. These historical events prove fascinating subjects to study in conjunction with your analysis of the novel. Historical research will enable you to see the novel in its historical context while also recognizing its status as a catalytic force for social change. Because the novel is so epic in its scope, the challenge of approaching this novel through its historical context is in isolating an idea or subject of manageable size. The notion of migration in the novel, for instance, is an important one for the Joads as well as a historical fact for the over 300,000 people who fled the dust bowl for California, but without some more limiting focal direction, "migration" is too big an idea for an essay. One way to limit the idea is to take one aspect of migration: Looking at how the idea of migration is rendered in the book as a distinctively American experience, for instance, would enable you to usefully limit an investigation of both the idea and the fact of migration. You might also study this novel in its sociological context. In the novel, the notion of what constitutes a hero and an outlaw is discussed through the story of bank robber Pretty Boy Floyd; seeking to understand the risky appeal of his story contributes to an understanding of how the characters think and, moreover, what the novel is saying about the social results of poverty and individual desperation. Still another historical context is that of vigilantism, the informal and often violent forms of popularly determined justice that the Joads witness and experience. The novel also refers to the incipient labor union organizing that was taking place at this time. For this last topic or any other historical topic, you would need to do some research to be able to consider knowledgeably what the novel is asserting about the world it describes.

Sample Topics:

1. **The migrant experience as the American experience:** How does the novel show how fundamentally American the migrants are in terms of their values and their goals? Analyze how Steinbeck emphasizes the American traits of his characters. In what ways does this technique encourage identification with the characters?

   This essay topic directs you to consider the novel's use of American identity reference points. After identifying some of these traits (e.g., pioneering, hard work, self-reliance, agrarianism), you could focus on one or two areas and track how those ideas are weaved into the plot and characterizations. The latter part of the topic suggests that Steinbeck intentionally tapped into these ideas in an effort to generate sympathy for and identification with the Joads. You would need to decide on the verity of that statement and demonstrate how you do or do not see it in action. Another approach to this topic could be to investigate how the unsympathetic characters in *The Grapes of Wrath* are dissociated from their American values.

2. **Migration and vigilantism:** How does *The Grapes of Wrath* speak out against an atmosphere of scapegoating and fear mongering? How does the novel analyze the conditions that contribute to vigilantism and other forms of popular anger?

This is a broad topic, and you would need to focus on a few key scenes and study closely how the novel seeks to understand the factors that culminate in vigilantism (such as when the Hooverville is set ablaze). This topic requires you to research the social climate of the time in order to understand examples of vigilantism outside this novel. One relevant example would be the "bum blockade" that the city of Los Angeles organized on the state's highways to prevent dust bowl refugees from joining the already flooded labor market. There are other examples of American vigilantism in the early 20th century that can be studied in history books and in other sources. An ambitious essay might draw connections to the more recent anti-immigration movements in California.

3. **Pretty Boy Floyd and the outlaw:** Ma Joad repeats the criminalization saga of the bank robber and folk hero Pretty Boy Floyd because she sees in his story a cautionary tale that Tom should hear. In what way does the story of Pretty Boy Floyd also operate as a cautionary tale for Steinbeck's audience?

Before writing this essay, you should research the story of how Pretty Boy Floyd became a bank robber, how his notoriety grew, and how he received popular support from the poor (who themselves felt robbed by the banks he was robbing). A good response to this topic would read closely the conversations in the novel about Floyd and especially how these relate to Tom, a man who has already served time in prison and does not want to return there (though his temper and parole violations put him at risk of this). What is the reader to conclude about Tom's farewell speech, in which he tells his mother that he will be "out there"? Does Tom Joad, whose experiences of injustice are coupled with his pride, symbolize a figure whom readers should fear?

4. **Labor unions and the novel:** The novel makes many references to labor unions and organizing as a response to the work-

ing conditions experienced by the Joads and others. How does Steinbeck use this contemporary movement in the novel? What purposes are served by this kind of historical reference?

A paper on *The Grapes of Wrath* and labor unions would require you to research the labor movement in America, paying particular attention to both the 1930s and agricultural workers (as opposed to industrial workers, who were considered easier to unionize). After doing this research, you would want to consider how Steinbeck uses the idea and practice of labor unions. In what specific ways does the book present labor unions as a commonsense solution for the challenges faced by the migrant workers? Consider what other significances are served by the idea of unions: How, for instance, are unions related to the idea of family? Your essay on this topic should discuss the blacklists mentioned in the book as a method used to inhibit labor organizing (see, for example, chapter 26).

Philosophy and Ideas

Another approach to forming an argument about *The Grapes of Wrath* is to identify and then analyze the philosophical ideas that circulate in the novel. This approach is related to the thematic approach discussed above in that it tracks an idea in the story, but this kind of an essay would demonstrate how you see the story as commenting on the idea in its more general form. For instance, many critics have debated the origin of the novel's philosophy of collectivity, which various critics see as rooted in biblical, Transcendental, Hindu, or Jungian philosophies. The notion of collectivity is a useful focus for thinking about *The Grapes of Wrath*; doing so reveals the inner dynamics of the novel's most prized social organization. Observing how the characters benefit from operating as a group and tracking the dominant arc of development for characters (from strict individuality to membership in the collective) enables you to understand how the general idea of a collective operates in the novel. You could locate evidence for the importance of this idea by looking at the presentation of sympathetic characters gaining awareness about the efficacy and fundamental humanity of working together toward common

goals. Other broad ideas in the novel include ownership, dehumanization, and social utopianism.

Sample Topics:

1. **The over soul:** How is Ralph Waldo Emerson's notion of an
   "over soul" related to Jim Casy's philosophy of the divinity of
   all men? How is Jim Casy's philosophy important to the novel's
   overall message?

   This topic guides you toward thinking about collectivity in a
   specifically Emersonian manner (as mentioned above, there
   are other ways to look at collectivity). The writer of this topic
   would need to acquire familiarity with Emerson's essay "The
   Over Soul" (which maintains that all humans are part of a
   single, divine soul) or with the Bhagavad Gita and its description of the *Paramatman* (supreme soul), a concept by which
   Emerson was deeply influenced. Once you have a working
   knowledge of the over soul or *Paramatman,* you could analyze how the notion operates in *The Grapes of Wrath.* Does the
   novel endorse this way of seeing the world? You will want to
   assess Jim Casy's preaching on this idea, as well as any actions
   you identify as being in keeping with the collective soul (i.e.,
   does Jim Casy practice what he preaches?). Are there other
   characters who likewise seem to embrace the divinity of all
   humankind?

2. **Ownership:** Ownership is a complex concept in this book, and
   for the Joads specifically it does not always bring out their best
   sides. Consider the positive and negative aspects of ownership
   as presented in the novel and reach a conclusion about what
   The Grapes of Wrath is ultimately saying about ownership. Is it
   natural and, more to the point, is it right?

   This is an evaluative topic about ownership as a concept and
   a practice, and it guides you to think about how ownership
   affects human relations in this book. *The Grapes of Wrath* presents owning property as engendering love of the land (chapter

5), but also as the source of a divisive I/we mentality (chapter 15). For this topic, you would want to identify both the positive and negative presentations of ownership and also reach a theory about what, ultimately, the novel is saying about ownership. Is there an amount of ownership that is ideal? Related concepts worth discussing might include greed and theft.

3. **Dehumanization:** Dehumanization, or the act of asserting the inferiority of a person or group of people, can be intentional or inadvertent. Where in this novel do you see intentional dehumanization, and for what goal do you see this dehumanization taking place? Consider also how dehumanized individuals work to maintain their humanity.

This is a topic that directs you to observe how a person or group of people are made to feel less than human. In a war, dehumanization has been observed to be a process by which the killing of an enemy seems less morally abhorrent (the thinking goes that since this enemy is not a man, killing him will not pack the sting of immorality). You would want to track the means by which dehumanization happens to the migrants and venture a theory on the sociological or psychological reasons that it takes place. Chapter 21 is worth reading closely because it gives voice to the people who think themselves superior to the migrants: "These goddamned Okies are dirty and ignorant." The readers know that the Joads are very human. Why might they be considered less than human? What purpose or outlook does dehumanization serve those who think in this belittling way? There are many scenes where you can observe dehumanization taking place, such as when Ma Joad is first called an "Okie" (chapter 18) or when the deputies invade the Hooverville (chapter 19).

4. **Social utopias and dystopias:** Under what conditions are people at their best and most heroic in this novel? Under what conditions are people at their worst and most base? Is the book

showcasing a specific social system as a panacea? What, in short, does the book want society to do?

This topic asks you to observe under what conditions in the novel we see the best and worst behavior. One approach to this topic would be to read closely the sections on the Hooverville shantytown and the Weedpatch government camp and observe what these disparate settings generate in terms of behavior. You should reach a conclusion on whether the novel is presenting a social mandate. Another question to consider: Is there any way in which the dystopic Hooverville is a judgment not on its occupants but on the society around it?

Form and Genre

Form and genre provide illuminating ways of analyzing many literary works. Form is defined as the shape and structure of a literary work; genre is defined as the kind, or classification, of a literary work. Though technically independent of the content of literature (love, for instance, is an idea that can be communicated in various forms), form and genre are used deliberately by authors to help further the ideas in, strengthen the dramatic impact of, and generally refine their stories. In *The Grapes of Wrath*, the genre is fiction and, more specifically, it is a novel. The novelistic form of *The Grapes of Wrath* is unusual in that it is composed of a conventional narrative intertwined with chapters that are not directly related to the plot. These less plot-directed chapters are called intercalary or interchapters and are themselves worthy of close study both for how they expand the novel's scope and for how they insert a different, often more lyrical voice into the highly realistic saga of the Joad family. Steinbeck felt that these interchapters would hit readers "below the belt," and his goal to engage the reader emotionally is worthy of analysis. You could, for instance, study how the interchapters complement the realistic novel and what emotional additions they offer. You could also study the interchapters as a text distinct from the Joad story. Seen together, what do the interchapters offer as a collection of texts on their own? What varieties of voices are included, and to what end? The question of form in this novel is an excellent approach to writing an essay. More traditional essay topics are also useful for *The Grapes of Wrath*. Consider, for example, the techniques by which the story is shaped or structured through discussions of narrative point of view, dialogue, or style.

Sample Topics:

1. **The form of the interchapters:** Analyze the form of the interchapters; pay special attention to the style in which they are written and the voices they include. Reach a conclusion about the effect of the interchapters on the overall narrative.

This topic asks you to consider the interchapters independently of the novel's plot. You would want to consider how the interchapters are constructed. What varieties of voices do we hear in them? In what style are they written? This last question asks you to note the different styles in which these chapters are voiced (e.g., lyrical, mythical, folkloric, supernatural). You would want to come to a conclusion about not only the effects the interchapters offer but also their overall function for the story. One idea to consider: How does the panoply of voices make this novel more expansive than a novel with a single protagonist or family?

2. **Protagonists and antagonists:** Who or what are the protagonists and antagonists of this novel?

This topic asks you to think about the dramatic form of this novel in terms of its protagonists and antagonists. Conventional fiction often features a single hero or protagonist around whom the story revolves and an antagonist, or character who presents conflict for the hero. One could argue that Tom Joad is the protagonist because he is the member of the Joad family whom the novel begins with and features most prominently. However, his character effectively leaves the story before the novel ends, and it is the family who concludes the action. Does this therefore mean that the family as a group is the true protagonist of *The Grapes of Wrath*? Or is the migrant community the protagonist? The question of an antagonist is likewise worth consideration, and to answer this question you should decide who or what the novel presents as the source of antagonistic force. Is it a group of people? Banks? Capitalism? Your essay's thesis will come from your ideas about the protagonists and antagonists of this novel.

3. **Biblical analogues in** *The Grapes of Wrath:* Analyze how a scene in the novel that contains clearly biblical resonances contributes meaning to the overall narrative. What does the story's specifically biblical provenance contribute to the scene as Steinbeck writes it?

There are a number of scenes in the novel that are clear analogues to stories from the Bible. This topic asks you to analyze how the story's inclusion contributes meaning to Steinbeck's narrative. You would need to locate and study the biblical story, understand the meaning of the story within the context of the biblical narrative, and then analyze how that story fits into the context of *The Grapes of Wrath*. One example of a biblical analogue is when Uncle John sets Rose of Sharon's stillborn baby adrift on the floodwaters. This act, in some of its details, is similar to the story of the baby Moses being set adrift on the waters of the Nile. The flood itself is another biblically significant story; in the Bible it is, after all, a flood that purifies the world by destroying it. This topic asks you to comment on this formal technique of referencing biblical stories (by studying how the inclusion of the Bible story works within the form of this novel) and to venture analysis of the meaning of the story within the novel's context. In the course of your analysis, also comment on how the stories differ.

Comparison and Contrast

Comparing components of a story in order to explain and analyze the similarities or differences between them is a useful approach to writing an essay. Remember to avoid the pitfall of merely creating a list of such similarities or differences in a work; instead, you must take the necessary step of commenting on these observations. To begin a comparison/

contrast essay, you might compare characters with each other: How does Pa Joad compare to Ma Joad? How does Tom Joad compare to Jim Casy? How does Jim Casy, as a spiritual character, compare to the zealot at Weedpatch? You could also compare characters (or other elements of the story, such as patterns of imagery or action) across different stories. For example, how do the depictions of labor compare in *In Dubious Battle* and *The Grapes of Wrath?* The challenge of this kind of essay is to decide what the similarities or differences you identify might mean. These are the questions that make essays interesting and the ones that will have different answers for each writer. To get to these questions, think about what kinds of effects Steinbeck achieves by producing either similarities or differences between elements of his stories. What, for example, does the difference between Tom Joad's and the one-eyed man's respective attitudes on perseverance do for our understanding of each character and his views of the world? It is not sufficient to identify a pattern and, to point to the existence of similarities or differences; you must also consider what purpose those similarities or differences might serve in the story overall.

Sample Topics:

1. **Compare the narrative voices within the novel:** Account for the various writing styles or narrative voices in the novel. Compare a few of them and discuss their formal differences while also theorizing on the connections between style and subject.

This is a comparative topic on form that asks you to study the different narrative styles in the novel and offer analyses about not only the form but also the relationship between its style and its content. One kind of narrative style sounds mythic, almost as if it were from a history passed down orally, as seen in chapter 5: "Men ate what they had not raised, had no connection with the bread." This chapter describes the financial practices that bankrupted the small farmers. These bankruptcies were effectively the downfall of the small farmers, and you might argue that the mythic voice used here emphasizes both the gravity of the event and the way the story will live on in the memories of the ruined farmers. Thus, the mythical style of the chapter's narration emphasizes the mythical weight of the event. Other narrative styles in the novel include a biblical voice, a down-home folksy voice, the fast-talking vernacular of salesmen, the "language of the roadsides" (chapter 2) in the banter among truck drivers and diner waitresses, and the voices of realism and naturalism. The panoply of voices is one of the appealing qualities of the novel, and the connections between style and subject are well worth exploring in an essay.

2. **Contrast the respective spiritual beliefs of Jim Casy and the zealous woman of Weedpatch:** These two characters have extremely different senses of the relationship between God and humans. How would you characterize their respective senses of holiness? Comment on what these differences might say about the novel's general position on God or religion.

This topic asks the writer to look carefully at the opinions of Jim Casy and the religious woman of Weedpatch and to evaluate the significance of their respective senses of God. Based on the way these characters are presented in the story, is one of their philosophies endorsed over the other's? What are the social and spiritual effects of the less vaunted spirituality? Based on your analysis, reach a theory on the novel's overall presentation of the ideal variety of religion or spirituality. Does one help while the other hinders?

3. **Contrasting Ma's and Pa's roles at the beginning and end of the novel:** Ma's and Pa's roles in the family undergo profound changes as the novel progresses. Identify what those changes are and, using the narrator's suggestions as evidence, offer a theory about why you think these shifts happen.

The focus here would be to track the changes that the roles of Ma and Pa undergo at the beginning and at the end of the novel. It would be important to consider how their authority within the family changes and to discuss what the novel presents as the reasons behind those transformations.

Bibliography and Online Resources for *The Grapes of Wrath*

Ashley, Leonard R. N. "*The Grapes of Wrath:* Novel by John Steinbeck, 1939." *Reference Guide to American Literature.* 3rd ed. Ed. Jim Kamp. Detroit: St. James, 1994. 985–86.

Bloom, Harold, ed. *John Steinbeck's* The Grapes of Wrath. Modern Critical Interpretations. New York: Chelsea House Publishers, 1998.

French, Warren, ed. *A Companion to* The Grapes of Wrath. New York: Viking Press, 1963.

The Great Books Foundation. "John Steinbeck: *The Grapes of Wrath, Of Mice and Men,* and *The Pearl.*" Retrieved 4 April 2007. <http://www.greatbooks. org/index.php?id=209>.

Heavilin, Barbara A., ed. *The Critical Response to John Steinbeck's* The Grapes of Wrath. Westport, CT: Greenwood Press, 2000.

Johnson, Claudia Durst. *Understanding* The Grapes of Wrath: *A Student Casebook to Issues, Sources, and Historical Documents.* Westport, CT: Greenwood Press, 1999.

Moss, Joyce, and George Wilson, eds. "*The Grapes of Wrath* by John Steinbeck." *Literature and Its Times: Profiles of 300 Notable Literary Works and the Historical Events That Influenced Them.* Vol. 3: *Growth of Empires to the Great Depression (1890–1930s).* Detroit: Gale, 1997.

Timmerman, John H. "The Squatter's Circle in The Grapes of Wrath." *Contemporary Literary Criticms.* Vol. 124. Detroit: Gale, 2000. 396–400.

Witalec, Janet. "The Grapes of Wrath: John Steinbeck." *Twentieth Century Library Criticism.* Vol. 135. Detroit: Gale, 2003. 240–364.

CANNERY ROW

READING TO WRITE

JOHN STEINBECK said that the largely whimsical *Cannery Row* (1945) was written at the urging of an American soldier, a young man who wanted to read something that would help him and his fellow soldiers forget the death and destruction they lived with every day on the European front during World War II. Steinbeck had traveled to Europe as a war correspondent, and his experiences with the soldiers moved him to recall what in life, in people, and in the world he cherished. *Cannery Row*'s mixed tones of humor, sadness, memory, loneliness, friendship, good nature, and humanity would have been evocative and familiar for a soldier fighting a war far away from home.

Cannery Row is a mixture not only in its tonal palette but also in its structure and content. In fact, mixture proves to be an important theme and the dominant pattern of imagery in the novel. This idea of mixture is communicated through the ecological metaphor of a tide pool. This idea is one that could prove interesting to write about in an essay, but whether you write on this or another topic, you must first grapple with the details and meanings of Steinbeck's prose. This section of the chapter will demonstrate how to read a particular passage—one that concerns this very idea of mixture—in preparation for writing an essay.

The first words of the novel introduce both the point of view and the ideas that are important in *Cannery Row:* "Cannery Row in Monterey in California is a poem, a stink, a grating noise, a quality of light, a tone, a habit, a nostalgia, a dream." This first sentence demonstrates the mixture of things that Cannery Row as a place will encompass in this story. Looking closely at the list given, you will notice that this place is rendered as an amalgam of things material and ineffable: It is an experience ("a grating noise") and an idea ("a nostalgia"), a reality ("a stink") and a fantasy ("a dream"), a work of art ("a poem") and a source of practical industry (the fish-canning industry that gives the place its name). Even noticing here that at its most obvious level Cannery Row is both beautiful and ugly is useful for literary analysis because this combination leads you to explore ways that the place is both things instead of just one. The remainder of the first paragraph further develops the idea of mixture:

> Cannery Row is the gathered and scattered, tin and iron and rust and splintered wood, chipped pavement and weedy lots and junk heaps, sardine canneries of corrugated iron, honky tonks, restaurants and whore houses, and little crowded groceries, and laboratories and flophouses. Its inhabitants are, as the man once said, "whores, pimps, gamblers, and sons of bitches," by which he meant Everybody. Had the man looked through another peephole he might have said, "Saints and angels and martyrs and holy men," and he would have meant the same thing.

You will notice that this first paragraph forms, in its entirety, a list or catalog. Most of the items on this list are conventionally thought of as negatives, but the narrator asserts that seeing "whores, pimps, gamblers, and sons of bitches" in a negative light might simply be a matter of attitude and perception, since these same people can be classified, according to the narrator, as "saints, angels, martyrs and holy men." By redirecting the reader's vision in order to question conventional expectations of people, the novel is urging us to question our values more broadly.

The acts of listing and classifying items and objects that are so prevalent here are worth analyzing in an essay. You might, for instance, explore reasons that the narrative includes so many lists. How are these lists related to the idea of nature and ecology in this book that takes place on the ocean? How are the societies on land compared to the societies in the tide pools? You might also consider how the nonjudgmental narration of the story emulates the tone and style of a scientific report and explore the effects of this narration on the reading of the story. Does the lack of narrative judgment prevent the reader from engaging with the story? These are the kinds of questions that the novel raises and that can become the core of an essay.

A slow and careful reading of *Cannery Row* will better allow you to identify and analyze the patterns, issues, and ideas in the stories. Reading slowly and taking notes in the margins of your book will make for a richer understanding of the novel, while also enabling you to gather the evidence you need to write a strong essay.

TOPICS AND STRATEGIES

This section of the chapter discusses various possible topics for essays on *Cannery Row* and general approaches to those topics. Remember that these are only starting points for your own analysis, not a comprehensive code to the novel. Every topic discussed here could encompass a wide variety of good papers.

Themes

Cannery Row treats many themes, ideas, and concepts that organize the action of the novel. The section above examined some of these: mixture, values, catalogs. Writers approaching the novel often begin by identifying a central theme they see as important and then deciding what the novel is saying about that theme. To identify a theme, you should look for ideas or even words that recur in the story. In the initial discussion, listing and classifying appear as central concerns in the first paragraph of the novel. Looking for the idea that underlies the act of classification will help you identify in what way or ways classification is also a theme. Catalogs and classifications are important to biology and ecology, two sciences that feature prominently in this novel. Ecology is probably the more apt of the two sciences, being concerned, as it is, with the relationships between living organisms and their natural environments. The next step is to decide what you think the novel is saying about the theme of ecology. How is this particular science important in this story, and in what ways does it speak to the events in the novel? Details such as those in the opening paragraph strongly suggest that the humans in this novel share traits with animals and that qualitative judgments about human activity are as irrelevant to human activity as they are to animal activity. Furthermore, the opening paragraph's presentation of the panoply of human existence in Cannery Row emphasizes the ecological diversity of life there. To study the theme of ecology, you would want to identify places where life forms are presented as interrelated and interdependent, just as they are in ecosystems. Other themes could be explored in similar ways—you could explore the theme of domesticity, for instance, by studying the novel's presentation of domestic situations for the Malloys and even Mack and the boys and by thinking about what the impulse of domesticity might be saying about human nature.

Sample Topics:

1. **Ecology:** How does the novel use the science of ecology to portray its subjects? In what ways is *Cannery Row* a meditation on ecology?

   Such an essay would need to look at those places in the novel that describe the interrelation and interdependence of the people, places, and animals of Cannery Row. One approach to this topic would be to look at instances of ecological interconnectedness, such as the connection between Cannery Row and Mack and the boys: Mack and his friends are represented as cynosures, or central figures, in the ecosystem that is Cannery Row. We see their influence on their ecosystem, for instance, when they fall out of general favor after the disastrous party; the malaise Mack and the boys suffer permeates the town and becomes a general atmosphere of bad luck and bad times. A broader essay on this topic could consider how the entire book is a meditation on the science of ecology. How does the biology of the tide pools, for instance, parallel the sociology of the neighborhood? In what ways are people represented as being like marine organisms? Taking another approach, you could study how the dispassion of science informs the presentation of individuals and events in this novel.

2. **Domesticity:** What is the nature or function of domesticity in this story? Does the novel present it as a threat to a good life or

the sign of a good life? What does it mean that so many characters demonstrate a desire for a domestic life?

To write an essay on this topic, begin by identifying where the novel reports on the impulses for domesticity and then assess what you think the novel is saying about the repeated examples of domesticity in such an unconventional place. You will want to examine the significance of Mr. and Mrs. Malloy's domestic impulses in their home, which is constructed from a cast-off industrial boiler. In what way are we to interpret Mrs. Malloy's desire for lace curtains in a home that has no windows? Is this an example of delusional or simply heartfelt domesticity? Mack and the boys demonstrate their own variety of domesticity when they begin to furnish their Palace Flophouse and Grill: What is the significance, do you think, of their domestic impulses? You could also approach this topic through its connection to gender roles. Mack and the boys are, for instance, represented as anathema to female domesticity in the scene with the captain during the great frog hunt. In what other ways do Mack and the boys represent a threat to female domesticity? Another approach to this topic could be to find connections between human and animal domesticity. The tide pools, for instance, are sites that demonstrate the need for a habitat. How are the Malloys implicitly compared to the hermit crabs that live in tide pools?

3. **Violence:** How does the novel represent and evaluate the use of violence? Does it judge the violent? Does violence serve a social function?

To write an essay such as this, begin by identifying where the novel either represents or discusses violence and then look at what kinds of reactions these instances inspire in Cannery Row. You could consider the fights that break out at parties, the beating that Doc gives Mack, and other examples (including nonhuman) of physically violent confrontation in this novel. From these scenes, a thesis can be developed about the role of violence in the story.

4. **Loneliness/alienation:** How does the novel present the effects of loneliness and alienation on individuals? If loneliness is so difficult for individuals, is the novel an effective call to community?

This topic invites the writer to explore the less sanguine events in this story, such as the suicides. In what ways are the suicides or experiences of outcasts (such as Frankie, William, and Horace) examples of distance or alienation from community? Another approach to this topic could consider how the community of Cannery Row can be seen as operating as a single unit, one that leaves no one behind. To discuss that idea, you might find it fruitful to discuss Dora's brothel as a beacon of community and human connection during the influenza epidemic that hits Monterey. Yet another approach to this topic would be to focus on the parable of the gopher near the end of the novel. What does the story about the gopher's leaving his idyllic home for the possibilities of flawed but companionable domesticity in the dahlia garden tell us about the book's presentation of the effects of loneliness and alienation on social creatures?

Character

Papers can focus on questions of character development (such as how Steinbeck distinguishes Mack from Lee Chong by their respective senses of ownership), means of characterization (such as the way we learn about Doc's habits and solitude from what Mack and the boys and other characters say about him), or interpretations of changes in a character as the novel proceeds (such as Frankie's burgeoning love for Doc taking excessive expression). To write an essay on character, you would need to approach the story by way of questions about how readers come to know various characters. An essay could center on the means by which Steinbeck builds the distinctive natures of his characters. How, for instance, does Steinbeck distinguish a character's manner? In the case of *Cannery Row*, Doc's wisdom, talent, and patient manner distinguish him as a naturally evolved, if isolated, individual. Mack has his own variety of wisdom, talent, and patience, and it is illuminating to compare the two characters in terms of these qualities: With close reading and reflection, you might recognize that Doc's qualities serve the greater community while Mack's are more self-serving. Though there is not a great deal of change within characters, there is plenty to say about them; many of the characters are unusual and strange and well worth discussing in an essay. To answer questions of character development, look closely at the details of language, action, or interactions with other characters. The ways characters behave with one another helps you understand who the characters are. Essays on character development assess not only the means by which characters are created but also what characters signify and represent for the story as a whole.

Sample Topics:

1. **Doc as a character:** What kind of figure is Doc? What does he value? What purpose does he serve in the community?

   Doc is a central figure in this novel, but his removal from society suggests that he remains somewhat unfathomable to the community at large; the narrator describes Doc as a "lonely and set-apart man." One approach to this topic would be to explore the ways in which Doc is perceived in the book. In what ways does the community of Cannery Row find Doc mysterious? You will want to discuss how the girls of the Bear Flag Restaurant, Mack and the boys, and Lee Chong perceive Doc. It would be worthwhile also to discuss the reasons that the community wants to throw Doc a party. In another approach to this topic, you might look at Doc himself, at what he says and does, as a means to ascertain what kind of figure he is. What does the episode with the beer milkshake, for instance, tell us about Doc? Whichever approach you take, you will want to discuss what purpose you see him serving in the larger community. What is his role in this ecosystem?

2. **Mack as a character:** What kind of figure is Mack? What purpose does he serve in the community?

Mack is as central to this story as Doc is, and the same kinds of questions can be applied to both characters. You might consider discussing how Mack is perceived by Doc, Lee Chong, and other characters (perhaps including himself, since Mack does ponder that subject). Doc, for example, considers Mack and his friends "true philosophers." Another source of information about Mack is the narration. The beginning of chapter 27, for instance, describes Mack and the boys as "the Virtues, the Beatitudes, the Beauties" and goes on to assert their centrality to the community's condition. Ultimately, you will want to reach a conclusion about Mack's role in the tide pool that is Cannery Row.

3. **Society and its outcasts:** Though this is a community of virtual outcasts from "respectable" society, there are in Cannery Row a number of eccentric characters, figures who are outcast from Cannery Row as well. Choose one or two characters and analyze what these outcasts reveal about the more central characters in the novel.

This is an evaluative topic requiring you to analyze what information the story offers about these important, somewhat strange, and sometimes mysterious characters. Some of the questions in the section above on alienation can be applied to this topic. You might consider analyzing William the pimp and his seeming inability to relate to other people. Frankie, the boy whose fondness for Doc becomes a fixation, is another figure who seems incapable of organic social affinity. The experience of both of these characters suggests that all societies, no matter what their station, develop values, expectations, and norms; these characters, furthermore, prove that life is difficult for those who cannot fulfill social expectations. Whichever outcasts you choose to analyze, be sure to discuss in your essay what they reveal about the novel's dramatic action, the society, or the other characters.

Philosophy and Ideas

Another approach to forming an argument about *Cannery Row* is to identify and analyze the philosophical ideas that circulate in the novel. This approach is related to the thematic approach discussed above in that it tracks an idea in the story, but this kind of an essay would demonstrate how you see the story as commenting on the idea in its more general form. In keeping with the fairly whimsical tone of the novel, among the pivotal ideas and events in the story is the throwing of parties. In chapter 30, the narrator meditates on the nature of parties: how they go wrong, how they go right, how they die. The novel's whimsical tone is made more complex by its undertones of melancholy; that the parties are occasions for both tragedy and comedy is, therefore, in keeping with the overall tone. The philosophy of parties, as described in this novel, could prove an interesting topic for an essay. You could, for instance, explore how parties emulate the biology of a natural organism. In what ways do they flourish or wither? How and why do they die? You might also explore the function of a party for society or, in the case of Mary Talbot, for an individual.

The ideas connected to mystery and the supernatural provide another source for good topics on this novel. You might analyze those moments of mystery in the novel to discover what they suggest about the residents of Cannery Row or the human impulse to understand what it cannot. Another idea that is important in this novel is the notion of success. Doc sees Mack and the boys as successful, and they seem generally content with their lives. An essay could explore how the novel presents the idea of success and, more specifically, the ways success is represented in *Cannery Row* as antithetical to American values.

Sample Topics:

1. **The philosophy of the party:** The book includes a number of examples of good and bad parties, but the apotheosis of Cannery Row is the rollicking party that is thrown for Doc. What is the function of a party to this society? What is the pathology of a party?

For this topic, you must consider how the novel presents the purpose and function of parties for the society of Cannery Row and, perhaps more broadly, humankind. One approach to this topic would be to consider the narrator's ruminations on parties. To that end, you would want to look at why one party is considered successful when another is a failure. You could, for instance, compare parties good and bad and assess the narrator's insights into their workings to reach a conclusion about the ingredients that together constitute party nirvana or party miasma. You could also consider the effect of successful or disastrous parties on the social world of Cannery Row. Another approach would be to assess what purpose parties serve for individuals; both Mary Talbot and Mack are characters who put a lot of themselves into parties, and you might consider how, though their guest lists are distinctive (e.g., Mack does not invite stray cats to his parties), the purpose of parties for both characters is similar.

2. **Mystery/the supernatural:** This novel is, overall, highly realistic, but there are mysterious moments that make considerable impressions on the residents of Cannery Row. What do the examples of mystery and the supernatural in this book reveal about this society?

An essay on this question will seek to illuminate how the mysterious moments in the story help us understand the culture of Cannery Row. Consider analyzing for social commentary the Chinese man who walks at twilight to the sea (especially the hallucinatory experience Andy from Salinas has when he tries taunting the man), the vision Henri the painter has of a ghostly murder in his boat (and Doc's refusal to come verify the vision), and even the role astrology plays in the timing of Doc's party. The role mystery plays for the individual is, perhaps, best exemplified by the general obsession that surrounds the flagpole skater. You could study the ways in which the skater fascinates and fixates the community and look to the individual reactions he inspires as a means to understand the mystery he poses. From that, you can deduce what this society values.

3. **Success:** Cannery Row is, literally and figuratively, on the other side of the tracks. The novel, however, presents its low- and no-rent residents as the true paragons of success in the world of Monterey (the city that surrounds Cannery Row) and beyond. If Mack and the boys, Dora and the girls, Doc, and the rest are examples of success, what is the novel saying about success?

This topic makes an assertion that your essay would need to explore. The first step would be to identify those sections where the narrator discusses success. You will certainly want to analyze the values asserted in chapter 2, where the narra-tor poses questions about blind ambition, including a para-phrase of Jesus: "What can it profit a man to gain the whole world and to come to his property with a gastric ulcer, a blown prostate, and bifocals?" After you identify passages that reveal the narrator's conceptions of success, you could discuss which characters most clearly embody those values. Taking another approach to this topic, you could demonstrate how *Cannery Row* is an indictment of American values that prize material success over other values. How does the novel's canonizing of society's cast-offs perform an indirect criticism of American society?

Form and Genre

Form and genre provide illuminating ways of analyzing many literary works. Form is defined as the shape and structure of a literary work; genre is defined as the kind, or classification, of a literary work. Though technically independent of the content of literature (love, for instance, is an idea that can be communicated in various forms), form and genre are used deliberately by authors to help further the ideas in, strengthen the dramatic impact of, and generally refine their stories. In *Cannery Row,* the genre is fiction and, more specifically, it is a novel. The novelistic form of *Cannery Row* is unusual in that it is composed of a conventional narrative intertwined with chapters that are not directly related to the plot; these less plot-directed chapters are called interchapters. Steinbeck had used this form before in *The Grapes of Wrath* and had experimented more generally with episodic story forms (to similar effect) in *The Red Pony* and *Tortilla Flat*. Steinbeck's utilization of interchapters in *Cannery Row* is worthy of close study both for how they expand the novel's scope and how they insert a different, often more lyrical voice into the more realistic events that take place on Cannery Row. You could, for instance, study how the interchapters complement the realistic novel and what poetic additions they offer to the text. You could also study the interchapters as texts distinct from the main story. The interchapters are often vignettes that speak to the larger ideas in the novel. Some examples of these include the stories featuring Mary Talbot, Doc's discovering the dead girl in the La Jolla tidepools, and the gopher's gallant though frustrated search for love. Examples of interchapters are found in the prologue and chapters 2, 4, 8, 10, 12, 14, 16, 19, 26, and 31. Seen together, what do the interchapters offer as a collection of texts on their own? What varieties of voices are included, and to what end? The question of form in this novel is an excellent approach to writing an essay. More traditional essay topics are also useful for *Cannery Row*. Consider, for example, the role of setting and tone.

Sample Topics:

1. **The form of the interchapters:** Analyze the form of the interchapters and consider how their themes and other significances relate to the larger story. Reach a conclusion about the effect of the interchapters on the overall narrative.

This topic asks you to consider the effect of the interchapters on the overall narrative of *Cannery Row*. You will want to explore whether the interchapters are different in form or content from the larger story. You might consider if, for instance, the tone of the interchapters is different from that of the larger story: Is one more melancholy or more comic? How do the interchapters help the reader more clearly understand the point of view of the narrator, of the characters, or of the story? For example, you could consider how the effects of social alienation are more developed in the interchapters (especially those having to do with Horace Abbeville or Frankie) and how these stories of lonely individuals stand as an implicit threat to individuals in the main story. In this case, do the interchapters about the outcasts of Cannery Row remind us that one of the attractions of social ties is the respite they provide from social isolation? You will want to come to a conclusion about not only the effects of the interchapters but also their overall function for the story.

2. **Setting:** In what ways is setting important to the novel? Consider setting as both an atmosphere and a powerful force in its own right.

To address this topic, you must consider in what ways the setting (time and place) of the story is important to the story. You could consider discussing either the time or the place. In what ways, for instance, does the post–World War I time period contribute to the conflicts in the novel? What about the recent repeal of Prohibition? You could also consider the ways in which the natural setting of the Monterey Peninsula is a force in this story. You would want to reach a conclusion about the role of the sea for Doc, both as a vocation and as a natural setting for him. It might also be worthwhile to consider how the animal culture echoes the human culture in this novel.

Language, Symbols, and Imagery

Language, symbols, and imagery are some of the creative means by which an author conveys certain feelings or ideas that would, if simply announced, be undermined in their imaginative and evocative power. All writers, and those of imaginative fiction especially, use language deliberately, and they choose words based on their connotative, or suggestive, meanings. As you read fiction in preparation for writing about it, you need to be alert to the connotative meanings of language, even as you register the literal meaning of language in order to follow the plot itself.

Symbols, usually used in conjunction with imagery, are objects, either animate or inanimate, that writers also use to convey ideas. In *Cannery Row*, repetitions of objects (such as alcohol and tide pools), of ideas (such as the natural desire for domesticity and the interdependence of life forms), and of settings (such as Lee Chong's grocery store or dawn and twilight times on Cannery Row) are significant. All of these things, by the very nature of their repetition and careful presentation, serve symbolic functions in the story. These things have meaning beyond their denotative definitions. The best essays on symbolism will look at the symbol and its affiliated imagery and consider these subjects in relation to the story's larger ideas. When you are asked to discuss symbolism, you are being asked to discuss what something signifies, means, and represents in light of the entire work.

Sample Topics:

1. **The tide pool as a symbol:** The tide pool is the vocation and fascination of Doc, and it also serves as the primary symbol in this novel. Consider how the tide pool serves as an analogue for the world of *Cannery Row*.

For this topic you must consider how the world of the tide pool is paralleled in the human world of Cannery Row and thereby becomes a symbol of the place. To address this topic, you would need to study the way that tide pools are represented in the narrative and locate ways in which the social world of *Cannery Row* is likewise represented. You will want to read closely the sections in chapter 6 that describe the tide pool at work. Within that chapter, you might note the impulse for domesticity that hermit crabs display (one that is repeated elsewhere in the novel). Another parallel between these animal and human societies is the proclivity for violence that both demonstrate. It would also be worthwhile to register ways in which the analogue falters: If there are ways in which the tide pool analogy breaks down, to what end does this happen? (In other words, what does the disconnect signify?) Taking another approach to this symbol, you might look at the diction affiliated with tide pools and analyze its tone. You will probably note that much of the language is essentially fond but objective, as in the description of the tide pool as "tranquil and lovely and murderous." By looking at the tone of the descriptions of this symbol, you could investigate how Steinbeck's scientific approach to his subject is evident.

2. **Collections/taxonomies:** In the beginning of the novel, the narrator describes the challenges of collecting delicate flat worms that, if handled directly, "break and tatter under the touch." He goes on to explain that the only method for collecting these worms is by allowing them to "ooze and crawl of their own will onto a knife blade." He describes this method as analogous to his writing approach for *Cannery Row*, where he decided to "open the page and to let the stories crawl in by themselves." Consider how the motifs of collecting and collections operate in this novel. You might expand the notion of collecting to include classifying and describing (also standard tasks for scientists). Explore how this pattern of imagery organizes the ideas and even the plot of *Cannery Row*.

This topic asks you to consider how collecting is a dominant motif, or pattern of imagery, in this novel. One approach would be to consider how the notion of collecting is represented as parallel to either the writing process or the plot of the novel. How does the episodic plot of *Cannery Row* function as a collection of stories, people, or even an era? Another approach would be to explore how the act of collecting is represented in the novel. You could, for example, read closely those passages in which Doc collects specimens in the tide pools or in which Mack and the boys collect frogs or cats. A third approach would be to consider the function of the many lists in the novel, such as the inventory at Lee Chong's grocery store, the waves of people who come down the hill to work in Monterey, or the animals that can be purchased at Doc's lab. These lists can be read as taxonomies, the lists that scientists use to classify objects. How do these lists contribute to either the atmosphere or action in *Cannery Row?*

Comparison and Contrast

Comparing components of a story in order to explain and analyze the similarities or differences among them is a useful approach to writing an essay. Remember to avoid the mistake of merely creating a list of similarities or differences in a work; instead, you must meaningfully comment on your observations about those connections or oppositions. To begin a comparison/contrast essay, you might compare characters with each other: How does Mack compare to Dora? How do the conformist characters compare with the nonconformist characters? You could also compare characters (or other elements of the story, such as patterns of imagery or plot) across different stories. For instance, how are philosophical characters compared in different works? How do the depictions of setting compare in *Cannery Row* and *The Pearl?* The challenge of this kind of essay is to decide what the similarities or differences you identify might mean. These are the questions that make essays compelling and the ones that will have different answers for each writer. After identifying patterns of similarity or difference, consider what purpose those similarities or differences might serve in the story overall.

Sample Topics:

1. **Compare unconventional families in different works:** Though there are few conventional families in *Cannery Row,* a great deal of sympathy and caring is demonstrated among informal collections of people, such as those at the Bear Flag Café or the Palace Flophouse and Grill. Choose one other work by Steinbeck that features an unconventional family. How are they alike or different? What kinds of commentary on family can be drawn from this comparison?

This topic asks you to consider how the families in Steinbeck's works can take unconventional forms. Other works that feature unconventional families include *Tortilla Flat, Of Mice and Men, The Grapes of Wrath, East of Eden* (where Lee is employed by the family he keeps together), and *The Red Pony* (where the family includes Billy Buck, the hired hand). One approach to this topic would be to observe how unconventional families in two or three works are represented as similar to, or different from, conventional families. For example, how does Dora's maternal personality create a family atmosphere in *Cannery Row* that is similar to the one that Ma Joad creates in *The Grapes of Wrath?* Taking another approach to this topic, you might explore how characters build, replace, or mimic family dynamics. You could consider how Lee in *East of Eden* or Billy Buck in *The Red Pony* both actively participate in the creation of a family. You could also consider how the all-male societies that Steinbeck writes of create their own families. Yet another approach would be to analyze the experience of those individuals who lack the human connection that families (conventional or otherwise) provide.

2. **Comparing philosophers in different works:** There are a number of philosophical characters in Steinbeck's works. From among *The Grapes of Wrath, Cannery Row, In Dubious Battle, East of Eden,* and *Of Mice and Men,* choose two or three philosophical characters and consider their roles in their respective stories.

This kind of essay would need to consider how a philosophical character operates in a particular work. In what ways does the philosopher promote a book's value system? In *Cannery Row,* Doc's observations about Mack and the boys enable the reader to see how the book appreciates and promotes the values of that fraternity. Jim Casy, in *The Grapes of Wrath,* is another character who helps the reader recognize that book's social message. One approach to this topic would be to assess how these philosophers serve as the voices for a book's ideology. Another approach would be to examine the experiences of characters who are philosophers. For example, are these characters always observers, or are there times when they become participants in the worlds they so assiduously watch? Must they always be lonely?

Bibliography and Online Resources for *Cannery Row:*

Alexander, Stanley. "*Cannery Row:* Steinbeck's Pastoral Poem." *Steinbeck: A Collection of Critical Essays.* Ed. Robert Murray Davis. Twentieth Century Views. Englewood Cliffs, NJ: Prentice Hall, 1972. 135–48.

Benton, Robert M. "The Ecological Nature of *Cannery Row.*" *Steinbeck: The Man and His Work.* Ed. Richard Astro and Tetsumaro Hayashi. Corvallis: Oregon State U P, 1971. 131–40.

Hintz, Paul. "The Silent Woman and the Male Voice in Steinbeck's *Cannery Row*." *The Steinbeck Question: New Essays in Criticism.* Ed. Donald R. Noble. Troy, NY: Whitson Publishing Company, 1993. 71–83.

March, Ray A. "Ed Ricketts and John Steinbeck's 'Doc:' Both Were Characters, Both Were Influential Marine Biologists." *Oceans* 19 (July–August 1986): 22.

The Martha Heasley Cox Center for Steinbeck Studies. "Cannery Row (1945)." Retrieved 27 February 2007. <http://www.steinbeck.sjsu.edu/works/Cannery%20Row.jsp>.

McEntyre, Marilyn Chandler. "Natural Wisdom: Steinbeck's Men of Nature as Prophets and Peacemakers." *Steinbeck and the Environment: Interdisciplinary Approaches.* Ed. Susan F. Beegel, Susan Shillinglaw, and Wesley N. Tiffney, Jr. Tuscaloosa: U of Alabama P, 1997. 113–24.

THE PEARL

READING TO WRITE

JOHN STEINBECK's long-standing attraction to and study of Mexico culminated in a number of his works being set in Mexico or featuring Mexican-American characters. Of these works, *The Pearl* (1947) is the most renowned. Studying Steinbeck's fascination with Mexico as a place and the Mexican (and Mexican-American) people as a culture could lead to an interesting analysis of Steinbeck's representations of things, people, and places Mexican. For example, a writer might notice that Steinbeck often represents Mexico's society as a welcome respite from the predatory atmosphere of capitalistic American society. Conversely, American capitalism is often represented in Steinbeck's works as a corrupting force that threatens the humane values of kindness, empathy, mercy, and selflessness. To write such an analysis, you could study the texts *The Pearl* (1947), "Flight" (1938), *Tortilla Flat* (1935), and *The Wayward Bus* (1947); you could also study the films—*Forgotten Village* (1941) and *Viva Zapata* (1952)—with which Steinbeck was directly involved. Whether you do this kind of broad, transtextual analysis or take a focused look at one element of a single text, you must wrestle with the nuances and details of Steinbeck's language. This section of the chapter will demonstrate how to read two passages in *The Pearl* in preparation for writing an essay.

The novella begins with an epigraph, a convention that is seen in many works of literature. Customarily, an epigraph is a brief quotation from another, usually familiar piece of literature that comments on the events in the work that follows the epigraph. While most writers cull their epigraphs from outside sources, Steinbeck here elected to write his own. The epigraph not only comments on the action to come but also establishes in the first sentence the style of the story: "In the town they tell the story of the great pearl—how it was found and how it was lost again." This opening sentence echoes the beginnings of folktales; it is thereby suggestive of the strong presence of an oral tradition in this fictional community where "they tell the story of the great pearl."

This opening is also suggestive of creation myths found all over the world, and that is no accident on Steinbeck's part. He was fascinated by folklore and creation myths that spoke to all readers. The story even comments on the fundamental power of these types of stories: "And because the story has been told so often, it has taken root in every man's mind." This quotation asserts that this story has, through reiteration, become both a part of general culture and a fundamental part of individual psychology ("taken root in every man's mind"). Note here how the narrator insists that individual experience transforms common experience. This observation could lead to an essay that analyzes the relationship between the individual and the group, as well as that between the group and the individual. To approach such an essay, you could examine the role of the community in the individual lives of Kino and Juana. Another approach could analyze how a small town is like a personified individual.

The remainder of the epigraph helps the reader anticipate not only the style but also the themes of the story:

> And, as with all retold tales that are in people's hearts, there are only good and bad things and black and white things and good and evil things and no in-between anywhere. . . . If this story is a parable, perhaps everyone takes his own meaning from it and reads his own life into it. In any case, they say in the town that . . .

The epigraph proclaims that the meaning in the story will be characterized as one of two things, "only good and bad . . . and no in-between anywhere." By asserting this, it invites the reader to expect a deliberately unrealistic style. This unrealistic style is presented here to be in keeping with the way humans understand folklore and legends ("retold tales"). This style could be an interesting topic for an essay. You could, for instance, track the ways that the style of the story stays true to the promises of the opening sentences. Do the characters remain only good or bad? Or do they take on the psychological complexity we expect from modern stories about individuals? Discussions on formal properties could also generate strong papers. The question of whether this story is a parable (as suggested by the epigraph) is one worth exploring. A parable is a story with a moral or a message, and an interesting essay could offer discussions of what the message of *The Pearl* might be.

With so much emphasis on the style of the story, and with the coy suggestion that this might be a parable, it is worth saying a bit more about how to interpret such tales. In such stories, realism is sacrificed for the larger goals, messages, morals, and purposes of the story. Scholars argue that the lack of realism or naturalness in parables fulfills the goal of being general enough for all hearers or readers of the story to identify with the tale. Parables have an ancient tradition; over the years many figures, including Jesus, have used parables to teach lessons. As a reader of such stories, you need to be sensitive to resonances of meaning that are carried by the literal events and characters in Steinbeck's novella. In a parable, the surface meaning of an event could appear straightforward, though the actions in the stories may have multifaceted meanings. Imagine, for example, a story about an overzealous hunter that would illustrate the saying, "a bird in the hand is worth two in the bush." Steinbeck uses the parable style in *The Pearl*, and the novella demonstrates how a particular character or action can carry abstract meaning. In the opening pages of the novella, for instance, the baby is stung by a scorpion. The particular actors here (the scorpion and Coyotito) can be interpreted as representative of abstract concepts (such as evil and innocence). As you read a story that announces at its inception that it might be a parable, you need to be attentive to the ancillary meanings that such a text invites; this is a variety of close reading that is necessary for all good essays on literature in general and on parables in particular.

A slow and careful reading of *The Pearl* will better allow you to identify and analyze the patterns, issues, and ideas in the stories. Reading slowly and taking notes will make for a richer understanding of the novella, while also enabling you to gather the evidence you need to write a strong essay.

TOPICS AND STRATEGIES

This section of the chapter discusses various possible topics for essays on *The Pearl* and general approaches to those topics. Remember that these are only starting points for your own analysis, not comprehensive codes to the novel. Every topic discussed here could encompass a wide variety of good papers.

Theme

The Pearl deals with many themes, ideas, and concepts that organize the action of the novella. The section above examined some of these: the power of stories, the role of community, culture, and good and evil, among others. The story also deals with such themes as harmony, social power, and violence. Writers approaching the novella often begin by identifying a theme that they see as central to the story and then analyzing what the novella is saying about that theme. To identify a theme, you would look for ideas or even words that recur in the story. You might notice that the story repeatedly refers to songs (of evil, of family, of the pearl itself) heard by Kino. This musical motif is important to the story, and one way to analyze it would be to consider music in terms of harmony. The next step would be to decide what the story is saying about the theme of harmony. Harmony has metaphorical ramifications when Juan Tomás observes that Kino is walking an unknown and "new ground"; keeping in mind that parables have ancillary meanings might lead you to observe that Kino's walking a "new ground" is akin to his breaking out of the harmonic order of the community's mores. To that end, you might notice that at the beginning and ending of the story Kino acts in accord with his world or, in keeping with the musical metaphor, in harmony with his world. Assessing when songs are heard and what they suggest about the action in the story might lead you to think about alternative thematic approaches to the musical motif. Other themes could be approached in similar ways—the theme of social power could be approached through the novella's depiction of which individuals in the story have power and how they use their power. You might also explore how the story characterizes the circumstances of those without social power. Thematic approaches also blend with the philosophical approaches described below.

Sample Topics:

1. **Music/harmony:** How are the notions of music and harmony integral elements of this story? Why do you think music is so important in this story?

To write an essay such as this, begin by identifying where the novella mentions music. Music is associated with tranquility when, in the beginning of the story, Kino listens to the "music" of the waves. Music is also associated with cultural history when we learn that "very long ago" Kino's people were great makers of songs. One approach to this topic would be to explore how music provides background messages about the actions or the feelings of the characters. You could explore, for instance, how Kino hears different "songs" at different times when he is considering the possibilities of the pearl itself. Another approach could be to explore how the notion of harmony is used in the story. You might, for example, look at how Kino's attempts to circumvent the prevailing socioeconomic system is understood to be an example of social discord; his desire to work around the corrupt pearl dealers is construed as cacophonous and chaotic by the community. The disharmonious result of his desire for justice seems, in some respects, to validate the community's fears of acting independently.

2. **Social power:** How does the novella represent the scepter of social power? In what ways do institutions maintain their power? In what ways are individuals prevented from gaining power?

This topic guides you to think about how *The Pearl* is implicitly critical of the social hierarchies in this Mexican town. One approach to this topic would be to consider how representatives of institutions are represented. The doctor, the priest, and the pearl buyers, for instance, all work to maintain and increase their power. You might explore, too, how the peasants in the village are prevented from gaining power. Based

on your analysis of the social hierarchy, you can reach a conclusion about the ways in which the novella is critical of the
distribution of social power.

3. **Knowledge:** How is knowledge represented in this novella? What
kind of knowledge is acquired over the course of the novella?

This is a topic that is very broad, and the first challenge would
be to decide how to focus your approach. You might consider how powerful individuals withhold knowledge about
the pearl's value (this would be a variant of the above topic
on social power). Kino himself provides another example of
the value of knowledge: One of his primary objectives for the
pearl is to parlay its economic value into an education for his
son. Another approach to a topic on knowledge could center
on how the novella depicts different varieties of knowledge.
Juana's intuitive knowledge, for instance, enables her to recognize before anyone else the threat that the pearl poses to
her family (chapter 3). How is Juana's knowledge characterized
by the narrator? How is Kino's eventual acceptance of Juana's
feminine variety of knowledge key to the survival of his family
(if not his son)?

Character
Essays can focus on questions of character development (such as how
Steinbeck distinguishes Kino from Juan Tomás by their distinctive
understandings of risk), means of characterization (such as the way we
learn about the doctor's values from what he says and thinks and from
what the other characters say about him), or interpretations of changes
in a character as the novella proceeds (such as Kino's initial contentment
being undermined by his ambition and finally replaced with resignation).
To write an essay on character, you would need to approach the story by
way of questions about how readers come to know various characters.
An essay could center on the means by which Steinbeck constructs the
distinctive natures of his characters. How, for instance, does Steinbeck
distinguish a character's manner? In *The Pearl,* Juana's facility with nur-
turance and the natural world distinguish her as an individual in accord

with her culture. The doctor, by contrast, is characterized as obsessed by things destructive, decadent, and European (his time in France long ago, for instance). His disapproval of the Mexican town that he works in and of the Mexican people themselves (whom he deems more appropriately served not by him but by a veterinarian) shows his antagonistic relationship with his world. The narrator's opinion also defines characters. To address questions of character development, look closely at the details of language, action, or interactions among characters. Essays on character development assess not only the means by which characters are created but also what characters signify and represent for the story as a whole.

Sample Topics:

1. **Kino's character development:** How does Kino change over the course of the novella? Why do these changes occur?

   This topic asks you to decide what kinds of changes happen in Kino's character. A successful approach to this topic would limit the scope of inquiry to a manageable one: You might consider, for instance, how Kino's appreciation of family is interrupted by his finding the pearl. Another narrow scope could be to focus on Kino's increasing aggression and violence in the face of the conflicts he experiences. Evidence for these topics (or other approaches to changes in Kino's behavior) can be drawn from scenes where Kino's behavior toward other characters or toward animals (such as the dog that lives near Kino's shack) demonstrates change. Finally, assess whether the changes you have identified represent growth for Kino. Do you think that his final recognition of Juana as a partner instead of an underling represents a kind of resignation or a kind of wisdom?

2. **The community as a character:** What kind of figure is the community in this story? What is its role in the life of Kino and Juana?

   This is an evaluative topic that asks you to analyze the community as a single entity. It is unusual for a community to act singly, as it so clearly does in *The Pearl*, such as in the passage that follows the stinging of Coyotito: "The screams of the baby brought the neighbors. Out of their brush houses they poured. . . . And those in front passed the word back to those behind—'Scorpion. The baby has been stung.'" You might approach this topic by observing how the community is both a group that responds to the family and an entity that affects the family, such as when their knowledge that the doctor will not come to the poor neighborhood guides Kino's revolutionary decision to take the baby to the doctor. Taking another approach, you could look at how the community functions in ways that are similar to a Greek chorus; this approach would require that you familiarize yourself with the definition of a Greek chorus. Finally, you must reach a conclusion about what the community's role is in the story. To do this, you will want to assess whether its role changes for Kino and Juana: Is the community as important to them at the end of the story? At the end, do Kino and Juana transcend the community or return to it?

3. **Juana and Juan Tomás:** Both Juana and Juan Tomás broaden our understanding of the experience of life in the world of *The Pearl*. How are these characters presented in the novella? How do they contribute to a greater understanding of the situation of the people and of Kino himself?

This essay would need to evaluate both characters and their respective roles in the novella. What qualities do these individuals embody? What qualities of Kino's do they enable us to perceive more clearly? This essay would need to bring in some discussion about the cautions both Juana and Juan Tomás offer to a resistant Kino (both about the pearl and about trying to circumvent the traditional sales process).

History and Context

Though not fixed in a specific time, the historical context of *The Pearl* still provides a worthwhile opportunity for strong analysis of the novella. The novella describes a world that has real-life connections to remote Mexican towns and villages in the early part of the 20th century and, many would say, today still. Though situated in the city of La Paz in Baja California, Mexico, the circumstances of the novella could have taken place in any number of small fishing villages in Mexico. One approach to writing about history in this work would be to consider the social and psychological results of Mexico's colonial past. How, for instance, does the novella portray European colonial powers as still exerting their power and influence, despite Mexico's ostensible independence? Does the novella imagine a Mexico that will be both ostensibly and actually free of Europe? Another historical element of the novella that could be usefully investigated is the Mexican peasant uprisings as a response to the systems of oppression that are evident in the book. How, for instance, does Kino's experience of economic and social injustice parallel the experiences of individuals who participated in the Mexican revolutions of the 19th and 20th centuries?

The atmosphere in which the novella was written is another worthwhile approach to history and context. The Mexican experience in California at this time was rife with conflict. The novel was penned in 1945 (published in 1947), and a look at California's political climate at that time reveals cogent connections to *The Pearl*. Steinbeck would have been very familiar with 1943's Zoot Suit Riots in Southern California. The riots describe a series of events in Los Angeles during World War II, when idle soldiers (stationed in Los Angeles, waiting for assignment), over a series of nights, attacked Mexican youths who were wearing zoot suits (voluminous suits that the soldiers interpreted symbolically as a flouting of wartime rationing and as a sign of gangsterism). The Zoot Suit Riots are, most historians now agree, misnamed; in fact, some historians now refer to the events as the Servicemen's Uprising, an appellation that more accurately describes the active players in this episode. Events like these were symptoms of larger social patterns—of mistrust and prejudice—that identified the relationship between the whites and the nonwhites in 1940s California: Parallels of these social relations are depicted in the setting of *The Pearl*. Steinbeck, having a lifelong fascination with Mexican and Mexican-American culture, as well as a love of California, would have avidly tracked the social situation in California. For this or any other historical topic, the writer would need to do some research to be able to consider knowledgeably what the novella is asserting about the world it describes.

Sample Topics:

1. **The colonial past of *The Pearl*:** The novella makes many references to Mexico's colonial past. How does Steinbeck use this history in the novella? What purposes are served by this kind of historical reference?

   A paper on *The Pearl* and colonialism would need to show some familiarity with Mexico's colonial history (e.g., the conquest and occupation by Spain, the thwarted invasion by France) in order to properly place colonialism in the social context of the novella. One approach to this topic would be to look at how the doctor is characterized as a proxy for colonialism. How, for instance, does his attitude toward and interest in the Mexican villagers echo the treatment of the Mexicans by the historical colonists? Ultimately, you will want to reach a conclusion about how the references to colonialism and Europe operate in this novel. You could, for instance, theorize about what Europe represents in a book that claims to see only the good and the bad of things. How might Europe's presence heighten the tensions around good and evil in this story?

2. **Peasantry and politics:** The novella is, in addition to being a parable, a very political story; as such it studies who has and who lacks power. In what ways does the novella demonstrate how oppression and disenfranchisement can lead to political uprisings? Consider discussing Kino's experience in conjunction with one of Mexico's revolutions.

   This is a broad topic, and you would need to focus on a few elements and evaluate the novella's position on them. You might consider assessing how Kino and his family are prevented from participating in even the most elemental forms of social power: Their poverty restricts them from receiving education, the sacrament of marriage (a sign of social respectability), or basic medical treatment. Even with the valuable pearl in hand, Kino's attempts to gain social power are obstructed. Historically, Mexico has been the site of many political revolutions, and generally speaking, these revolutions have been precipitated by tremendous oppression, especially of the rural landless Indians. At the time he was working on *The Pearl,* Steinbeck was also researching (for a later screenplay) Emiliano Zapata, a political leader who galvanized the peasantry of southern Mexico during the Mexican Revolution (1910). An approach to the topic of peasantry and politics would be to track how Kino's growing awareness of his powerlessness leads to his outrage and then his search for power. You might also consider how he seeks ways to acquire power (i.e., to become politicized); to do this, you would want to do close readings of his realizations about his social position. Ultimately, you will want to gauge whether Kino's experience (especially at the novella's end) bespeaks either hope or doom for the peasantry.

3. **The Mexican experience in California:** The novella describes a Mexican experience that could very easily have been transposed onto California social history. What historical contexts was Steinbeck writing out of? In what ways is *The Pearl* an answer to the experience of Mexicans in 1940s California?

This is a broad topic, and you would need to research the Mexican experience in California to be able to answer it judiciously. One approach would be to analyze the historical events briefly described in the introduction to this section (e.g., the Zoot Suit Riots). You could approach this topic by looking at the particular varieties of injustice and exclusion these events in Southern California embody. These events articulated systems of persecution that parallel, in important ways, the experiences of the dust bowl refugees whom Steinbeck wrote about in *The Grapes of Wrath.* You might consider Steinbeck's American audience and how *The Pearl* could be a means by which the author sought to humanize the experience of a people he admired and thought persecuted by the American people.

Form and Genre

Form and genre provide illuminating ways for thinking about and describing many literary works. Genre describes the general variety of literature; in *The Pearl,* the genre is fiction. Form describes one of two things: It is either a specific category within genre, such as a novella, which falls within the category of fiction, or it can describe the shape or structure that the text takes. Form and genre prove especially interesting to discuss in conjunction with *The Pearl* because its form is so unusual for a 20th-century piece of fiction. When the narrator announces that this is a "retold tale" that contains "only good and bad things and black and white things and good and evil things and no in-between anywhere," he is telling us about the form that the story will take. Furthermore, he is telling us to expect that this will be a story similar to one from the oral tradition ("a retold tale that [is] in people's hearts"), a story that will, by its nature, lack a kind of realism. This lack of realism for the sake of a tale could make for the basis of an interesting essay. How, for instance, does Steinbeck's story deliberately use the style of a folktale? How does the lack of realism contribute to the story's meaning? The narrator also raises the possibility that *The Pearl* is a particular kind of folktale, a parable (a story that teaches a lesson). Assessing whether the story performs the function of a parable could also form an interesting essay. You could approach such an essay by considering what lesson *The Pearl* is teaching.

Sample Topics:

1. *The Pearl* **as folklore:** John Steinbeck thought of *The Pearl* as folklore and said that he tried to "give it that set-aside, raised-up feeling that all folk stories have." Where do you see this folkloric technique being used in the story? What is the effect of this "raised-up feeling"?

This topic asks you to consider the story as an example of folklore and to assess what effect its folkloric nature has on the reading of the story. The first step in addressing this topic would be to identify how *The Pearl* resembles a folktale. You could research some conventions of folktales (in an encyclopedia, for instance) to ascertain what they are. Some classic conventions include absolutism (characters are either good or bad), repetition (often of numbers, such as combinations of three), and poetic justice (the bad are punished and the good are rewarded). Any deviations from the folktale tradition that you identify in *The Pearl* would also generate valuable analysis. You will certainly want to discuss the end of the story, where Juana and Kino's characters both seem larger than life. Ultimately, you will want to reach some conclusions about the folkloric atmosphere in this story. Do characters remain absolutes, or do they take on gradations of good and bad? Does the use of folklore add or subtract meaning from the story?

2. *The Pearl* **as parable:** The opening of the novella suggests that it might be a parable. Argue whether it is and, if so, what this story teaches.

This topic asks you to argue whether or not this story is an example of a parable (a story that teaches a lesson). This is discussed in the "Reading to Write" section above. The first step in addressing the topic would be to decide what Kino learns from his experiences and what, by extension, the reader is supposed to learn from Kino's experiences. Based on your conclusions about the overall lesson of this story, you will be able to analyze how this lesson is conveyed.

Language, Symbols, and Imagery

Language, symbol, and imagery are some of the creative means by which an author conveys certain feelings or ideas that would, if simply announced, be undermined in their imaginative and evocative power. All writers, and those of imaginative fiction especially, use language deliberately, and they choose words based on their connotative, or suggestive, meanings. As you read fiction in preparation for writing about it, you need to be alert to the connotative meanings of language even as you register the surface meaning of language in order to follow the plot itself.

Symbols, usually used in conjunction with imagery, are objects, either animate or inanimate, that writers also use to convey ideas. In *The Pearl* repetitions of imagery (such as music and song), of ideas (such as the importance of the natural world for humans), and of objects (such as the pearl) are significant. All of these things have meaning beyond their denotative definitions; by nature of their repetition and careful presentation, these objects serve symbolic functions in the story. In an analysis of a parable-like story such as *The Pearl*, you will also want to be prepared for characters to represent ideas; Coyotito is an example of a character functioning as a symbol (of innocence) in this story. The best essays on symbolism will look at the symbol and, perhaps, its affiliated imagery and consider these subjects in relation to the story's larger ideas. When you are asked to discuss symbolism, you are being asked to discuss what something signifies, means, and represents in light of the entire work.

Sample Topics:

1. **Coyotito as symbol:** In many ways, Coyotito represents the hope of a new life for his family and his community. With the education his father wants Coyotito to have, the boy would bridge the traditional and modern worlds. What other symbolic functions does Coyotito serve in the story? What is the symbolic meaning of his death?

   This topic asks you to analyze how the character of Coyotito functions in the story as a symbol and to consider what he might represent symbolically. You could consider discussing why Coyotito is stung by the scorpion, why he is poisoned by the doctor, and how he is associated with the pearl itself. This last point deserves special attention because the story presents the value of the pearl as dependent on the boy (that is to say, without the boy, the pearl has no value for Kino and Juana). Another connection between the pearl and the boy: Both are passive objects that meaning is projected onto. This relationship between the pearl and Coyotito suggests that the story is, in many ways, a story of Coyotito. Why do you think Coyotito dies at the end of the story? What does his death symbolically signify for the story?

2. **The symbolism of the pearl:** What symbolic purposes does the pearl serve in this novella? Does it have different meanings for different characters? Ultimately, what does it represent to Kino and Juana?

   For this topic, you must analyze the symbolic meanings of the pearl. One way to approach this topic would be to consider the meanings of the pearl relative to the characters in the story. You could focus your approach further by concentrating on a pair of characters, such as Juana and Kino. Juana, for instance, is initially desirous of the pearl, but she soon realizes the pitfalls that such an object represents for her family. To her, it symbolizes promise and then doom. Kino's realization of the pearl's dangers is delayed by his hopes for it. Another way to approach this story is to focus on the pearl itself. Does it have an existence outside of the characters' projections of meaning onto it? Is it an animate or inanimate object? The pearl is represented as changing: In the beginning of the story it is described as "gloating and triumphant," but at the end of the story the pearl is described as "gray and ulcerous." Whatever approach you take to this topic, you will want to reach a conclusion about the pearl's symbolic function in the story overall. What does it signify? Why do Kino and Juana return it to the sea?

Comparison and Contrast

Comparing components of a story in order to explain and analyze the similarities or differences among them is a useful approach to writing an essay. Remember to avoid the mistake of merely creating a list of similarities or differences in a work; instead, you must take the necessary step of commenting on these observations. To begin a comparison/contrast essay, you might compare characters with each other: How does Juan Tomás compare to Kino? How do the male characters compare with the female characters? You could also compare characters (or other elements of the story like patterns of imagery or action) across different stories. For example, how do the depictions of place compare in "Flight" and *The Pearl?* How is the notion of family depicted differently in *The Pearl* and *The Grapes of Wrath?* The challenge of this kind of essay is deciding what the similarities or differences you identify might mean. These are the questions that make essays interesting and the ones that will have different answers for each writer. It is not sufficient to identify a pattern and to point to the existence of similarities or differences; you must also consider what purpose those similarities or differences might serve in the story overall.

Sample Topics:

1. **Comparing male and female characters:** How are male and female characters characterized in this story? Does this story argue for feminine and masculine "types"? What are they?

   This topic asks you to compare the masculine and feminine characters in this story. One approach would be to assess whether the story presents men and women as having essential character types, or fundamental traits. What, in this story, does it mean to be a woman or a man? You will want to discuss how Juana seems to be aware of things that Kino is not, while she also remains deferential to the role she believes the man needs to play in a couple. At the end of the story, they return to La Paz "not walking in single file, Kino ahead and Juana behind, as usual, but side by side." What does it mean that Kino ultimately acknowledges Juana's equal importance in the couple? Some critics believe that this partnered return to the village represents Kino's accepting of the idea of the feminine. Are there other signs that support this interpretation?

2. **Contrasting the Old and New Worlds:** How does *The Pearl* represent the New (American, native) and Old (European, conqueror) Worlds? Does it prefer one over the other? Is one dominant at the end, or are they joined?

   For this topic, you must consider how actions and materials associated with the Old and New Worlds are represented in the novella. This juxtaposition of cultures is first established in the treating of Coyotito's scorpion sting; you will want to compare how the narrator presents the traditional remedy versus the modern one. Methods for settling disputes are also instructive moments for contrasting the Old and New Worlds; Kino, for instance, becomes as "cold and deadly as steel" and a "killing machine" when he is defending his family against the trackers. Steel's association with European manufacturing helps us recognize that Kino is using the tools of the Old World (tools that, perhaps ironically, subjugated his people during the conquest). You will need to reach a conclusion about the state of the world in La Paz at the end of the story. Is it an equal mixture of both worlds, or does one still dominate the other?

Bibliography for *The Pearl*:

Johnson, Claudia D. *Understanding* Of Mice and Men, The Red Pony, *and* The Pearl: *A Student Casebook to Issues, Sources, and Historical Documents.* Literature in Context. Westport, CT: Greenwood Press, 1997.

Lisca, Peter. "Escape and Commitment: Two Poles of the Steinbeck Hero." *Steinbeck: The Man and His Work.* Ed. Richard Astro and Tetsumaro Hayashi. Corvallis: Oregon State UP, 1971. 75–88.

Morris, Harry. "The Pearl: Realism and Allegory." *Contemporary Literary Criticism.* Vol. 21. Ed. Sharon R. Gunton. Detroit: Gale, 1982. 370–72. Originally published in *English Journal* 52 (October 1963): 487–505.

"*The Pearl*." *Novels for Students.* Vol. 5. Ed. Diane Telgen. Detroit: Gale, 1999. 305–23.

EAST OF EDEN

READING TO WRITE

MANY CRITICS think of *East of Eden* (1952) as Steinbeck's second-greatest work. Though *Grapes of Wrath* (1939) continues to be considered his masterpiece, *East of Eden* was the novel closest to the author's heart. Steinbeck might have had such fondness for the novel in part because it includes so much of his own family history: The majority of it is set in the region in which he was born and raised; his mother's family members play important character roles; his childhood home is described and featured in the action; and John Steinbeck himself, as a young boy, makes some cameo appearances. Studying the mixture of personal history and fictional creation would be a worthwhile approach for an essay; you could, for instance, assess whether this mixture contributes to a sense of authenticity or, instead, blurs the narrative focus in the novel. Though the presence of announced autobiography is a somewhat unusual circumstance for a work of fiction, it makes organic sense for a novel that is about the intense relationships among family members (Steinbeck's and otherwise) and the legacies that families pass down to later generations.

Legacies provide the conflict and energy of the novel because, the novel argues, legacies provide the genesis of all human individuality, identity, and anguish. The novel focuses on the lingering effects of the deeds and misdeeds of biblical characters, providing variations on the theme of the Cain and Abel story from the Bible. To write insightfully about this novel, therefore, the writer must have some familiarity with the story of Cain and Abel, the first children of the first humans, Adam and Eve.

The book in the Bible from which all these firsts come is Genesis, which, as the title implies, accounts for the beginnings of the world and humankind. The inception of humanity is described as fraught with conflict and paradox: The aftermath of the first sin marks the beginning of humankind and the love of a parent for a child (which echoes that of God for his children), but it also marks the beginning of shame, pain, and mortality. So, at the moment of expulsion from the Garden of Eden, there is the simultaneous origin of life and death. Shame, sadly, does not end with God's disappointment with Adam and Eve; their sons, Cain and Abel, figure in a second punitive expulsion. In this story Cain and Abel each present God with a gift: Cain, a farmer, gives the bounty of the land; Abel, a herdsman, gives the sacrifice of an animal. For unexplained reasons, God favors Abel's present, and an enraged Cain, jealous of God's preference for his brother, kills Abel. When God questions Cain about his brother's whereabouts, Cain infamously denies knowledge and petulantly answers God with another question: "Am I my brother's keeper?" For the transgression of murder (the world's first, according to the Bible), God banishes Cain and sends him to the land of "Nod, east of Eden."

The novel's title strongly suggests that the action takes place in a world away from, but not beyond, God's grace and purview. One approach to an essay on this novel would be to study how the narrative incorporates and modifies the Cain and Abel story. You could, for instance, track how the events in the story echo the fateful gifts, the mystery of love and favor, or even the lonely consequences of filial alienation. Since there is no literal fratricide in the novel, you could analyze how that variety of murder is replaced with hostility and loathing, or, sometimes, love and acceptance.

The novel's opening describes the principal groups of characters and the landscape in which the primary action takes place. This opening echoes those of creation stories. Just as Genesis describes how things came to be as they are, so *East of Eden*'s assertions about people and places in the beginning describe things as they prove to be in the novel itself. This analogue could form the basis of an essay on the novel. For instance, how are the opening chapters an homage to Genesis? You could assess in what ways the novel adopts the genealogical aspects of Genesis to move the novel's action to the two families (Trask and Hamilton) featured in the novel.

No matter what topic you choose to analyze, you must first contend with Steinbeck's use of language. This section of the chapter will demonstrate how to read closely an early passage in *East of Eden* in preparation for writing an essay. As you read closely, you need to be aware of details of language, character, setting, and dramatic conflicts and look for what these details are telling you about the story. In the first chapter of *East of Eden*, the land and the people both are given symbolic, as well as literal, existences. As you read the following paragraph, look for the literal and figurative details that will help you understand what is being established about the story to come:

> I remember that the Gabilan Mountains to the east of the valley were light gay mountains full of sun and loveliness and a kind of invitation, so that you wanted to climb into their warm foothills almost as you want to climb into the lap of a beloved mother. They were beckoning mountains with a brown grass love. The Santa Lucias stood up against the sky to the west and kept the valley from the open sea, and they were dark and brooding—unfriendly and dangerous. I always found in myself a dread of west and a love of east. Where I ever got such an idea I cannot say, unless it could be that the morning came over the peaks of the Gabilans and the night drifted back from the ridges of the Santa Lucias. It may be that the birth and death of the day had some part in my feeling about the two ranges of mountains.

In terms of patterns of figurative language, there is considerable personification here: The foothills of the eastern Gabilan Mountains are compared to "the lap of a beloved mother." The diction extends these affectionate associations: "light," "gay," "full of sun," "loveliness," and "invite." By contrast, the mountains to the west are "dark," "brooding," "unfriendly," and "dangerous." What is particularly revealing about this passage is less the mapping of the landscape than the narrator's characterization of it. From what the narrator asserts about place, we deduce that he interprets the world around him as having essential, fundamental qualities (here, eastern mountains are represented as fundamentally good, while the western mountains are represented as fundamentally bad). Furthermore, he portrays the world as featuring opposed forces. Ascertaining the outlook of the narrator will help us understand more fully the story that he will tell us.

Steinbeck places himself (or a fictive version of himself) in the story by asserting "I remember." In fact, his maternal relatives, the Hamiltons, are significant characters in the story. This biographical fact and the corollary narrative tracks of memoir and family biography that run through this book present opportunities for productive analysis about the role of the narrative in the novel. An essay could explore the persona of the narrator and assess whether it affects the events in the story. What does he value, understand, overlook?

A slow and careful reading of *East of Eden* will better allow you to recognize the patterns, issues, and ideas in the novel. Reading slowly and taking notes will make for a more enriched understanding of this epic story, while also enabling you to gather the evidence you need to write a strong essay.

TOPICS AND STRATEGIES

This section of the chapter discusses various possible topics for essays on *East of Eden* and general approaches to those topics. Remember that these are springboards for independent interpretation, not a road map to the novel. Every topic discussed here could support a wide variety of good papers.

Themes

East of Eden includes many themes, ideas, and concepts that fuel the action. Some of these ideas include ideality/reality, legacy, love, and identity. Writers approaching the novel often begin by identifying a central theme they see as important and then arguing what the novel is saying about that theme. You can identify a theme by tracking the ideas, symbols, or even words that recur in the story. In the beginning of this novel, for instance, the particulars of the Hamilton family's legacies are described. As was discussed above, all origins and histories generate significant conflict in this novel and prove to be important themes. Next, decide what you think the story is saying about the theme of legacies—either historical or material. Both Adam Trask and his brother Charles, for instance, argue about the legacy (i.e., material inheritance) bequeathed to them by their father, Cyrus. Of the two brothers, Charles is the more preoccupied by the misdeeds that their father may have committed to generate this inheritance (that is, he is interested in the origin of his father's wealth). This observation could lead to a discussion of morality as exemplified by the characters: Charles, who is painfully aware of his own moral imperfections, is obsessed with his father's morality. Analyzing the legacy of a moral outlook proves to be an interesting approach to this story because so many characters discuss what it means to have flawed parents. This sense of legacy is one that Caleb Trask (Charles's possible natural son, though the novel does not dwell on what would be the miraculous paternity of twins fathered by different men) is deeply sensitive to; his belief in his own sense of moral inadequacy causes him to question in what ways he might be his wicked mother's son. You could approach other themes in similar ways: You might approach the theme of ideality/reality through the novel's depiction of a character's struggles with preconceived notions and then offer an analysis about what the role of ideality/reality might be in the novel. Thematic approaches also blend with the philosophical approaches described below.

Sample Topics:

1. **Legacy:** What is the nature or function of legacy in this novel? In what ways does the novel present it as powerful? Are there any ways in which legacy is characterized as inconsequential?

   For this topic you must consider the role of legacy in the novel. The entire novel could be considered a meditation on legacy because it analyzes how Cain's acts and persona have trickled down to all humans. This, however, is too sweeping a scope for an essay of reasonable length; the challenge of this topic, then, is to limit its focus. One way to limit the focus would be to specify the idea of legacy. You could, for instance, consider legacy in the material sense of the world. A number of valuable inheritances are passed down in this novel: Cyrus's, Charles's, and Cathy's. An essay could consider the consequences of these legacies for the recipients: In what ways are these legacies gainful, and how are they destructive? You could skew this approach to include the notion of gifts; the giving of presents is, after all, an act common to the biblical Cain, Charles Trask, and Cal Trask. In none of those cases is the gift received in the way hoped for. Another approach to the notion of legacy is to analyze the more congenital variety, in the sense of family tradition or history. Cal, for instance, once he knows his mother's identity, worries that he is as bad as she is. Are there ways that Cal tries to make his legacy a self-fulfilling prophecy? Ways that he fights it? You might also consider how (and why) characters such as Adam and Abra appear far less invested in their pedigree.

2. **Love:** How does the novel depict the nature of love? How does it present the general phenomenon of love? What are some particular effects of love on characters?

This topic asks you to consider the qualities and effects of love. One approach to this topic could center on familial love. A writer could track how the drive for love can have destructive consequences, as in the case of Charles Trask, whose desire for love from his father generates a murderous hatred for his brother. This dynamic is repeated, to a lesser degree, in Cal's feelings for his father and brother. One of the interesting aspects of love in this book is the preponderance of unrequited love, both filial and romantic: This is seen in Charles, Caleb, and Adam. One approach to this topic could be philosophical; you could consider how love is not dependent on the beloved but is an individually held feeling more than a quality of a mutual relationship. You might look for examples of mutual love (perhaps with Cal and Abra at the end of the novel) to ascertain what conditions the novel presents as necessary for mutual and simultaneous love. Another approach would be to look for examples of platonic love, such as those provided by Lee or Samuel Hamilton.

3. **Identity:** How does the book present the process by which identity is created? What makes us who we are?

Does *East of Eden* present nature or nurture as the strongest marker of character? The novel contains a number of characters whose backgrounds are described, but perhaps the most useful individuals to discuss for this topic would be the twins, Caleb and Aron. You will want to locate places in the novel where the differences between the twins are discussed, such as in chapter 24, where Lee explains the twins' distinctions to Samuel Hamilton; you should reach some conclusions about how and why their identities are created. Another approach to this topic would be through the figure of Cathy Trask, a character whose nature is strong and fixed: She is born, in the words of the narrator, a "psychic monster," and the loving care she receives as a child has no discernable effect on her monstrousness. What do you think the book is suggesting about identity in general with a character such as Cathy? Ultimately, you should offer an analysis about whether the novel presents human identity as elective or inborn.

4. **Ideality/reality:** How does this novel represent and evaluate the opposing concepts of ideality and reality? How do preconceived notions affect characters?

To write an essay such as this, begin by identifying characters who most struggle with their preconceived notions of other characters. You could look at Adam, Aron, or even Charles or Cathy. Adam's image of Cathy, to take one example, prevents his registering not only her desires (such as when she tells him that she is going to leave him) but also her lack of humanity (a trait that other characters quickly recognize). You would want to analyze the later scene where he confronts her and, by so doing, is freed from his misguided ideals of her. A strong analysis will offer some theory explaining why Adam is so blind to her for so long. Is there something in him that is desperate to deny her wickedness? These questions could also be applied to Aron's idealizing of Abra, a tendency that Abra resents. Charles has a strong desire to idealize his father; Cathy has a compulsion to generate negative ideals of the people around her. Idealizing becomes, for Charles, Adam, and Cathy, a kind of self-imposed blindness.

Character

Good essays can focus on questions of character development (such as how Steinbeck distinguishes Cal from Aron Trask by their distinctive manners with Abra), means of characterization (such as the way the reader learns about Adam Trask from his thoughts and the discussions about him by other characters), or interpretations of changes in a character as the novel proceeds (such as the evolution of Cal Trask from petulant to humbled). To write an essay on character, you would need to approach the story by way of questions about how readers come to know various characters. How, for instance, does Steinbeck distinguish a character's manner? In *East of Eden*, Cathy Trask's malevolence is underscored by her penchant for sexual sadism. Adam Trask's restlessness is demonstrated by his years of pointless wandering: To some extent, we better understand his desire for domesticity with Cathy when we take into account his long search for a home. To analyze questions of character development, look closely for distinguishing traits of physicality, language, action, or interactions with other characters. The ways characters behave with one another can help you understand the means by which characters are created and assess what characters signify and represent for the novel overall.

Sample Topics:

1. **Cal Trask's character development:** How does Cal change over the course of the novel? Why might these changes occur?

To argue a thesis on a topic such as this, you must first decide (based on a careful reading of the second half of the novel, where Cal appears) what changes happen in Cal's character. Evidence for this can be drawn either from his actions with other characters or from his meditations on himself and others. The scenes where Lee counsels Cal to rise above his baser impulses could provide you with evidence explaining reasons behind changes in Cal's character.

2. **Cathy (Kate) Ames as a character:** What kind of figure is Cathy (later, Kate)? In what ways is her malevolence made manifest, and how do you think her wickedness functions for the characters in the novel? What role does her evil play in the story overall?

This is an evaluative topic that requires you to analyze what information the novel offers about this important but somewhat elusive character. Because her malevolence is such a clearly stated aspect of her persona, it would not be analytically worthwhile simply to discuss the different ways in which she is shown to be bad. Instead, it would be better to consider her evil at work: That is, how does her evil function in the story? One approach would be to consider how the fascination she inspires parallels that of the serpent's in the Garden of Eden. So, in the broader sense, in what ways is Cathy characterized in the novel as a source of forbidden knowledge, sexual shame, and chaos? Another approach to an essay on Cathy would be to consider her essential mystery and unfathomability. To address this aspect of her character, you would want to analyze those sections where the narrator reveals how baffling he finds her and reach a conclusion about what it means that she is unknowable to him.

3. **Character development in general:** How does the story present characters to the reader? What techniques does the novel use?

A paper on this topic would observe how Steinbeck gives insight into character. A possible technique would be to look carefully at a pair of characters or a set of techniques and attempt to show what effects they have. You could discuss the way that two characters deal differently with the prospect of travel or immigration, for instance. What might these reactions tell us about each character? About the meaning of home? Other subjects would also be fruitful for this topic. Analyzing the techniques of dialogue and physical description, for instance, are other ways of writing about character development.

4. **Samuel Hamilton and Lee:** How are these characters presented in the novel? Are they complementary figures, or do they represent significantly different kinds of people?

This essay would need to describe and evaluate both characters and their relationship to each other. What qualities do they share, and in what ways do they conflict? It would be worthwhile to consider what these men offer to Adam Trask in terms of knowledge, wisdom, and inspiration. A strong essay might consider the significance of their both being from socially marginalized groups.

History and Context

History and context can provide compelling approaches to the analysis of *East of Eden*. The novel relies so heavily on biblical stories that a basic understanding of that particular context is essential for comprehending the events in the novel at all. One way to approach an essay on the biblical context would be to study the brief relevant passages of the Bible in order to familiarize yourself with the analogues with which Steinbeck was working when he conceived of and wrote this novel. The story of Cain and Abel is presented in the novel as being the most revealing tale in the Bible: It is the one that, the novel strongly suggests, reveals to us our human proclivities for jealousy and anger while also serving as a cautionary tale about what happens to us when our uglier tendencies go unchecked. The use of the story of the first brothers is so broad in scope that the challenge of approaching this novel in terms of its biblical context is to limit an idea or subject to a manageable size. An essay could explore, for instance, how characters cope with the inheritance of Cain and Abel's story, where good and evil are both demonstrated. Aron, for example, is incapable of assimilating the simultaneous impulses of good and evil that he sees in himself and others; Cal, in contrast, accepts and is later transformed by his understanding and assimilation of good and evil. One of the primary mysteries of the Cain and Abel story remains mysterious to scholars still: Why does God prefer Abel's gift over Cain's? You might explore how this enigmatic preference is handled in the novel: Does the novel explain the preference? Or, might preference just be a natural idiosyncrasy? An essay could assess whether this mystery of the Cain and Abel story is left intact in *East of Eden*. Another approach to a topic that looks at biblical context would be to focus on Cathy Ames and explore how her characterization resembles that of dubious women in the Bible. Such a study would yield greater understanding of the sorority of villainous women in ancient contexts. Another topic could look at the historical world in which the latter half of the novel is set. For example, studying the experience of the Chinese-American Lee would enable a greater understanding of this singular individual. For any historical topic, the writer would need to do some research in order to consider knowledgeably what the novel is asserting about the world it describes.

Sample Topics:

1. **The Cain and Abel story in the novel:** The novel's action and characters are rooted in the story of Cain and Abel as described in the opening chapters of Genesis. What elements of the novel seem most analogous to the events in the story? How are the mysteries of the Cain and Abel story left intact in the novel?

   A paper on Cain and Abel in the novel would need to include an examination of the contents and morals of the biblical story. What, for instance, does the story suggest about human nature and the legacy of the first murder? To investigate the resonances of the story in the novel, you will want to consider chapter 22, where Adam, Lee, and Samuel Hamilton debate the meaning of the story. Another approach would be to analyze Lee's later report of what the council of wise men he consults in Chinatown has to say about Cain and Abel. A strong essay on this topic will answer the final question in the topic about the mystery of the story. Do you think that *East of Eden* resolves the mystery of God's preferential attention to one brother? What, ultimately, does *East of Eden* conclude about the human and cultural legacy of Cain and Abel?

2. **Cathy Ames and her biblical predecessors:** The novel's characterization of Cathy Ames as an evil figure is clear, but the fact
that evil is sexed as female in the story is a provocative aspect
that harkens back not only to Eve but also to Lilith, Delilah, and
Jezebel. How do the stories of these ancient characters help us
better understand Cathy Ames?

This essay would require an investigation of a number of
women from the Bible, including Eve, Delilah, and Jezebel—
female characters associated, to greater and lesser degrees,
with deceit, destruction, and sexuality. The figure of Lilith is
an especially interesting one to consider in conjunction with
Cathy: Both are women who abandon an Adam for goals of
profound sexual depravity, and both are indifferent mothers.
The story of Lilith is controversial, and she is not included in
the standard Bible. Some stories present Lilith as Adam's wife
before Eve is created. Lilith is infamous for deserting Adam
when she is asked to be sexually submissive to him; she later
consorts (with no apparent regrets) with demons and devils.
One source of information on this story is presented in the
anonymous medieval text *Alpha-Bet of Ben-Sira*. A study of
Cathy and Lilith or any of the other female figures mentioned
would enable a better understanding of traditions that associate women with sex, chaos, and destruction.

3. **Lee in his Chinese-American context:** Lee shares the story of
his parents' immigration and his own struggles with prejudice
and exclusion in his home country. Based on your research into
Lee's story, what conclusions can you draw about the significance of Lee's experience for this novel?

This topic would require you to research the history of the
Chinese in California in the late 19th and early 20th centuries. You should familiarize yourself with the Chinese Exclusion Act (1882) and its effect on Chinese immigrants who
were brought to California to work in the mining camps and
in the construction of railroads. One approach to this topic

would be to analyze how Lee's experiences seem to suit him for his eventual life in the Trask household. You might discuss in what ways he transcends the prejudice he experiences. How, for instance, does he maintain his dignity in the face of this hostility and prejudice? Later, how does his wisdom and dignity benefit the Trask family? Ultimately, what role does his Chinese background play in the ideas and events in the novel?

Philosophy and Ideas

Another approach to forming an argument about *East of Eden* is to identify and then analyze the philosophical ideas that circulate in the novel. This approach is related to the thematic approach discussed above in that it tracks an idea in the story, but this kind of essay would demonstrate how you see the story commenting on the idea in its more general form. The philosophical question of free will, for example, resonates in the story for many of the characters; tracking how characters struggle with what they identify as their fate or their free will would enable you to understand how the general idea of free will operates in the novel. You could locate evidence for the importance of this idea by looking at how the action presents sympathetic characters as gaining awareness about their elective identities and, further, fostering their humanity by choosing to transcend their petty tendencies. Other broad ideas in the novel include the universality of the human soul, good, evil, and love.

Sample Topics:

1. **Fate and free will:** How does this novel present the opposing notions of fate and free will?

   This kind of essay would need to focus on the ways that the novel represents the notions of fate and free will. One approach to an essay on this topic would be to focus on a small number of characters and to assess to what degree they believe in or exercise their free will. Do characters believe themselves fated, by blood and nature, to be a certain kind of being or not? The characters most interested in free will include Lee, Samuel Hamilton, and Cal: The older men's disquisitions, indeed, influence Cal's later decision to rise above the perceived shortcomings of his parentage. Another approach to this topic would be to focus on fate and theorize why so many characters in the novel seem to be seduced by powers that are beyond their control. Yet another approach would be to limit your discussion to *timshel*, the Hebrew term taken from the Cain and Abel story that is translated in the novel as "thou mayest." Does the novel present *timshel* and its implicit choice as an answer to the questions about identity? An ambitious essay on this topic might include discussions of Cathy Ames, a character who appears to lack a will to exercise, though her will is powerful. Do you think that *timshel* could apply to Cathy or that, instead, *timshel* applies to other characters' reactions to Cathy?

2. **The universality of human experience:** The novel represents people as sharing fundamental traits and tendencies. In what ways does this universality materialize in the novel, and what is the significance of this phenomenon for the story?

This topic makes an assertion about the novel's representations of humanity. The first step in approaching this topic would be to locate passages in the novel that demonstrate the validity of the assertion. One example is in chapter 24, where the story of Cain and Abel is described as the "story of mankind." This chapter also features a scene of quaintly convoluted biblical study: Chinese scholars studying Hebrew in order to understand the biblical text so they can assist a Chinese-American man, who himself will later discourse on the scholars' findings for an Irish man and an American man. That Cain and Abel could have identical meanings for all cultures strongly suggests that different traditions are no impediment to understanding. It also implies that humans are the same the world over. You will want to theorize about what role this universality plays in the ideas in the novel. You could consider how, by invoking the Cain and Abel story, the dramatic action in *East of Eden* is rendered that much more broadly in its scope. Another question to consider in this light: Does this universalism make this story more mythic? You might consider how the novel is, by its use of these universal issues and ancient texts, conversing with the mythic texts that inform and underlie it.

Form and Genre

Steinbeck never stopped experimenting with the forms that his stories took. Form and genre therefore present ample opportunities for literary analysis in his fiction. *East of Eden* is so unusual that one approach to an essay could be to analyze what genre it most embodies. The novel combines elements of allegory, memoir, legend, myth, Bible stories, modern fiction, and postmodern fiction. Metafiction is customarily associated with postmodern literature, and some critics see *East of Eden* as demonstrating many of the technical forms that were later categorized as postmodern. Metafiction is defined as fiction that comments on its own fictiveness. Literally, it means literature about literature. We see examples of meta-art when a cartoon character comments on how artificial a cartoon can be, or when a playwright has a character comment on the play that the character is featured in. In literature, metafiction is demonstrated when a story draws attention to either its constructedness or its active creation of a story. In *East of Eden* the narrator speaks in a way that reminds the reader of the artifice of the book, the figure of the author, and, perhaps, his personal opinions on the characters whom he is recounting (if a biographical anecdote) or creating (if a fictional anecdote). We are reminded of the act of creating stories when the narrator expresses confusion about his own assessments about characters (particularly with Cathy Ames, a character he finds puzzling). Examples of metafiction are found in many places in the novel. More conventional essay topics are also useful for analyses of *East of Eden*. Consider, for example, the techniques by which the story is shaped or structured through discussions of narrative point of view, dialogue, or style. The topics below guide you to consider the elements and categories of metafiction, allegory, fiction, and nonfiction.

Sample Topics:

1. ***East of Eden* and metafiction:** In what respects does *East of Eden* use the technique of metafiction? How does the story's nods to its own artifice affect the reading of this novel?

For this topic, you must analyze examples of metafiction in the novel and assess what effect these moments of artistic transparency have on the reading of the story. One approach to the topic would be to assess how the metafictive examples interrupt the narrative flow and then to explore what significance these interruptions might serve in terms of thematic purpose. Another approach to this topic would be to analyze how the metafictional moments further the novel's discussion of the creation of art. Consider, for instance, how the narrator comments in chapter 17 on his uncertain understanding of Cathy Ames: Does this make the narrator seem more or less reliable? How does it show that creating art is a series of choices? A more ambitious approach would be to familiarize yourself with the definitions of postmodern literature (in a dictionary of literary terms) and assess whether this novel fulfills the precepts of postmodernism.

2. ***East of Eden* as allegory:** Does the fact that *East of Eden* is known to use allegorical conventions change the way we understand its characters or their actions? How do the characters change or subvert their roles in this avowed allegory?

An allegory is a story that is based on, and often parallels, another story or event. George Orwell's *Animal Farm*, for instance, is an allegory: It tells a story ostensibly about a society of barnyard animals, but it is more meaningfully a story about a human society and totalitarianism. The allegorical foundation of *East of Eden* is the Bible's rendering of Cain and Abel. For this topic, you need to think about how the allegorical underpinnings affect the reading of this story. One approach to this topic would be to analyze the novel's use of biblical motifs such as scars (the "mark of Cain"), gifts, paternal and fraternal relationships, initials, and names. You will want to discuss how the levels of meaning either add to or interrupt the dramatic action in the novel. Another approach to the topic would be to consider the ways that the allegory breaks down in the novel. Consider, for instance, the ways that Cal's role in the Cain and Abel myth is changed in the novel.

254 Bloom's How to Write about John Steinbeck

Though his gift is rejected by his father (much like God rejects Cain's gift), Cal is later redeemed and forgiven and reincorporated into his society (not at all like Cain).

3. **Intersections of fiction and nonfiction:** Steinbeck mixes the saga of his real-life family, the Hamiltons, with that of a fictional family, the Trasks. What are the narrative roles of these respective families? What is the effect of this mixture of fiction and nonfiction?

For this topic, you need to think about the symbolic significance of the Trasks and the Hamiltons in *East of Eden* and, furthermore, about the effect of mixing fictional and real-life characters. To address this topic, you might find it worthwhile to assess what you think the general thrust of the book is. Once you identify a main theme or purpose of the novel, you will be able to determine what role each family serves for the furtherance of that theme. Ultimately, this topic guides you to consider how the interplay of fiction and nonfiction affects the narration of *East of Eden.*

Comparison and Contrast

Comparing components of a story in order to explain and analyze the similarities or differences between them is a useful approach to writing an essay. Remember to avoid merely creating a list of such similarities or differences in a work; instead; you must take the necessary step of commenting on these observations. To begin a comparison/contrast essay, you might compare characters with each other: How does Cal compare to Charles? To Aron? How does the wise Samuel Hamilton compare to the wise Lee? You could also compare characters (or other elements of the story like patterns of imagery or action) across different Steinbeck novels. For example, how do the depictions of morality compare in *East of Eden* and *The Grapes of Wrath?* The challenge of this kind of essay is to decide what the similarities or differences you identify might mean. These are the questions that make essays interesting and the ones that will have different answers for each writer. To get to these questions, you might find it helpful to think about what kinds of effects Steinbeck achieves by producing either similarities or differences between elements of his stories. What, for example, does the difference between Cal and Aron's respective tolerance for human imperfection do for our understanding of each character and his views of the world? It is not sufficient to point to the existence of similarities or differences; you must also consider what purpose those similarities or differences might serve in the story overall.

Sample Topics:

1. **Contrast a dualism in *East of Eden*:** There are a number of opposing categories at work in this story: These dualities include love/hate, beauty/ugliness, good/evil, material/spiritual. Track one of these dualities and assess its status over the course of the novel. Does the opposition remain constant in the novel?

   For this topic, you need to look carefully at the ways in which dualistic categories operate in the novel and to evaluate their significance. One approach to an essay on this topic would be to notice how an opposition changes over the course of the story. You might notice that the opposition provides energy and conflict for one or more of the characters. Cathy Ames is an interesting character to discuss in light of her dualistic nature: She is both beautiful and ugly, at times almost simultaneously. An essay on love/hate might discuss how often these distinctions switch places (that is, love can turn to hatred very quickly). Another approach to this topic could compare the prevalence of dualism in the beginning of the novel and then assess whether the dualisms collapse. Are things so opposed at the end?

2. **Comparing moralistic characters in different novels:** Lee is one of many characters in Steinbeck's works who are philosophical and moralistic. Compare Lee's philosophy with another character in a work by Steinbeck.

   This kind of essay would need to begin by assessing the philosophical beliefs of Lee. You might consider what he values as a means to identify his personal philosophy. Consider, for example, what he believes is the role of the individual. Isolating one idea, such as the role of the individual, would be a useful way to set up a contrast with another character. Jim Casy (from *The Grapes of Wrath*) and Doc Burton (from *In Dubious Battle*), for instance, also meditate on this concept in their respective novels. Another interesting philosophical concept, one that is integral to the events and characters in *East of Eden,* is sin. Jim Casy proclaims in *The Grapes of Wrath* that "maybe there ain't no sin and there ain't no virtue. There's just stuff people do." Would Lee agree with this assessment of sin? Your answer to that question could form the basis of an interesting comparative essay on moralistic characters.

Bibliography and Online Resources for *East of Eden*:

Ditksy, John. *Essays on* East of Eden. Muncie, IN: John Steinbeck Society of America, 1977.

"John (Ernst) Steinbeck, 1902–1968." *Contemporary Literary Criticism.* Vol. 45. Ed. Daniel G. Marowski and Roger Matuz, Detroit: Gale Research Co., 1977. 368–85.

The Martha Heasley Cox Center for Steinbeck Studies. "The Women of East of Eden: Cathy." Retrieved 28 February 2007. <http://www.steinbeck.sjsu.edu/works/women.jsp>.

Timmerman, John H. *John Steinbeck's Fiction: The Aesthetics of the Road Taken.* Norman: U of Oklahoma P, 1986.

INDEX